Acknowledgments

Grateful acknowledgment is given authors, publishers, photographers, museums, and agents for permission to reprint the following copyrighted material. Every effort has been made to determine copyright owners. In case of any omissions, the Publisher will be pleased to make suitable acknowledgments in future editions.
Acknowledgments continued on page R2.

The **McGraw·Hill** *Companies*

 Glencoe

Send all inquiries to:
Glencoe/McGraw-Hill
8787 Orion Place
Columbus, OH 43240-4027

·

ISBN: 978-0-07-889996-6
MHID: 0-07-889996-6

Printed in the United States of America.

4 5 6 7 8 9 10 110/055 11 10 09

Table of Contents

Table of Contents

UNIT 3   What makes life good? _____ 124

Table of Contents

Whom can you count on?

As you read the following selections, you'll discover a variety of ways in which to think about the question: **Whom can you count on?** Some of the situations and characters may help you come up with your own answer to that question.

Lou Gehrig:

The Luckiest Man on the Face of the Earth

New York City, July 4, 1939

The legendary New York Yankee Lou Gehrig was forced to quit baseball in May of 1939 due to a rare disease. He spoke to a full house at Yankee Stadium on Lou Gehrig Day that July.

Fans, for the past two weeks you have been reading about a bad break I got. Yet today I consider myself the luckiest man on the face of the earth. I have been in ballparks for seventeen years and have never received anything but kindness and encouragement from you fans. ❶

Look at these grand men. Which of you wouldn't consider it the highlight of his career just to associate with them for even one day?

Sure, I'm lucky. Who wouldn't consider it an honor to have known Jacob Ruppert; also the builder of baseball's greatest empire, Ed Barrow; to have spent six years with that wonderful little fellow Miller Huggins; then

> ❶ **Determine Main Idea/ Supporting Details** Why is Lou Gehrig grateful?

to have spent the next nine years with that outstanding leader, that smart student of <u>psychology</u>—the best manager in baseball today—Joe McCarthy!

Sure, I'm lucky. When the New York Giants, a team you would give your right arm to beat, and vice versa, sends you a gift, that's something! When everybody down to the groundskeepers and those boys in white coats remember you with trophies, that's something.

When you have a wonderful mother-in-law who takes sides with you in <u>squabbles</u> against her own daughter, that's something. When you have a father and mother who work all their lives so that you can have an education and build your body, it's a blessing! When you have a wife who has been a tower of strength and shown more courage than you dreamed existed, that's the finest I know.

So I close in saying that I might have had a tough break; but I have an awful lot to live for! ○

Answer the BIG Question

When you do the following activities, consider the Big Question:
Whom can you count on?

WRITE TO LEARN Who were the people in Lou Gehrig's life that he could count on? Who were some of the people who could count on him? Write your responses in your notebook.

PARTNER TALK Meet with another student who has read Lou Gehrig's speech. Discuss how Lou Gehrig handled the news of his illness and his forced retirement from baseball, a sport he loved. What might he have been feeling? What character traits made Lou Gehrig a great man as well as a great ballplayer?

Vo•cab•u•lary

psychology (sy KAWL eh jee) the study of the emotional and behavioral characteristics of a person or group
squabbles (SKWAB ulz) minor disagreements

Through these poems, you will meet different people who can be counted on.

TO LOU GEHRIG

by John Kieran

"To Lou Gehrig" is a tribute to one of the most talented baseball players of all time.

We've been to the wars together;
We took our foes as they came;
And always you were the leader,
And ever you played the game.

Idol of cheering millions,
Records are yours by <u>sheaves</u>;
Iron of frame they hailed you,
Decked you with <u>laurel</u> leaves.
But higher than that we hold you,
We who have known you best,
Knowing the way you came through
Every human test.

Let this be a silent <u>token</u>
Of lasting friendship's gleam
And all that we've left unspoken—
Your pals of the Yankee team.

Vo•cab•u•lary

sheaves (sheevz) bundles of items, as in papers
laurel (LOR el) leaves from trees often woven into wreaths; used by ancient Greeks to crown winners
token (TOH ken) a sign or symbol of something

Sister/Friend

by April Halprin Wayland

A sister provides comfort and understanding.

If I ever forget
how much you
feel
know
sense

may I remember
this April night
and you,
listening to my breaking voice
and blowing softly on my wet cheeks

POEM

by Langston Hughes

The following poem makes a statement about a lost friend.

I loved my friend.
He went away from me.
There's nothing more to say.
The poem ends,
Soft as it began—
I loved my friend.

Answer the BIG Question

When you do the following activities, consider the Big Question:
Whom can you count on?

WRITE TO LEARN In your notebook, write a couple of sentences retelling the message or story of each poem. Then in one or two sentences, write what you've learned from these poems.

PARTNER TALK Work with a partner who has read these poems. Discuss the different people the speaker in each poem counted on. Then, if you feel comfortable, share a story with your partner about a time in your life when you counted on someone.

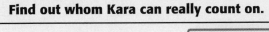

TALES OF A Seventh Grade NADA
by Bizet Kizcorn

Find out whom Kara can really count on.

If only I could come up with comebacks like these, Laura would stop making fun of me.

Maria said that I wasn't a total dork. I just hang out with nerds too much.

"Shut up, Laura!"

No. Too stupid.

"Everyone thinks you're mean, Laura."

What am I, a baby?

Sara, you talk so much your telephone melted!

Wait! I can just write these down!

Montel, your mouth is so big Batman thought it was his cave!

Perfect!

WRITE TO LEARN

A graphic novel tells a story in comic format. Each scene is called a "cell." Write a scene (or two) that illustrates what Kara finds out about herself and her friends. Include dialogue.

from THE

FELLOWSHIP
OF THE RING

by J. R. R. Tolkien

The Fellowship of the Ring is the first book in the *Lord of the Rings* trilogy. At this time, the hobbit Frodo Baggins and his companions are traveling to the place where the Ring of Power can be destroyed.

---

from **The Fellowship of the Ring**

Frodo rose to his feet. A great weariness was on him, but his will was firm and his heart lighter. He spoke aloud to himself. 'I will do now what I must,' he said. 'This at least is plain: the evil of the Ring is already at work even in the Company, and the Ring must leave them before it does more harm. I will go alone. **❶** Some I cannot trust, and those I can trust are too dear to me: poor old Sam, and Merry and Pippin. Strider, too: his heart yearns for Minas Tirith, and he will be needed there, now Boromir has fallen into evil. I will go alone. At once.'

> **❶ Draw Conclusions**
> Why does Frodo decide to "go alone"?

He went quickly down the path and came back to the lawn where Boromir had found him. Then he halted, listening. He thought he could hear cries and calls from the woods near the shore below.

'They'll be hunting for me,' he said. 'I wonder how long I have been away. Hours, I should think.' He hesitated. 'What can I do?' he muttered. 'I must go now or I shall never go. I shan't get a chance again. I hate leaving them, and like this without any explanation. But surely they will understand. Sam will. And what else can I do?'

Slowly he drew out the Ring and put it on once more. He vanished and passed down the hill, less than a rustle of the wind.

The others remained long by the river-side. For some time they had been silent, moving restlessly about it; but now they were sitting in a circle, and they were talking. Every now and again they made efforts to speak of other things, of their long road and many adventures; they questioned Aragorn concerning the realm of Gondor and its ancient history, and the remnants of its great works that could still be seen in this strange borderland of

Vo·cab·u·lary

realm (relm) land, kingdom
remnants (REM nentz) small parts remaining

the Emyn Muil: the stone kings and the seats of Lhaw and Hen, and the great Stair besides the falls of Rauros. But always their thoughts and words strayed back to Frodo and the Ring. What would Frodo choose to do? Why was he hesitating?

'He is debating which course is the most desperate, I think,' said Aragorn. 'And well he may. It is now more hopeless than ever for the Company to go east, since we have been tracked by Gollum, and must fear that the secret of our journey is already betrayed. But Minas Tirith is no nearer to the Fire and the destruction of the Burden.

'We may remain there for a while and make a brave stand; but the Lord Denethor and all his men cannot hope to do what even Elrond said was beyond his power: either to keep the Burden secret, or to hold off the full might of the Enemy when he comes to take it. Which way would any of us choose in Frodo's place? I do not know. Now indeed we miss Gandalf most.'

'Grievous is our loss,' said Legolas. 'Yet we must needs make up our minds without his aid. Why cannot we decide, and so help Frodo? Let us call him back and then vote! I should vote for Minas Tirith.' **2**

2 Draw Conclusions Why does Legolas think the group should take a vote?

'And so should I,' said Gimli. 'We, of course, were only sent to help the <u>Bearer</u> along the road, to go no further than we wished; and none of us is under any oath or command to seek Mount Doom. Hard was my parting from Lothlorien. Yet I have come so far, and I say this: now we have reached the last choice, it is clear to me that I cannot leave Frodo. I would choose Minas Tirith, but if he does not, then I follow him.'

'And I too will go with him,' said Legolas. 'It would be faithless now to say farewell.'

'It would indeed be a betrayal, if we all left him,' said Aragorn. 'But if he goes east, then all need not go with him; nor do I think

Vo•cab•u•lary

bearer (BAIR er) keeper; one in posession of

that all should. That <u>venture</u> is desperate: as much so for eight as for three or two, or one alone. If you would let me choose, then I should appoint three companions: Sam, who could not bear it otherwise; and Gimli; and myself. Boromir will return to his own city, where his father and his people need him; and with him the others should go, or at least Meriadoc and Peregrin, if Legolas is not willing to leave us.'

'That won't do at all!' cried Merry. 'We can't leave Frodo! Pippin and I always intended to go wherever he went, and we still do. But we did not realize what that would mean. It seemed different so far away, in the Shire or in Rivendell. It would be mad and cruel to let Frodo go to Mordor. Why can't we stop him?'

'We must stop him,' said Pippin. 'And that is what he is worrying about, I am sure. He knows we shan't agree to his going east. And he doesn't like to ask anyone to go with him, poor old fellow. Imagine it: going off to Mordor alone!' Pippin shuddered. 'But the dear silly old hobbit, he ought to know that he hasn't got to ask. He ought to know that if we can't stop him, we shan't leave him.'

'Begging your pardon,' said Sam. 'I don't think you understand my master at all. He isn't hesitating about which way to go. Of course not! What's the good of Minas Tirith anyway? To him, I mean, begging your pardon, Master Boromir,' he added, and turned. ❸ It was then that they discovered that Boromir, who at first had been sitting silent on the outside of the circle, was no longer there.

❸ **Draw Conclusions**
Which character knows Frodo best?

'Now where's he got to?' cried Sam, looking worried. 'He's been a bit queer lately, to my mind. But anyway he's not in this business. He's off to his home, as he always said; and no blame to him. But Mr. Frodo, he knows

Vo•cab•u•lary

venture (VEN chur) a risky undertaking

he's got to find the Cracks of Doom, if he can. But he's afraid. Now it's come to the point, he's just plain terrified. That's what his trouble is. Of course he's had a bit of schooling, so to speak— we all have—since we left home, or he'd be so terrified he'd just fling the Ring in the River and bolt. But he's still too frightened to start. And he isn't worrying about us either: whether we'll go along with him or no. He knows we mean to. That's another thing that's bothering him. If he screws himself up to go, he'll want to go alone. Mark my words! We're going to have trouble when he comes back. For he'll screw himself up all right, as sure as his name's Baggins.'

'I believe you speak more wisely than any of us, Sam,' said Aragorn. 'And what shall we do, if you prove right?'

'Stop him! Don't let him go!' cried Pippin.

'I wonder?' said Aragorn. 'He is the Bearer, and the fate of the <u>Burden</u> is on him. I do not think that it is our part to drive him one way or the other. Nor do I think that we should succeed if we tried. There are other powers at work far stronger.'

'Well, I wish Frodo would "screw himself up" and come back, and let us get it over,' said Pippin. 'This waiting is horrible! Surely the time is up?'

'Yes,' said Aragorn. 'The hour is long passed. The morning is wearing away. We must call for him.' **4**

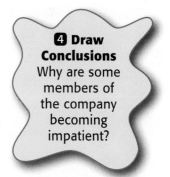

4 Draw Conclusions
Why are some members of the company becoming impatient?

At that moment Boromir reappeared. He came out from the trees and walked towards them without speaking. His face looked grim and sad. He paused as if counting those that were present, and then sat down aloof, with his eyes on the ground.

'Where have you been, Boromir?' asked Aragorn. 'Have you seen Frodo?'

Vo•cab•u•lary

burden (BUR din) load

Boromir hesitated for a second. 'Yes, and no,' he answered slowly. 'Yes: I found him some way up the hill, and I spoke to him. I urged him to come to Minas Tirith and not to go east. I grew angry and he left me. He vanished. I have never seen such a thing happen before, though I have heard of it in tales. He must have put the Ring on. I could not find him again. I thought he would return to you.'

'Is that all that you have to say?' said Aragorn, looking hard and not too kindly at Boromir.

'Yes,' he answered. 'I will say no more yet.'

'This is bad!' cried Sam, jumping up. 'I don't know what this Man has been up to. Why should Mr. Frodo put the thing on? He didn't ought to have; and if he has, goodness knows what may have happened!'

'But he wouldn't keep it on,' said Merry. 'Not when he had escaped the unwelcome visitor, like Bilbo used to.'

'But where did he go? Where is he?' cried Pippin. 'He's been away ages now.'

'How long is it since you saw Frodo last, Boromir?' asked Aragorn.

'Half an hour, maybe,' he answered. 'Or it might be an hour. I have wandered for some time since. I do not know! I do not know!' He put his head in his hands, and sat as if bowed with grief.

'An hour since he vanished!' shouted Sam. 'We must try and find him at once. Come on!'

'Wait a moment!' cried Aragorn. 'We must divide up into pairs, and arrange—here, hold on! Wait!'

It was no good. They took no notice of him. Sam had dashed off first. Merry and Pippin had followed, and were already disappearing westward into the trees by the shore, shouting: Frodo! Frodo! in their clear, high, hobbit-voices. Legolas and Gimli were running. A sudden panic or madness seemed to have fallen on the Company.

'We shall all be scattered and lost,' groaned Aragorn. 'Boromir! I do not know what part you have played in this mischief, but help now! Go after those two young hobbits, and guard them at the least, even if you cannot find Frodo. Come back to this spot, if you find him, or any traces of him. I shall return soon.'

Aragorn sprang swiftly away and went in pursuit of Sam. Just as he reached the little lawn among the rowans he overtook him, toiling uphill, panting and calling, Frodo!

'Come with me, Sam!' he said. 'None of us should be alone. There is mischief about. I feel it. I am going to the top, to the Seat of Amon Hen, to see what may be seen. And look! It is as my heart guessed, Frodo went this way. Follow me, and keep your eyes open!' He sped up the path.

Sam did his best, but he could not keep up with Strider the Ranger, and soon fell behind. He had not gone far before Aragorn was out of sight ahead. Sam stopped and puffed. Suddenly he clapped his hand to his head.

'Whoa, Sam Gamgee!' he said aloud. 'Your legs are too short, so use your head! Let me see now! Boromir isn't lying, that's not his way; but he hasn't told us everything. Something scared Mr. Frodo badly. He screwed himself up to the point, sudden. He made up his mind at last—to go. Where to? Off east. Not without Sam? Yes, without even Sam. That's hard, cruel hard.'

Sam passed his hand over his eyes, brushing away the tears. 'Steady, Gamgee!' he said. 'Think, if you can! He can't fly across rivers, and he can't jump waterfalls. He's got no gear. So he's got to get back to the boats. Back to the boats! Back to the boats, Sam, like lightning!' **5**

Sam turned and bolted back down the path. He fell and cut his knees. Up he got and ran on. He came to the edge of the lawn of Parth Galen by the shore, where the boats were drawn up out of the water. No one was there. There seemed to be cries in the woods behind, but he did not heed them. He stood gazing for a moment, stock-still, gaping. A boat was sliding down the bank all by itself. With a shout Sam raced across the grass. The boat slipped into the water.

> **5 Determine Main Idea/Supporting Details**
> How does Sam figure out where Frodo went?

'Coming, Mr. Frodo! Coming!' called Sam, and flung himself from the bank, clutching at the departing boat. He missed it by a yard. With a cry and a splash he fell face downward into deep swift water. Gurgling he went under, and the River closed over his curly head.

An exclamation of dismay came from the empty boat. A paddle swirled and the boat put about. Frodo was just in time to grasp Sam by the hair as he came up, bubbling and struggling. Fear was staring in his round brown eyes.

'Up you come, Sam my lad!' said Frodo. 'Now take my hand!'

'Save me, Mr. Frodo!' gasped Sam. 'I'm drownded. I can't see your hand.'

'Here it is. Don't pinch, lad! I won't let you go. Tread water and don't flounder, or you'll upset the boat. There now, get hold of the side, and let me use the paddle!'

With a few strokes Frodo brought the boat back to the bank, and Sam was able to scramble out, wet as a water-rat. Frodo took off the Ring and stepped ashore again.

'Of all the <u>confounded</u> <u>nuisances</u> you are the worst, Sam!' he said.

'Oh, Mr. Frodo, that's hard!' said Sam shivering. 'That's hard, trying to go without me and all. If I hadn't a guessed right, where would you be now?'

'Safely on my way.'

'Safely!' said Sam. 'All alone and without me to help you? I couldn't have a borne it, it'd have been the death of me.'

'It would be the death of you to come with me, Sam,' said Frodo, 'and I could not have borne that.'

'Not as certain as being left behind,' said Sam.

'But I am going to Mordor.'

'I know that well enough, Mr. Frodo. Of course you are. And I'm coming with you.'

'Now, Sam,' said Frodo, 'don't <u>hinder</u> me! The others will be coming back at any minute. If they catch me here, I shall have to argue and explain, and I shall never have the heart or the chance to get off. But I must go at once. It's the only way.'

'Of course it is,' answered Sam. 'But not alone. I'm coming too, or neither of us isn't going. I'll knock holes in all the boats first.' **6**

Frodo actually laughed. A sudden warmth and gladness touched his heart. 'Leave one!' he said. 'We'll need it. But you can't come like this without your gear or food or anything.'

> **6 Respond**
> What is your opinion of Sam?

'Just hold on a moment, and I'll get my stuff!' cried Sam eagerly. 'It's all ready. I thought we should be off today.' He rushed to the camping place, fished out his pack from the pile where Frodo had laid it when he emptied the boat of his

Vo•cab•u•lary

confounded (kawn FOWN did) confused
nuisances (NOO suns uz) annoying persons or things
hinder (HIN dur) to hold back, to get in the way

companions' goods, grabbed a spare blanket, and some extra packages of food, and ran back.

'So all my plan is spoilt!' said Frodo. 'It is no good trying to escape you. But I'm glad, Sam. I cannot tell you how glad. Come along! It is plain that we were meant to go together. We will go, and may the others find a safe road! Strider will look after them. I don't suppose we shall see them again.' **7**

7 Synthesize
What qualities does Frodo show?

'Yet we may, Mr. Frodo. We may,' said Sam.

So Frodo and Sam set off on the last stage of the Quest together. Frodo paddled away from the shore, and the River bore them swiftly away, down the western arm, and past the frowning cliffs of Tol Brandir. The roar of the great falls drew nearer. Even with such help as Sam could give, it was hard work to pass across the current at the southward end of the island and drive the boat eastward towards the far shore.

At length they came to land again upon the southern slopes of Amon Lhaw. There they found a shelving shore, and they drew the boat out, high above the water, and hid it as well as they could behind a great boulder. Then shouldering their burdens, they set off, seeking a path that would bring them over the grey hills of the Emyn Muil, and down into the Land of Shadow. ○

Answer the BIG Question

When you do the following activities, consider the Big Question:
Whom can you count on?

WRITE TO LEARN Frodo and Sam both put each other's needs and safety ahead of their own. When was the last time you did something truly selfless? In your notebook, write about a time when you put the needs of another before your own.

PARTNER TALK With a partner, discuss the qualities of someone you know you can count on.

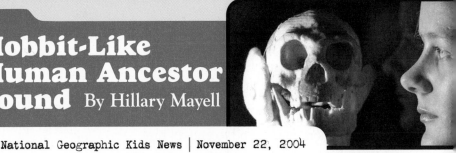

Hobbit-Like Human Ancestor Found By Hillary Mayell

National Geographic Kids News | November 22, 2004

Read about a startling discovery made on an island in Indonesia.

Scientists have found skeletons of a hobbit-like <u>species</u> of human that grew no larger than a three-year-old modern child. The tiny humans had skulls about the size of grapefruits and lived on a remote island in Indonesia 18,000 years ago.

The scientists discovered bones of the miniature humans in a cave on the island of Flores. Scientists named the new species *Homo floresiensis*, after the island.

But dig workers called them hobbits after the tiny creatures from the *Lord of the Rings* books. ❶

> ❶ **Respond**
> Why is this discovery important?

One female skeleton stood just 3.3 feet (1 meter) tall, weighed about 55 pounds (25 kilograms), and was around 30 years old at the time of her death.

"They [the hobbit-like species] had slightly longer arms than us. . . . they had hard, thicker eyebrow ridges than us, a sharply sloping forehead, and no chin," scientist Richard Roberts said.

"While they don't look like modern humans, some of their behaviors were surprisingly human," scientist Peter Brown said.

The "hobbits" used fire in <u>hearths</u> for cooking and hunted stegodon, a primitive dwarf elephant found on the island.

The hobbit-like creatures lived on Flores as recently as 13,000 years ago, which means they would have lived at the same time as modern

Vo·cab·u·lary

species (SPEE sheez) a category of living organisms consisting of similar individuals capable of interbreeding
hearths (harths) fireplace floors

humans, scientists say.

But it is unknown whether the creatures lived alongside modern humans. ❷

Still, rumors, myths, and legends of tiny creatures have swirled around the isolated island for centuries. It's certainly possible that they <u>interacted</u> with modern humans, according to the researchers.

❷ **Respond**
What question about the "hobbits" would you like to see answered?

Researchers are also anxious to study how and why the creatures came to be so small.

There is no record of human adults ever being that small. Modern Pygmies from Africa are considerably taller at about 4.6 to nearly 5 feet (1.4 to 1.5 meters) tall.

"I could not have predicted such a discovery in a million years," said Chris Stringer of the Natural History Museum in London. "This find shows us how much we still have to learn. . . ."

The study was published in the October 28, 2004, issue of *Nature*. ○

Answer the
BIG Question

When you do the following activities, consider the Big Question:
Whom can you count on?

WRITE TO LEARN In some ways these tiny creatures are similar to modern humans, and in other ways they differ. Write a brief entry in your notebook describing the main similarities and differences.

LITERATURE GROUPS Scientists were amazed to discover the skeletons of hobbit-like creatures in Indonesia. Join a couple of students who have read this selection. Discuss one or two other recent scientific discoveries that may have surprised you.

Vo•cab•u•lary

interacted (in tur AK ted) acted with others

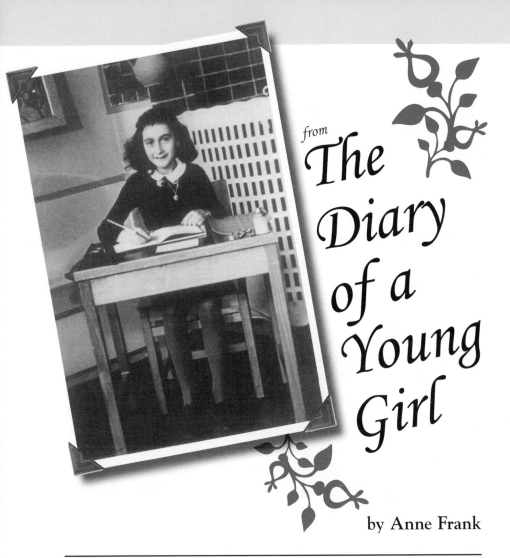

from

The Diary of a Young Girl

by Anne Frank

Anne Frank creates an unusual close friend in order to share her deepest feelings.

I haven't written for a few days, because I wanted first of all to think about my diary. It's an odd idea for someone like me to keep a diary; not only because I have never done so before, but because it seems to me that neither I—nor for that matter anyone else—will be interested in the unbosomings of a thirteen-year-old schoolgirl. Still, what does that matter? I want to write, but more than that, I want to bring out all kinds of things that lie buried deep in my heart.

from The Diary of a Young Girl

There is a saying that "paper is more patient than man"; it came back to me on one of my slightly melancholy days, while I sat chin in hand, feeling too bored and limp even to make up my mind whether to go out or stay at home. Yes, there is no doubt that paper is patient and as I don't intend to show this cardboard-covered notebook, bearing the proud name of "diary," to anyone, unless I find a real friend, boy or girl, probably nobody cares. And now I come to the root of the matter, the reason for my starting a diary: it is that I have no such real friend. ❶

❶ Determine Main Idea
What is the main point Anne is making in this paragraph?

Let me put it more clearly, since no one will believe that a girl of thirteen feels herself quite alone in the world, nor is it so. I have darling parents and a sister of sixteen. I know about thirty people whom one might call friends—I have strings of boy friends, anxious to catch a glimpse of me and who, failing that, peep at me through mirrors in class. I have relations, aunts and uncles, who are darlings too, a good home, no—I don't seem to lack anything. But it's the same with all my friends, just fun and joking, nothing more. I can never bring myself to talk of anything outside the common round. We don't seem to be able to get any closer, that is the root of the trouble. Perhaps I lack confidence, but anyway, there it is, a stubborn fact, and I don't seem to be able to do anything about it.

Hence, this diary. In order to enhance in my mind's eye the picture of the friend for whom I have waited so long, I don't want to set down a series of bald facts in a diary like most people do, but I want this diary itself to be my friend, and I shall call my friend Kitty. No one will grasp what I'm talking about if I begin my letters to Kitty just out of the blue, so albeit unwillingly, I will start by sketching in brief the story of my life.

My father was thirty-six when he married my mother, who was then twenty-five. My sister Margot was born in 1926 in

Vo•cab•u•lary

melancholy (MEL en kawl ee) sad

Frankfort-on-Main, I followed on June 12, 1929, and, as we are Jewish, we <u>emigrated</u> to Holland in 1933, where my father was appointed Managing Director of Travies N.V. This firm is in close relationship with the firm of Kolen & Co. in the same building, of which my father is a partner.

The rest of the family, however, felt the full impact of Hitler's anti-Jewish laws, so life was filled with anxiety. In 1938 after the <u>pogroms</u>, my two uncles (my mother's brothers) escaped to the U.S.A. My old grandmother came to us, she was then seventy-three. After May 1940 good times rapidly fled: first the war, then the <u>capitulation</u>, followed by the arrival of the Germans, which is when the sufferings of us Jews really began. Anti-Jewish decrees followed each other in quick succession. Jews must wear a yellow star, Jews must hand in their bicycles, Jews are banned from trains and are forbidden to drive. Jews are only allowed to do their shopping between three and five o'clock and then in shops which bear the placard "Jewish shop." Jews must be indoors by eight o'clock and cannot even sit in their own gardens after that hour. Jews are forbidden to visit theaters, cinemas, and other places of entertainment. Jews may not take part in public sports. Swimming baths, tennis courts, hockey fields, and other sports grounds are all prohibited to them.

Vo·cab·u·lary

emigrated (EM ih grayt ud) moved or migrated out of one country or region to another

pogroms (POH grumz) organized massacres of helpless people

capitulation (kuh pih chuh LAY shun) surrender

Jews may not visit Christians. Jews must go to Jewish schools, and many more restrictions of a similar kind. **2**

So we could not do this and were forbidden to do that. But life went on in spite of it all. Jopie used to say to me, "You're scared to do anything, because it may be forbidden." Our freedom was strictly limited. Yet things were still bearable.

2 Synthesize
How did Hitler's treatment of the Jews affect Anne?

Granny died in January 1942; no one will ever know how much she is present in my thoughts and how much I love her still.

In 1934 I went to school at the Montessori Kindergarten and continued there. It was at the end of the school year, I was in form 6B, when I had to say good-by to Mrs. K. We both wept, it was very sad. In 1941 I went, with my sister Margot, to the Jewish Secondary School, she into the fourth form and I into the first.

So far everything is all right with the four of us and here I come to the present day. ○

Answer the BIG Question

When you do the following activities, consider the Big Question:
Whom can you count on?

WRITE TO LEARN Think about a time when you wanted to confide in a friend but found it difficult. What did you want to say? Why was it difficult? Make an entry explaining the situation in your notebook.

PARTNER TALK With another student who has read this selection, discuss the restrictions placed on Jews during the Nazi occupation of Holland. Discuss whether it is possible for something like this to happen again.

Baby Hippo Orphan Finds a Friend

By Catherine Clarke Fox

Find out what happens to a baby hippo when it no longer has its mother to count on.

Have you noticed that sometimes the most unlikely pairs form the best friendships? Late last December, flood waters in the East African country of Kenya swept a herd of hippopotamuses down the Sabaki River and into the Indian Ocean. After a few days, most of them struggled to shore and returned inland.

Then, right after the Asian <u>tsunami</u> hit on December 26, local people spotted a baby hippo in the rough surf, apparently left behind by the herd. They were worried.

Hippos live around fresh water, and the people figured the salt water wasn't good for the little fellow. Besides, he had no mother to look out for him.

After hours of effort, they caught the big baby (about 600 pounds, or 270 kilograms). They named him Owen after one of his rescuers. ❶

> ❶ **Determine Main Idea/ Supporting Details**
> What is the main idea of this section? What details help explain the main idea?

Vo•cab•u•lary

tsunami (soo NAH mee) an enormous, potentially destructive wave caused by an earthquake or a volcano erupting on the bottom of the ocean

Baby Hippo Orphan Finds a Friend

Wildlife officials took Owen the hippo to the safety of Haller Park, a <u>sanctuary</u> for wild animals in the port city of Mombasa. To their surprise, Owen, about a year old, trotted right up to a giant gray tortoise.

Tortoises are among the longest-living creatures on Earth. This one's name is Mzee, which means "old man" in the Swahili language. He is more than a hundred years old.

"Mzee hissed, lifted himself up off the ground, and tried to run," reported Paula Kahumbu, an ecologist in charge of Haller Park. (Ecologists study how living things relate to their surroundings.) "But by the next morning, they were together!"

They have been together ever since, even staying close and touching when they sleep.

Owen could weigh more than 6,000 pounds (2,700 kilograms) when he is grown—heavier than a minivan. Eventually he will be introduced to Cleo, an adult hippo, so he can be with his own kind.

But Kahumbu said Owen and Mzee will still spend time together if they wish. ❷ ○

> ❷ **Synthesize**
> What makes friendships like this one so appealing?

When you do the following activities, consider the Big Question:
Whom can you count on?

WRITE TO LEARN Think about the unlikely friendship in this article. Then write a brief entry in your notebook about an unlikely friendship you have observed.

PARTNER TALK Work with a partner to discuss what hardships people might experience during a natural disaster. Then focus on one hardship; discuss some possible ways that people might help each other through a difficult time.

Vo•cab•u•lary

sanctuary (SANK choo air ee) a safe place for birds and wild animals

Finding a Way

by Jan Klinkbeil

Support can come from surprising sources.

Drew!

Honestly, Julie, you've been moping about this for days. What's wrong?

McCloud wants to see your extracurriculars.

They're big into literature and journalism and Julie doesn't have any writing extracurriculars and *all* her friends are going to get in and she *won't*.

Gee, *thanks,* Trish.

Don't call me Trish, Jules.

And what's your damage? I'm agreeing with you!

Well, gee, since you put it *that* way...

So get with it!

Not how I would've put it, but Tricia has a point. It's what you can accomplish—not what you think you can — that'll help you.

Extracurricular activities are important, but it's still grades that'll make the difference.

If you want this, apply yourself. Work for it. No one's going to hand it to you.

You've got to *deserve* it.

Heh, too bad for *you, Jules.*

Oh, yeah, no big deal, he was *only* the editor of the *Clarion!*

Not to mention his regional prize! I have, like, *no* extracurricular activities!

Yeah, but *he's* still lame, and you're *good.*

You're *freaky* good. It was meant to be, Julie!

Don't sweat it.

Keep your grades up, like you always do, and you're a shoo-in.

Hey, speaking of grades, how did you all think you did on that test in Western Civ?

Pfft, piece of *cake.*

I don't know. I don't think it's that *simple.*

But why doesn't anyone else seem worried?

Am I taking it all way too seriously?

Later, in Tae Kwan Do class...

Sound off.

Hwa-Rang of *Tae Kwan Do Hyung.*

How many movements?

29.

What was the Hwa-Rang?

A youth group in the Silla Dynasty.

They helped unify the three Kingdoms of Korea.

You seem a little distracted tonight, Julie.

Oh. I'm sorry.

No need to be sorry. But you're usually very *Focused*.

I'm working on a problem.

Anything I can help with?

No, I - *wait.* Could Tae Kwan Do count as an extracurricular on an application for a magnet school?

Certainly. Would you like a letter of recommendation as well?

Sure! Um, but this is for a writing course...

Well, I can vouch for what a singular student you are.

How simple answers never satisfy you - how you always need to know *why,* and don't stop till you understand.

WRITE TO LEARN
Think about different people who support you in your goals at home, at school, or in your neighborhood. Who do you feel comfortable counting on for support? Why? Write about it in your notebook.

When the Rattlesnake Sounds

by Alice Childress

Harriet Tubman helped more than 300 slaves reach freedom on the Underground Railroad. The "stations" on this railroad were houses where escaping slaves could hide.

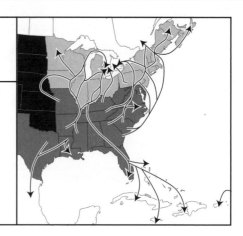

Underground Railroad Key:

← Approximated flight routes

Free states

Slave states

Territories

Characters

Harriet Tubman. An experienced leader who knows how to handle people with firmness . . . and love.

Lennie. A strong, determined, no-nonsense kind of young woman.

Celia. A young woman who has the tendency to get fed up when the going is grubby and ordinary.

Setting

Time. Very close to the end of legal slavery.

Place. Cape May, New Jersey.

Scene

A hotel laundry room. Harriet, Lennie, and Celia are washing clothes. Harriet and Lennie work <u>vigorously</u>, absorbed in the task. Celia is slowing up and finally stops.

Celia. (*cautiously watching* Harriet *and* Lennie) Lord, I'm tired. (*others keep working*) Seem like we workin way past our dinnertime, don't it? Harriet? Lennie?

Lennie. Not much past dinner. It feels like about one o'clock.

Harriet. We're gonna stop and eat by 'n by. We'll put out five

---

Vo•cab•u•lary

vigorously (VIG ur us lee) in a way that shows physical strength

bundles of wash today. Yesterday was only four.

Celia. Only four? When I went to bed last night, I cried, I was so bone-weary. Only? How can four bundles of wash be only?

Harriet. Just a while longer, Celia. Let's sing. When you singin, the work goes fast. You pick a song, Lennie.

Lennie. (*decides to pick one that will annoy* Celia) Wadin in the water, wadin in the water (*children*). Wadin in the water, God gonna trouble the water. (Harriet *joins her in singing.*)

Celia. (*drying her hands on her apron*) I want my dinner now. I'm hungry.

Lennie. We all hungry, Celia. Can't you hold out a little more?

Celia. If we all hungry, why don't we all eat? We been up since seven this mornin . . . workin. For what? Why?

Lennie. You know why! We got to finish five bundles.

Celia. (*to the heavens above*) Five bundles for what?

Lennie. For a dollar and a quarter, that's what! (*grumbling*) I'm tellin you . . . some people.

Harriet. (*Sensing trouble, she stops washing.*) Celia is right, Lennie. It's not good to kill yourself workin.

Lennie. (*her eyes on* Celia) Did you fix it again, Harriet? We suppose to take turns. I take a turn, you take a turn, then . . .

Harriet. (*hastily cutting her off*) I got some nice corn bread and some side meat. The coffee should be ready. (*handing out paper parcels to the girls*) We need to rest awhile. Here, Celia, and that's yours Lennie. (*going back to her tub*) I'll just wash out these few more pieces before my water turns cold. ❶

❶ Draw Conclusions Why does Harriet say they should rest?

Lennie. I ain't restin unless you rest too. Not like some people I know.

Celia. She keep sayin some people.

Vo•cab•u•lary

parcels (PAHR selz) packages

Wonder who she means?

Harriet. *(with a sigh)* I'll stop too.

Celia. *(looking at the pile of unwashed clothes as she unwraps her lunch)* White folks love white clothes and they love to sit in the grass too . . . and I'm sick of scrubbin grass stains.

Harriet. Well, we need the money.

Celia. *(puts down her lunch and snatches up a <u>flouncy</u> white dress)* Look at all the money they got. This cost every bit of twelve dollars. *(imitating the hotel guests)* Spendin the summer in a big hotel, ridin round in carriages. *(drops her airy act and goes back to anger)* If just one of em give us what she spend in a week . . . we wouldn't have to work two months in no hotel laundry.

Lennie. I got a life-size picture of them givin you that much money. They ain't gonna give you nothin, so you better be glad you got the chance to earn some.

Celia. Scrubbin! Ain't that a damn somethin to be glad about? Excuse me Harriet, I meant to say dern or drat.

Harriet. Celia got somethin on her mind, and she need to talk, so let her talk, Lennie. But no dammin, dernin, or drattin either. All here got more manners than to cuss.

Lennie. *(as she looks at* Harriet's *food)* Is that your dinner? You ain't got no meat on your bread, Harriet.

Harriet. I don't too much like meat.

Lennie. I know who do. Some people.

Celia. *(bursting out at* Harriet*)* Stop sayin that! You do too like meat! Stop makin out like you don't. You goin without so you can save another nickel. ❷ Yall drivin me outta my head. Maybe I'm just not suited for this kind of thing.

> ❷ **Respond**
> What do you think of Celia?

Vo•cab•u•lary

flouncy (FLOWN see) like decorative material that is gathered or pleated; frilly

Lennie. But I am, huh?

Harriet. (*quietly and seriously*) You tired of this bargain we made? You sorry about it and don't know how to quit?

Lennie. (*flaring with anger*) She promised and she got to stick by it! Your father is a <u>deacon</u> of the church . . . and if you don't keep your word, you gonna bring disgrace down on him and every member of your family.

Harriet. Lennie, don't be so brash. Mother and father is one thing . . . child is another. Each one stands upon his own deeds. She don't have to stay. Celia, you can go if you want.

Celia. I don't really want to get out of it. But I want some of my money for myself. I'm tired of sleepin three in a room. I want to spend a little of the money . . . just a little, Harriet. Buy a few treats.

Lennie. She's jealous of them rich white ladies . . . cause they got silk <u>parasols</u> to match they dresses. I heard her say it. "Wish I had me a silk parasol."

Harriet. We eatin and sleepin. We spend for that and nothin more . . . that was the bargain.

Celia. (*to Lennie*) I could own a silk parasol and carry it . . . without actin like a field hand.

Harriet. I been a field hand, children. Harness to a plow like a workhorse.

Celia. Scuse me, I'm sorry.

Lennie. (*really sarcastic*) Celia, that don't sound nothin like them big speeches you used to make in church meetin. (*mocking Celia*) "I'll die for my freedom!" . . . Had everybody whoopin and hollerin every time you open your mouth, whole church stompin and shoutin amen.

Vo•cab•u•lary

deacon (DEE kun) a church officer who is not an ordained minister
parasols (PAR eh sawlz) light umbrellas used for protection from the sun

Celia. *(sadly)* I remember how it was. *(The women remove their aprons and Harriet takes her place center stage. Church music in from off-stage or recording of "The Old Ship of Zion," or any of the A.M.E. Zion songs. Harriet Tubman was a member of that church. She addresses the audience as though they are the* <u>congregation</u>.*)*

Harriet. *(Music and humming are in low as she speaks.)* God bless you, brothers and sisters, bless you, children.

Offstage Voices plus Lennie and Celia. Amen . . . Amen . . . Bless God.

Harriet. I thank the good Lord for the support of the African Methodist Episcopal Zion Church in the freedom struggle. There is comfort and good fellowship here.

Church Voices. Yes, Lord. Amen.

Harriet. Not like hidin in the bitter cold, with the huntin dogs followin you down with no restin place in sight.

We had to give the little babies <u>paregoric</u> so they wouldn't cry and let the paddy-rollers know where to find us. We crossed some lonely roads and rivers . . . the dark of the night around us, the clouds cuttin off the sight of the North Star. But everything was all right cause where I go . . . God goes . . . and I carry a gun . . . two guns . . . a hand pistol and a shoulder rifle . . . just in case the Lord tell me I got to use it!

Church Voices. Amen! Speak! Praise the holy name! Amen!

Harriet. I thank the Father for the help and assistance of the Society of Friends and the <u>abolitionists</u>, and all well-wishers.

Vo•cab•u•lary

congregation (kawn greh GAY shun) a gathering of people for worship

paregoric (pair eh GOR ik) medicine that causes drowsiness in most people

abolitionists (ab uh LI shun ists) people who favor abolishing, or getting rid of, a particular law or custom; specifically those who favored abolishing slavery

Church Voices. Amen, Amen, Amen.

Harriet. But as I put my hand to the plow to do the work of Freedom, so I also put my money into the work. I have none now, so I will spend my summer washin and ironin so that when the fall come I have some of my own to put . . . to buy food, medicine, paregoric for the babies, and ammunition for the pistol . . . Lord grant I never use it. Any ladies here want

People dug tunnels to hide slaves until they could be moved to freedom.

to go with me to wash clothes and give the money to free our slave brethren?

Lennie. (*stands by* Harriet's *side*) If you would have me, Mrs. Tubman, it would be the greatest honor, a great honor indeed.

Harriet. Thank you, my daughter.

Celia. (*stands up and throws her arms out in a Joan of Arc gesture*) I'll die for my freedom! Take me, Sister! I'm ready to fight the good fight. Hallelujah!

Church Voices. (Celia *has set the church to rocking.*) Glory! Glory! Hallelujah! Fight the good fight! Amen! (*Music fades out as women don their aprons again.*)

Celia. I remember how it was, Lennie, and the promise I made. But how much can we get like this? Maybe if everybody worked and gave their money to the Underground, it would mean somethin. This way I just can't see it, but I believe in freedom and I understand.

Harriet. Ain't no such thing as only "understandin." Understandin mean action. ❸ You have to look after what Celia does . . . and if nobody else do nothin, you got to. Freedom is just a baby, and you its mother. You don't stop lovin and carin for it just cause others don't care.

❸ **Determine Main Idea/ Supporting Details**
What does Harriet mean when she says, "understandin mean action"?

Celia. Maybe it's easy to talk like that when you Moses. It's easy to kill yourself for somethin when thousands of people be cheerin you on. Lennie and Celia don't mean nothin to nobody. We could die here and nobody would know or care.

Lennie. Don't you talk for me! Ain't nothin greater to me than to be able to say . . . "I, Lennie Brown, scrubbed clothes side by side with Moses." If you lookin for praise, you don't belong here.

Harriet. Children, let us keep peace. We act like we hate each other worse than we hate the slaveowner.

Celia. I know what I sound like . . . *(falls at Harriet's feet and holds out her hands)* Oh, Harriet, my hands are skinned sore.

Lennie. Do, Jesus, look at Celia's hands.

Harriet. *(turns Celia's head and searches for the truth)* But it ain't your hands that's really botherin you. It ain't food, it ain't sleepin three in a room, and it ain't about silk parasols. What's botherin you, Celia?

Celia. I'm so shame for feelin the way I do. Lord knows I'm shame.

Harriet. Tell it. Speak your shame.

Celia. I'm scared. If these people in this hotel knew who you was. Forty thousand dollars' reward out for you! ❹

Lennie. *(dashes to the door to see if anyone is around to listen)* Hush your fool mouth! Moses got the charm. Slave holder will never catch Moses.

> ❹ **Determine Main Idea/ Supporting Details** What scares Celia most?

Celia. I'm so shame. All those other things just lies. I ain't so terrible tired. I'm just scared and shame cause I'm afraid. Me talkin so big. Sure, I'd work all summer and give the money to the Underground. It did sound so good in the meetin where it was all warm and friendly. Now I'm scared of gettin into trouble. I never been no slave. And I'm scared of nothin round me but white folks.

Lennie. We ain't got no room for no rabbity, <u>timid</u> kinda women in this work.

Harriet. Oh, yes, Lennie, we got room for the timid and the brave. Poor little Celia. Child, you lookin at a woman who's been plenty afraid. When the rattlesnake sounds a warnin . . . it's time to be scared. Ain't that natural? When I run away was nobody to cheer me on . . . don't you think I was scared?

Vo•cab•u•lary

timid (TIM id) fearful

Lennie. But you got to freedom.

Harriet. *(The feeling of a "meeting" begins.)* Oh, but when I found I'd crossed that line! There was such a glory over everything. The sun came shinin like gold through the trees.

Lennie. *(feels like she is at church meeting)* You felt like you was in heaven! You was free!

Harriet. But there was no one to welcome me in the land of freedom. I was a stranger in a strange land. My home, after all, was down in the old cabin quarters with the ones I knew and loved . . . my slave mother and father, brothers, sisters, and friends. Aunt Day . . . she used to be <u>midwife</u>, tend the sick, bury the dead. Two field hands I knew, they used to ease some of the work off the women who was expectin. There I was standin on free land, with my heart back down there with them. What good is freedom without your people?

Lennie. Go on, Harriet!

Harriet. And so to this solemn <u>resolution</u> I come: As I was free . . . they would be free also.

Lennie. Praise God, that's Harriet Tubman!

Harriet. Sometimes I was scared in the icy river. Chilled to the bone and just might drown.

Lennie. But you got cross.

Harriet. I was scared in the dark and the swamp . . . but I came to the light. Most times I was full of hatred for the white folks.

Lennie. And you came to the Friends.

Harriet. And I came to John Brown. *(offstage music . . . soft violin . . . sound of voices ad-libbing at a reception)* There was this big, fine affair. A reception. Abolitionist reception. The ladies were all dressed in lovely gowns, made by free labor.

Vo•cab•u•lary

midwife (MID wyf) a person, usually a woman, trained to assist women in childbirth

resolution (rez uh LOO shun) a firm decision to take a certain course of action

I was in my best too . . . but that wasn't too much better than what I'm standin in. They had pretty cakes and a punch bowl . . . the grandest party. Violin music . . . what you call elegant. There was a goodly crowd, and I was way on the other side of the room, away from the main door where the people would enter. Everybody called him Captain Brown . . . Captain. (Harriet *moves to the far side of the stage and turns toward the opposite door to illustrate the distance between her and Captain Brown.*)

Captain John Brown

Harriet. The whisper started way down the hall and came through the room . . . "It's Captain Brown. He's here. Captain Brown is about to enter." Then he came in the door. He was a fine, stern-lookin gentleman . . . goodness glowed from his face like a burnin light. The room got quiet. He looked all around until he saw me. Mind now, we had never met. The ladies and gentlemen were all tryin to meet him . . . Oh, it was Captain, Captain, Captain. He held up his hand. There was silence, then he said . . . "The first I see is General Tubman. The second is General Tubman. The third is General Tubman." He crossed the room and bowed to me . . . and I shook his hand.

Lennie. And he died for us, didn't he?

Harriet. Celia, he was a brave man, but I believe he must have been scared sometimes. But he did what he had to do.

Celia. I guess he was just brave. Some folks braver than others.

Harriet. I was with hundreds of brave black men on battleground. I was there, Celia. We saw the lightning and that was the guns, then we heard the thunder and that was the big guns, then we heard the rain falling . . . and that was the drops of blood. And when we came to get the crops, it was dead men we reaped.

Lennie. Fightin for us to be free. I guess they musta been scared sometimes.

Harriet. Give me your hand, Celia. Look, see the skin broken across the knuckles. Counta you some man or woman gonna have warm socks and boots to help em get to freedom. See the cuts the lye soap put in your skin. Counta you some little baby is gonna be born on free soil. It won't matter to him that you was afraid, won't matter that he did not know your name. Won't nothin count ceptin he's free. A livin monument to Celia's work. (Celia *cries.*) You go to the room and rest. Maybe you might want to stay here after you think about it.

Lennie. Sure, Celia . . . think bout it. We can manage. And if you want to go home, we won't hold it against you. I ought not to have said what I did. Sometimes I get scared myself . . . but it

Allen Chapel African Methodist Episcopal (A.M.E.) Church

makes me act evil and brave, you know? **5**

5 Synthesize
How has Lennie changed?

Celia. I don't want to go home. Guess there's worse things than fear. I'm glad to know I don't have to be shame about it.

Harriet. That's right. If you was home doin nothin, what would you have to be fraid bout? That's when a woman oughta feel shame, shame to her very soul.

Celia. (*Gathers up clothes, places them in tub, starts working. Harriet goes to her tub.*) If we sing, the work goes faster.

Lennie. (*goes to her tub*) Your time to pick a song, Celia.

Celia. (*Celia starts scrubbing. They all work for a few moments. Celia has decided on a song. She sings out.*)

Oh, Lord, I don't feel no ways tired
Children, Oh, Glory Hallelujah
For I hope to shout Glory when this world is all on fire
Oh, Glory, Hallelujah
(*The others join her on the second round.*)
Oh, Lord, I don't feel no ways tired . . .

CURTAIN ○

Answer the BIG Question

When you do the following activities, consider the Big Question:
Whom can you count on?

WRITE TO LEARN Celia once claimed that she would die for her freedom. Later, she expresses fear and complains about the physical demands of her work. Think about a time when you made a difficult commitment and people were counting on you. Write about your experience in your notebook.

LITERATURE GROUPS Get together with two or three other students who have read this selection. Discuss a struggle against injustice that you see in the world today. What are some people doing to change the situation?

Why do you read?

They are everywhere you look: on signs, in newspapers and magazines, on video games and television, and game instructions, in books, and on the Internet.
What are they? Words!
Why do you read? *You read for information, entertainment, adventure—to learn and to enjoy!*

THE CALAMITY KIDS IN:

THE BERMUDA TRIANGLE TERRARIUM!

by Jerzy Drozd and Sara Turner

Reading is the key to solving a dangerous mystery in the fourth dimension.

WRITE TO LEARN
Think about the ways reading could save your life in the real world. List them in your notebook.

to young readers

by Gwendolyn Brooks

Grab a key to the treasures that are hidden in books.

Good books are
bandages
and voyages
and <u>linkages</u> to Light;

are keys and hammers,
ripe <u>redeemers</u>,
dials and bells and
healing <u>hallelujah</u>.

Good books are good nutrition.
A reader is a Guest
nourished, by riches of the Feast,
to lift, to launch, and to applaud
      the world.

Vo•cab•u•lary

linkages (LING kij ez) connections
redeemers (rih DEE murz) rescuers
hallelujah (hal eh LOO ya) an expression of joy

INVITATION

by Shel Silverstein

What are you invited to do?

If you are a dreamer, come in,
If you are a dreamer, a wisher, a liar,
A hope-er, a pray-er, a magic bean buyer…
If you're a pretender, come sit by my fire
For we have some <u>flax</u>-golden tales to spin.
Come in!
Come in!

Answer the BIG Question

As you do the following activities, consider the Big Question:
Why do you read?

WRITE TO LEARN Think about the title of the poem "Invitation." In what way is a book an invitation? Write a response in your notebook.

LITERATURE GROUPS Meet with two or three other students who have also read these poems. Choose two or three images from the poem "To Young Readers." How do these images help the writer get across the message of the poem?

Vo·cab·u·lary

flax (flaks) a plant whose stems are used to produce pale yellow fiber that is woven into linen

REAL SPIDER SUPERPOWERS

Reported by Cameron Walker
and written by Sarah Ives

Read to discover how spiders can outjump, outspin, and generally outpower the superhero!

Spider-Man appeared in movie theaters to fight villains with his many superpowers—but real spiders have some tricks of their own.

Real spiders may not be able to fight Doc Ock, the criminal in *Spider-Man 2*, but some spiders *can* jump as much as 50 times their body length.

U.S. long jumper Mike Powell holds the world's record with a jump of 29 feet, 4.5 inches (8.95 meters). Powell is 6 feet,

2 inches (1.9 meters) tall. If he had a spider's jumping ability, he might be able to leap 300 feet (90 meters). That would definitely bring him the gold medal in the Olympics!

Spiders jump to catch insects. "They hunt down prey, and then they'll pounce on it," said Andrew Martin, from the University of Applied Sciences in Germany.

But that's not all spiders can do. In the movies, Spider-Man walks up buildings. Some real spiders can also walk upside down on smooth surfaces.

Some spiders' feet are covered with tiny hairs. These hairs give spiders the strength to hold 170 times their body weight before coming unstuck. That would be the same as Spider-Man carrying 170 people from danger while clinging to a building with his fingers and toes, Martin said.

Scientists hope that they can use the secret of spiders' stickiness to make better sticky notes, gloves for soccer goalies, and even boots for astronauts.

Spiders can also spin as many as seven different kinds of silk. Some of the silk is so strong that it rivals the strength of steel! With skills like that, spiders could give Superman, the Man of Steel, a run for his money!

Spiders use the silk for many different purposes, like catching insects in webs, traveling from place to place, parachuting, forming egg sacs, and wrapping up prey.

According to Todd Blackledge of the University of California, Riverside, the first *Spider-Man* movie had some realistic webs. "They had such a great variety of webs," he said. "Somebody had really done their homework." ❶

❶ Review
What "super-powers" do real spiders have?

Real Spider Superpowers

- There are more than 37,000 described spider species in the world, but only about 25 are thought to have <u>venom</u> that can affect people.

- The largest known spider is the Goliath birdeater tarantula. This South American spider can be as big as a dinner plate. The spider has even snatched birds from their nests!

- The smallest known spider is the mygalomorph (MIG-uh-low-morf) spider from Borneo. Its body is the size of a pinhead.

- Most spiders have eight eyes. But some don't have any eyes, and others can have as many as 12.

- A spider eats about 2,000 insects a year.

- Some people eat spiders. In the South Pacific, some people say spiders taste nutty and sticky like peanut butter. ○

Answer the BIG Question

As you do the following activities, consider the Big Question:
Why do you read?

WRITE TO LEARN Think about the author's purpose in writing this article. Then, write a brief entry in your notebook about your reason for reading the article.

LITERATURE GROUPS With a small group of students who have also read this selection, list or describe the types of spiders you have seen. What information in the article surprised you the most?

Vo·cab·u·lary

venom (VEN um) a poison

BLUES FOR BOB E. BROWN

by T. Ernesto Bethancourt

Can Roberto Moreno, a. k. a. Bob E. Brown, make it as a blues singer?

Upper West Side, New York, New York

I was just getting home from my after-school delivery job at the Big Apple Market. It was about eight-thirty. I heard Mama and Papa going at it right through our apartment door. I stood outside in the hall of our second-floor walkup and tried to make out what was going on inside. 1

> **1 Set a Purpose for Reading**
> What do you expect to get out of reading this story?

No sense in walking into an argument unless you already know whose side you're supposed to be on. That's the trouble when you're the last kid left at home. They always want you to take sides. Ever since my older brother, Lou, left to join the Navy, it's been this way. My married sister, Margie, lives in Queens now. She's too far from West Eighty-eighth Street in Manhattan, where we live, for Mama to get her involved in her hassles with Papa.

"I don't care!" I heard Papa say. "I won't have him in my house."

"But Juanillo," I heard Mama counter, "he's your own father. Your flesh and blood . . ."

I knew Mama was trying the soft approach with Papa. When she's really pleased with him or wants something, she calls him Juanillo. Any other time, it's plain old Jack. But actually, my father's name *is* Juan—meaning "John"—and *Juanillo* means "Johnny" or "Johnny-boy."

All us kids have traditional Latino names, too. My brother Lou is really Luis Alfredo, my sister Margie is Margarita Dolores, and I'm Roberto Ernesto, although everyone calls me Bobby. I couldn't imagine anyone calling me by my middle name. Or, worse yet, *Ernie!*

My dad speaks some Spanish; so does my mom. But us kids only know a few words—me least of all, being the youngest. To give you an idea how little, I almost failed Spanish in my junior year at Brandeis High School.

The hassle was still going on inside the apartment. "My mind's made up, Helen," I heard Papa say. "If he's so interested in seeing his grandchildren after all these years, that's tough. I want nothing to do with him."

Now I knew what was going on. We had heard from my grandfather. I didn't even know he was still alive. My dad never talks about him. Seeing as how my parents' fight wasn't about me, I put my key in the door and went inside.

The hall door opens right into the kitchen of our apartment. Then comes the living room and two bedrooms. But most of the time if we aren't watching TV in the living room, most of our family life is in the kitchen.

Mama was seated at the table with her ever-present cup of Café Bustelo coffee with milk. Papa, still wearing his Transit Authority uniform, was having one of his two daily bottles of Schaefer beer. I kissed Mama and got a hug from Papa. "Hi, guys," I said. "What's happening?" As if I didn't know.

"Nothing—nothing at all, Bobby," Papa said.

"Pretty loud nothing," I said. "I heard you two down the hall."

"Oh, *that*," my dad said with a wave of a hand. "Just between your mama and me. A family matter."

"Jack!" said Mama. "You mean you aren't going to mention it?"

"Mention what?" I said, still not letting on.

My dad shook his head in a funny mix of disgust and dismay. "You might as well know, Bobby. Your grandfather has decided he's still part of our family. After all these years. We got a letter from him today."

"Grandpa's here in New York? Last time I heard you mention him, he was in California."

"He's still out there," Mama said. "But his letter says he's coming here this week. He says he wants to see us—*all* of us." Mama looked pointedly at Papa, who looked away.

"How did he even know where to find us?" I asked.

"It was your brother, Lou. He's stationed in Oakland now—"

"I know, but—?"

"Let me finish," put in Papa. "Your brother took it upon himself to track the old man down. He had some family records of my mother's that *someone* gave him." Papa looked angrily across the table at Mama. "So Lou found him—a man he'd never seen in his life—a man who didn't even come to his son's wedding."

"We know, Juanillo," Mama said softly.

"Then why should you care about a man you've never met?" my dad demanded of my mom.

"Because no matter what you say, he's your father. Yes, I know. He left when you were ten years old. But that was thirty-five years ago, Juanillo. In a way, you don't know him, either."

"I know all I need to know. My mother told me, God rest her soul."

I could see they were going to be at this for a while. I opened the fridge and took out a frozen dinner and popped it into the microwave. Then I walked down the hall to my bedroom.

I took my guitar off the chair and sat down to practice. I had an audition on Saturday night, downtown in the SoHo section of town.

I started with some simple blues changes and scales. That's my thing: traditional blues and jazz. No amplifiers—just straight acoustic. I was really getting into my solo on "Beale Street Mama" when I heard the microwave beeping.

When I came into the kitchen, Mama and Papa weren't quite so upset. Papa looked at me and said, "Well, what about it, Bobby? Do you want to meet the old man?"

"We decided it's up to you kids," Mama said. "Your father has his mind made up. He won't see your grandpa. But if you want to meet him, that's okay with us."

"What does Margie say?" I asked.

"I'm going to call her in a little while and ask."

"That's not the point," my dad said. "It's what *you* say about meeting him."

I looked at both my parents. Here I was, on the hook again. If I said yes, probably Papa would feel I was letting him down. If I said no, Mama would think I was cold. After all, I see *her* father and mother every month when they come in from Long Island. And we always have Thanksgiving dinner at their place in Oceanside. Now what was I going to say? They were looking at me, expecting some answer.

"Can I think about it?" I asked.

"Sure, honey," Mama said, ignoring Papa's look. "Take your time. He won't be coming to town until next Monday."

I took my TV dinner out of the microwave and brought it to my room. While it was cooling, I put on an old album of blues artists that I had found in a secondhand store downtown. It was made in the 1960s. The record company doesn't even exist anymore. But there sure was some good stuff on it. That record was where I learned "Beale Street Mama" from.

The guy who played and sang it was terrific. His name was Ivan Dark. I tried to find out more about him, but it seemed like this was the only recording the guy ever made. Too bad. They didn't even have a picture of him on the album cover. All it said about him was he came from New York.

But I kind of liked the idea. Almost all the great acoustic blues players came from down South, or from the South Side of Chicago. But here was a New York blues man. I had played his album track so many times, it was old and scratchy.

I ate my Budget Gourmet sirloin tips while I listened to Ivan Dark. Then I practiced until ten o'clock and went to bed. I had a full day of pedaling the delivery cart for Big Apple the next day—Saturday. And eleven-thirty that night, at Mary's Grill in SoHo, was my live audition.

Saturday at ten, I checked myself out in the bathroom mirror. I was wearing my all-black outfit: suit, shirt, tie, and shades. I debated with myself whether I should wear the black <u>fedora</u> hat. Then I decided I'd look too much like one of the Blues Brothers.

Vo•cab•u•lary

fedora (fih DOR uh) a soft, felt-brimmed hat with a crease along the crown

But I did want to look older than eighteen. My brother Lou is lucky that way. He was fifteen when he grew a moustache. I could get away with shaving twice a week. I think it's because Lou is like my dad: dark curly hair, medium complexion and build. Papa has always had a moustache, far as I can remember.

To look at me, you wouldn't think we were related. I'm tall and thin, with straight, light brown hair and hazel eyes. I took a lot of heat from kids in school about that. "Some Puerto Rican *you* are," they'd say. Called me *huero,* and a lot of other names not too choice. A lot of them just couldn't get next to a guy named Roberto Moreno who looks like I do. Mama says there's blondes on her side of the family. Maybe that's where I get my looks.

I looked at myself in the mirror and shrugged. "You are who you are, man," I told my reflection.

Then I went to my room and packed up my guitar. It's an old Gibson arch-top acoustic. The <u>pawn shop</u> guy I bought it from said it was made in the 1930s. I can believe it. But man, does that ax have a tone—a full bass and a treble that could cut glass. Just right for blues.

Mama and Papa were watching the ten o'clock news on Channel 5 as I left. We did the usual going-out-late stuff. *Yeah, I'll be careful, Mama. Papa, I know it's dangerous out there. I'll walk near the curb and away from dark doorways. Yeah, Mama, I'll call if I'm going to be late . . . .* I finally got out the door. Jeez, you'd think I was still a kid!

I hailed a cab at Amsterdam and Seventy-ninth Street. I'd been saving my tips so I could cab it both ways. You get on the subway at a late hour, and you're just asking for it. And if you're wearing a suit and carrying an instrument—well, you might as well wear a sign saying "Take me."

Mary's was in full cry when I got there. It had started out years ago as a neighborhood place that served lunches and drinks

---

Vo•cab•u•lary

pawn shop (PAWN shop) a place where money is lent in exchange for personal property

to the factory workers. But now all the factory lofts are full of artists and sculptors. The little luncheonettes and neighborhood bars changed with the times. Now they got sidewalk tables and hanging plants inside, and they serve fancy food.

Mary's is a little different, though. They kept the old, crummy plastic-covered booths and the big, long bar. About all they changed was, they put in a little stage and a sound system. And behind the bar, they got a bunch of autographed pictures of jazz and blues musicians who played there. Some names you might know, if you're into my kind of music.

Brutus, the guy at the door, knew me and passed me in without checking any I.D. Just as well. I was using Lou's old driver's license. He gave it to me when he went into the Navy.

The place was heavy with smoke and the smell of stale beer. It's one of the few places in SoHo where they don't put the cigarette smokers in some kind of sinner's jail room. But by the late hours, the air gets so you can chew each lungful before you inhale it.

The trio onstage was tearing up a jazz number I recognized— an old Dave Brubeck tune called "Take Five," on account of it's in 5/4 time. It's the house policy at Mary's that they don't play anything there newer than bebop. I spotted Mary behind the bar, right away.

She's hard to miss. Five four and easily two hundred pounds, with a flaming red wig that was probably new when the Beatles were big. She gave me a huge grin and waved me over. "Bob E. Brown, you rascal!" she hollered over the trio and the crowd noise. "I was wondering if you was gonna show. You're on in fifteen minutes."

Maybe I ought to explain about that Bob E. Brown. See, when I decided to be a blues man, Roberto Moreno didn't sound right for that line of work. I was already Bobby, and Moreno means brown in Spanish. And because there's already a rock singer named Bobby Brown, I came up with Bob E. Brown—the "E" being for Ernesto. It sounds the same as Bobby. It's just spelled different. It's no sin or anything to change your name. After all, Muddy Waters's real name was McKinley Morganfield. ❷

I took the empty stool at the end of the long bar. Mary drew me a Coke with a piece of lime in it. "Try and act like it's a Cuba Libre, rascal," Mary said. "Don't want to give the customers the wrong idea." Mary knew I was underage, and I don't drink, anyway. But she's in the business of selling drinks.

❷ Set a Purpose for Reading
Has your purpose for reading this story remained the same?

She leaned across the bar, and a lot of Mary rested on the hardwood. "Best you tune up in the kitchen, rascal," she said. "The group will want the downstairs dressing room when they get off. You ready?"

"As I'll ever get." I didn't want to admit I felt shaky. Sure, I had played at neighborhood places and at assemblies in school. But this was different. This was *professional.*

Even when I had performed for Mary, it was in the daytime. And Mary's easy to be with and play for. It's like she's everyone's mama. I took a quick sip of my drink, then went into the kitchen to tune up.

When I came out, the trio was just finishing up. There was a light dusting of applause. It seemed like the crowd was more interested in each other than in what was happening onstage. Mary got up and announced, "Let's have a nice hand for the Milt Lewis Trio, folks." A little more clapping was all that got her.

"Tonight," Mary went on, "we have a special treat for you. A young man who's making his first appearance here at Mary's, the home of good jazz and blues. Please welcome a new generation blues man—Bob E. Brown!"

I swallowed a lump in my throat the size of a baseball and got onstage to some indifferent applause. "Go get 'em, rascal," Mary whispered to me. I adjusted the mike in front of the chair on the stage—I work sitting down—and went right into a Bessie Smith tune, "Gimme a Pig's Foot."

Halfway through, I realized I was making as much impression as a snowball on a brick wall. I started to feel dribbles of sweat creep down my back. *What am I doing here?* I thought. *I must have been crazy to try this!* I finished the chorus and went into my vocal.

That was when it happened. Something clicked in my mind. If these people didn't want to listen, that was okay. What I was doing was between me and my guitar. If they liked it—swell. If they didn't, I still had my music.

I threw back my head, not caring and sang, "Gimme a pig's foot and a bottle of beer. Send me gate, 'cause I don't care . . ." The damnedest thing happened. The house got quieter. Every now and then, when I looked up from the finger board of my ax, I could see heads turning and faces looking at me. The sweat on my back and on the palms of my hands started to dry out.

When I got to the last line, "Slay me 'cause I'm in my sin . . . .," they began clapping. They applauded all the way through the last four bars I played solo to finish the tune. I couldn't believe it. They liked me!

The next two tunes were a blur in my mind. Oh, I know what songs I did. I just don't remember paying attention to *how* I did them. All the hours and years of practice took over. I didn't watch my hands, like I usually do. I watched the faces of those people watching me. I sang *to* them, not at them. ❸

The great blues man, Josh White, said that he didn't sing songs, he told stories. And every song is a story. I told those folks my story—but in the words of the blues I sang.

I glanced over and saw Mary. She had come out from behind the bar and was standing only a few feet away. She was smiling

❸ **Review**
How did Bob E. Brown gain the crowd's applause?

like it would bust her face. She waved and put one index finger across the tip of the other to form a letter T. That meant it was time for me to do my last number. I finished the tune I was playing, and the house really came apart.

For the first time, I spoke directly to the crowd. "Thank you very much," I said, my voice a lightly shaky. "I'd like to finish up with a tune I learned from a recording by a New York blues man, Ivan Dark. It's called 'Beale Street Mama.'"

I went into the intro, and they were already clapping. I played the first chorus and went into the vocal: "'Beale Street Mama, won't you come on home . . . .'" As I did, I was startled by the sound of the upright bass from behind me. I almost missed a chord change. Out of the corner of my eye, I saw that the Milt Lewis Trio had come onstage behind me.

Then we really started to cook. Milt Lewis plays alto sax, and with the bass and a drummer added, we did I don't know how many choruses. I dropped into rhythm playing while everyone took his solo, then we all finished together.

In my entire life, I never felt anything like that. Nothing compared. Not even Angela Ruiz in the hall outside her folks' apartment. When we played the last note, there was a moment of silence, like the crowd wanted to make sure we were finished. Then the place blew up with clapping, hollers, and whistles.

Suddenly, Mary was at my side. "Let's hear it for Bob E. Brown!" she shouted over the din.

"Let's hear more!" somebody in the house hollered. "Yeah, more!"

another voice said.

"We got all night, folks," Mary said. She put a huge meaty arm around my waist. "We gotta let this rascal get some rest. Don't worry. He'll be back . . . Bob E. Brown, ladies and gentlemen. Remember that name!"

I got offstage on a cloud. As Mary led the way to the bar, people applauded as I went by. Some of them reached out and shook my hand. Lots of them said nice things as I went by.

Back at the bar, Mary drew a Coke with lime and set it in front of me. "Well, rascal, seems like you got the stuff," she said. "And if you want a gig, you got one here. Milt and the guys start a road tour in two more weeks.

"But I like the sound you made together. Can you pick up a trio to work with?"

I almost fell off the bar stool. "I don't know any other musicians," I admitted, my face feeling warm.

Mary frowned. "Bet you don't have a union card, either," she said. I shook my head. Then she smiled that five-hundred-watt grin. "Then you gotta get busy, rascal. You get your little butt up to the union hall. Tell them you got a contract here. They can call me to check it out.

"Pay them the fee. You'll have your card fast enough, if I know that local. And believe me, I know that local. You start in two weeks. I'll book a trio to back you."

It wasn't until I was in a cab headed home after one more show that Mary's words sank in. A fee? How much did it cost to join the musicians' union, anyway? But I was too tired and too happy to think about it that night. I was somebody. I was Bob E. Brown—a real blues man!

I nearly died when I found out on Monday what the union initiation fee was. I called Local 802 and spent about twenty minutes on the phone. If I drew every cent from my savings account, I was still five hundred dollars short. Half a thousand: all the money in the world!

I put down the phone and stared at the kitchen walls. Mama

and Papa were still at work. I had thirty minutes to get over to the Big Apple Market, and I still hadn't eaten a thing. I went to the fridge and saw the note from Mama on the door.

Bobby, your grandfather called. He wants you to call him at his hotel, the Waldorf-Astoria. He's in Room 1620. The decision is yours.

I took some spiced ham from the fridge and made myself a quick sandwich. There was no Pepsi left, so I got a glass of water to wash it down with. As I ate, I thought, *So he's in town, huh? Guess I gotta make up my mind.*

But to tell the truth, all that was on my mind was that five hundred bucks. How in the name of anything was I going to raise that in two weeks? I had finally gotten a professional gig, and now I was in danger of losing it. It was driving me nuts.

More to get my mind off it than anything else, I dialed the hotel. After two rings a woman's voice said, "Waldorf-Astoria Hotel. How may we help you?" **4**

4 Review
What was on Bobby's mind when he phoned his grandfather's hotel?

I couldn't believe it. I'd only walked past the Waldorf. My grandfather was actually staying there, at one of the ritziest places in town. I gave the switchboard operator the room number. It rang for a while before anyone picked up and a man's voice said hello.

"Mr. Moreno, please," I said.

"Which Mr. Moreno?"

All of a sudden, I had to think of what my grandfather's first name was. Then it came to me: same as Papa—Juan. That's who I asked for. "Just a moment," the voice said.

"This is Juan Moreno," a new voice said.

"This is Bobby, your grandson, I think. My mother left me a note to call you."

The voice warmed. "Bobby! How are you, kid? Yeah, this is your grandpa. Where are you? When can we get together?"

"Uh—I don't know. I'm home right now, but I got to go to work in a few minutes."

"I thought you were still in school, kid."

"I am. I work afterward."

"Until when?"

"Eight o'clock."

"Good enough. We'll have dinner. Get a cab. I'll leave money with the doorman. You know where I am?"

"The Waldorf-Astoria?"

"That's right. But I'm in the Waldorf *Towers*. That's the side entrance, not the Park Avenue one. Tell the cabbie; he'll know. See you about eight-thirty, okay?"

"I ought to clean up and change, right?"

"Okay, then. Nine o'clock. I'll be waiting, Bobby."

When I arrived at the hotel, I was wearing the same outfit I did at the Mary's audition, but with a white tie. I figured if I was going to have dinner at a place like this, I'd need one.

My grandfather had taken care of business. The doorman had money for my cab and even tipped the driver for me. And when he showed me into the lobby and what elevator to take, he called me Mister Moreno! I'd been having quite a different kind of life, lately. First I was Bob E. Brown, the blues man. Now I was *Mister Moreno*.

I rang the bell at my grandfather's door, and a guy about twenty opened it. He was my size and build, with dark hair and eyes. He was wearing a designer shirt and slacks, with a pair of shoes that would cost me a month's pay at the Big Apple. "Come in," the guy said, extending a hand for me to shake. "You must be Bobby. I'm your Uncle Jim."

It wasn't a hotel room he led me into. It was an apartment like I never had seen, even in a movie. "Dad!" my "Uncle Jim" called out. "Bobby's here."

A man came out of the next room, and I went into shock. If someone had given me a magic mirror to show me what I'd look like in fifty-five years, here I was!

He had a full head of straight white hair. He was thin and

over six feet tall and had a deep suntan that made his hair look silver. His eyes were the same color as mine, too. He was wearing a lightweight suit that screamed money, and a conservative tie.

As he extended his arms to give me an *abrazo*, I saw, from beneath the white cuff of his shirt, the glint of a gold Rolex. This was my grandpa?

He threw a bear hug around me, then stepped back and held me at arm's length. "So you're Bobby, huh?" he said. "I'd have known you anywhere, kid. Same as I'd know myself.

"Here, sit down," he said, waving me to a chair. "You want something to drink? Jimmy, get Bobby what he wants," he told my "uncle." "You've already met Jimmy, right?"

I just nodded. I was numb. Finally, I said, "He's my uncle?"

My grandpa laughed. "Yeah, he is. Not much older than you, though." He looked at me and

laughed again. "I've been married a few times since your grandma, kid. Jimmy's from the latest edition. What can he give you?"

"A Coke would be fine, sir."

"Sir? What is that crap? Call me Grandpa. I kind of like it." Jimmy came over and handed me the soda. I thanked him.

"What about I leave you two alone, Dad?" Jimmy asked. "I have to get downtown, anyway."

"Have a good time, Jimmy," Grandpa said. "You got enough money?"

"I'm fine, Dad."

"And don't forget. If they won't let you tape the group, I want a full report on what you think."

Jimmy had put on a leather jacket from a closet near the door. I know guys on West Eighty-eighth that would kill for one like it. "Come on, Dad," he said. "If I don't know the business by now…"

"How do you run it when I step down?" Grandpa finished. "Okay, boy. Have a good time."

Jimmy left and Grandpa focused in on me. He sat down on the sofa facing my chair and leaned forward. "But tell me about yourself, kid," he said, "and about your family. I know a lot from your brother, Lou. Your sister isn't going to see me. And your mom has to side with your father. That I can understand. You're the only family I got here that's talking to me, it seems."

I thought I saw a far-off look of sadness in the old man's eyes. I don't know why, but I started to talk. He was a good listener. He didn't break in, and I could tell from the expression on his face that he was interested in what I had to say.

I told him everything: my dreams, the gig at Mary's coming up, my feeling about being a blues man. All except the money for the musicians' union. I could see the old man was rich, but I didn't want him to think that that was why I had come to see him.

When I'd finished talking, he went over to the bar in the corner and poured himself a tall glass of tonic water with ice. He saw me watching him and smiled. "I don't drink anymore," he said. "Not my idea. It's the doctors. I stopped smoking, drinking, and eating Caribbean cooking. I may not live a long time," he said, taking a sip of the tonic water, "but it sure as hell will *feel* like it." He set the glass down by the bar. "Stay here," he said. "I'll be right back." He went into the other room.

I sat there trying to digest all that had happened. My grandpa was something else. He had to be almost seventy—sixty-five at the youngest. Yet he was so *alive*. Not like my mama's dad, who really looks tired.

And what really knocked me out was that this guy didn't have a trace of an accent. My other grandpa talks like Ricky Ricardo on *I Love Lucy*. He didn't even have a New York accent like Mama and Papa. He came back into the room with a flat-top acoustic guitar, and I nearly fell off the chair.

It wasn't nylon strung, either. It was a Martin, model D-28. I knew it right away. That's how come I'd bought the Gibson. I couldn't afford one like this. He held it out to me and said, "It's already in tune, kid."

He went over to the bar and brought me one of the stools. "No straight-back chairs here," he said. "This will have to do. Okay, play for me."

"Play what?"

"Whatever you think I'd like best. Or better yet, what *you* like best. Please yourself enough, you'll please your audience." He sat down on the couch.

I played "Beale Street Mama," naturally. I'd already told him how well it had gone down when I played at Mary's. When I finished, he reached inside his back pocket and took out a hankie that looked like it was silk. He blew his nose like a trumpet playing an A natural. He gave me a look that had no name on it and said, "You got the stuff, kid."

"That's what Mary said," I replied.

"She would. Mary and me go back thirty-five years. When her husband was still alive and ran the Jazz Stop on Hudson Street."

"How do you know Mary?"

"Give me the guitar, kid," he said. I handed the Martin over. And he played. "Beale Street Mama."

A creepy feeling came over me. Every last lick I had practiced for hours just flowed from under his fingers. Then he sang the first chorus. The voice was deeper and darker, but the phrasing was there. I started to feel like I was in the middle of a *Twilight Zone*.

When he finished, I couldn't say a word. I just looked at him. My other grandpa is a retired garment worker. His idea of music runs to old-time stuff like you hear in the black-and-white musicals on Televisa, the Spanish-language network on UHF.

"You know the record, too!" I finally got out.

"Kid, I *made* the record," Grandpa said. "If your Spanish was better, you could have figured that out. Moreno doesn't mean brown, like you think. It means *dark*. In Russian, Juan is *Ivan*. That's how I became Ivan Dark. Who ever heard of a blues man from New York named Juan Moreno?"

"But how come you never made any more records?"

"I did. Lots of them. Just not as Ivan Dark. Got into Latino jazz. It's where I really belonged to begin with."

"But you were—are so good."

"Doesn't matter, Bobby. Sure I was good. I learned from the best. They were still alive in the late fifties and early sixties. Josh White, the Reverend Gray Davis, Mississippi John Hurt, Muddy Waters. I worked with all of them and learned by watching and listening.

"But good isn't great. And those men were great. There were other young guys who hung around and played blues. They're all gone, most of them.

"A guy I knew in nineteen fifty-seven is still at it. His name's Dave Van Ronk. He had his thirty-year anniversary in the music business this weekend. That's part of what brought me to town. They had a big blowout at the Village Gate. I was there on Sunday."

"But why did you stop playing blues?" I insisted.

"I finally figured it out, Bobby. Even though my folks learned their English from Black people—that's the neighborhoods we lived in after they came here from San Juan, and that's the first 'American' music I heard—it's not our culture.

"I could play rings around lots of Black kids my age. That didn't matter. I wasn't accepted, really.

"Dave Van Ronk is a white man from Astoria, Queens. I don't know if Dave was too dumb or too stubborn to quit. But I heard him last night. And he's a blues man down to his toenails."

"And so you quit?"

"I never quit!" said the old man, sitting up straight. "I went into my Latino roots. I found a way to meld Latino and jazz music. And I did well. I've got a club in Oakland, my own record label, and I do just fine."

"I'm sorry," I said. "I didn't mean to make you mad, Grandpa." But I knew I had said the wrong thing. I got up. "Well, I guess I have to go now."

"Why? We didn't even have dinner. I can call room service. Look, kid. I don't want to lose touch with you. We hardly started to know each other."

I came out and said what was on my mind. "Look, Grandpa. Maybe it was different when you were coming up. But there's lots of kids of all backgrounds who play blues, jazz, even soul. ❺

"That's the great thing about music. It cuts across all lines today. The Milt Lewis Trio is Black; they never said anything but how much they liked what I did. Mary is Black, and she's gonna give me a job at her club. And are you gonna tell me that Joe Cocker, a white Englishman, has no soul?

❺ **Review**
How has the blues scene changed since Ivan's day?

"What brings us all together is the music. And it don't matter where you come from or where you're at. You're Juan Moreno. I'm gonna be Bob E. Brown."

The old man stood up and smiled. "Maybe your Uncle Jimmy is right, kid," he said. "It's time for me to step down. Us old guys think we know it all. Maybe we can learn a lot from you kids. If we're smart enough to listen. I wish you well."

I got up and headed for the door. "It's getting late, Grandpa,"

I said. "And I got school tomorrow."

"I'll give you cab fare," he said.

"That's okay," I replied. "The subway's still running." I knew I was taking a chance wearing a suit, but I didn't want to ask the old man for anything more.

"You sure?" he asked.

"You already gave me 'Beale Street Mama,'" I answered. "Thanks, *abuelo*." I took an *abrazo* from him and left.

I get regular letters from him now. I write when I can. The first letter I wrote was a thank-you. He got in touch with Mary the next day. He also paid my whole initiation fee to Local 802. When I got my union card, it was already made out. In the space that reads "Member's Name" it said Roberto Moreno. But there's another space on the card for the name you play under: your stage name. In that space, Grandpa had had the clerk put in *Ivan Dark II*.

I was really grateful for what Grandpa did. And I love the old man for it. But to hell with that *Ivan Dark II*. I'm Bob E. Brown, and I'll show the world I am. **6** ○

6 Review
How has Roberto changed since the beginning of the story?

Answer the BIG Question

As you do the following activities, consider the Big Question:
Why do you read?

WRITE TO LEARN Bob E. Brown discovers what makes his heart sing. Make a brief entry in your notebook about what makes your heart sing. How can you take the first step in finding out who you are?

LITERATURE GROUPS Get together with two or three others who have also read this story. Discuss the role Bob E. Brown's grandfather played in his career. Do you think Bob E. Brown would have succeeded without his grandfather's help?

HURRICANE EMILY BAD NEWS FOR ENDANGERED TURTLES

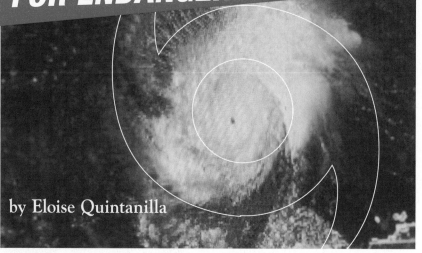

by Eloise Quintanilla

Read to discover how Hurricane Emily affected turtles on the beaches in Mexico.

Storm sweeps away 84,000 eggs on Mexican beach ❶

❶ Preview
What do the photos and the subhead tell you?

AKUMAL, Mexico — When Hurricane Emily tore through the <u>Yucatan Peninsula</u> on July 17, 2005, it destroyed nearly all the eggs that had been laid that season by endangered sea turtles on the white sand beach of Xcacel.

On the Gulf Coast of Mexico about 60 miles south of Cancun, the stretch of beach near Akumal is one of the most

---

Vo•cab•u•lary

Yucatan Peninsula (YOO kah tahn puh NIN suh luh) stretch of land that extends into the Gulf of Mexico

important nesting grounds in Mexico for green and loggerhead sea turtles. Alejandro Arenas Martinez, director of the Xcacel sea turtle conservation program, said that more than 84,000 eggs were swept away.

"In all of the 15 years I have been working here, a hurricane has never hit so hard, so early in the season," he said. The effect of the loss of the eggs will be felt several years down the line, he said, when this summer's generation was set to lay their own eggs. Arenas said that an average of 80 percent of the eggs, or 67,000, would have hatched.

A sea turtle off the coast of Mexico

Looking down at the lone surviving nest—of more than 700—Arenas sighs. "These eggs were laid on July 16, one day before the hurricane hit. Except for this one nest, every egg laid after May 17 was lost." ○

Answer the BIG Question

As you do the following activities, consider the Big Question:
Why do you read?

WRITE TO LEARN Think about the author's purpose in writing this article. In your notebook, jot down what you learned about endangered sea turtles in Mexico.

PARTNER TALK Meet with a partner who has also read this selection. Discuss how the eggs were lost. Could this have been prevented?

NAKED ANIMALS

by David George Gordon

Read to discover how some animals have adapted to their environments.

Without fur or hair, most mammals would be pretty uncomfortable. That's because a furry covering shields mammals' bodies from the weather, keeping them warm and dry—sort of like your clothes do for you.

Of the 5,000 kinds of wild mammals, only a few are nearly hairless. These creatures developed other ways to thrive comfortably.

Furless Pets ❶

A few animals, such as the sphynx cat and the Mexican hairless dog, are practically hairless because people bred them that way.

They're bred as pets.

A sphynx generally feels like <u>suede</u> to the touch. Some sphynxes have very fine, hard-to-see body hair. They feel like warm, fresh peaches!

> ❶ **Preview**
> What do the subheads on this page and the next page tell you?

Vo•cab•u•lary

suede (swayd) soft leather with a velvetlike feel

Many Animals Thrive in Their Near-Nakedness.

Elephants, rhinos, and hippos don't have fur. They all live in hot places, where the trick is to keep cool. Being practically hairless is one way these animals deal with the heat. They use mud, dust, and water to protect their skin from sunburn.

Whales spend all of their time underwater. Their body fat keeps them warm, so they don't need fur coats. Naked mole rats live entirely underground, where the temperature stays warm year-round. No need for hair there!

Hair has a special importance for some animals. If it's long and colorful, or short and cropped in different shapes, it can attract lots of attention from the opposite sex. Think about that the next time you see a male lion's mane at the zoo or a teenager with a spiked Mohawk hairstyle at the mall!

Are We Naked?

Some people call humans "naked apes." That's not entirely accurate, though. An adult human's body is covered with about five million hairs—the same number that an adult gorilla has. However, human hair is generally shorter and thinner than gorilla hair. You may have to look closely to see the hairs on most of your body. **2** ○

> **2 Review**
> What do some animals use as a substitute for fur?

Answer the BIG Question

As you do the following activities, consider the Big Question:
Why do you read?

WRITE TO LEARN Think about the author's purpose in writing this article. Then, write a brief entry in your notebook about your reason for reading the article.

LITERATURE GROUPS Join two or three other students who have read "Naked Animals." Discuss your reaction to hairless animals, particularly pets.

ANIMAL HOUSE

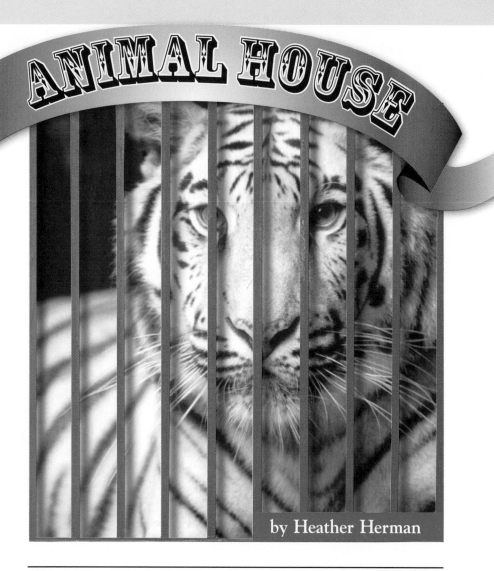

by Heather Herman

Should circuses be allowed to include animals in their shows?

Fifteen-year-old Heather Herman is fighting to free animals from performing in circuses and parades. She just might win. 1

> **1 Preview**
> What do you expect to learn about circus animals?

P eople have come up to me and said, "The circus is a Denver tradition:"—there's a neighborhood here named for

P.T. Barnum—"how can you try to stop the circus?" Or, "You're a kid, you're supposed to love the circus!" But this isn't about the circus; it's about the animals. There are so many people in our generation who believe that using wild animals for entertainment is just wrong. If we do something about this now, watching elephants, tigers, and other animals perform won't be a tradition by the time we grow up. We'll have a new tradition, our own tradition.

I've been learning and thinking about animals since I was in fourth grade, when my dad showed me some <u>brochures</u> about animal cruelty that he'd gotten from a co-worker. I looked at them and thought, *This is so awful. I want to do something to help.* Over the years I wrote letters to the local newspaper and did some research on the Web to find organizations that would send me information, like the Humane Society, but somehow I didn't feel I was making a real difference. I was especially upset by what was going on in circuses. I'd always thought animals in the circus were just like pets performing tricks. I didn't realize you had to train them with physical force and that they travel in really small cages. The trainers often do things that you would never do to your dog or cat—you wouldn't strike your puppy with a whip if he didn't do what you asked! Or leave your cat in a cage so tiny she couldn't even turn around. I couldn't believe this was happening and that nothing was being done about it.

I asked different groups what I should do when the circus came to town. They told me to go out and protest. I thought, *Well, that doesn't help the animals.*

So, two years ago, when I was thirteen, I began to wonder about trying to make a change. At first, people didn't take me seriously—they just thought, *Oh, there goes Heather again.* In the past, I had started crazy little neighborhood-club things—a church newspaper, volunteer work here and there—and never really followed through on any of them. But when I learned

Vo•cab•u•lary

brochures (broh SHOORZ) small booklets containing information about a product or particular interest

that the city of Boulder, Colorado, had already outlawed animal circuses, I thought it'd be great to do something like that in Denver. (There are at least 20 circuses touring the country that don't feature animal acts.)

I got in touch with a group called the Rocky Mountain Animal Defense (RMAD) to find out how I could get Denver to ban animal circuses too. I learned that I needed to call the city's Election Commission, which is in charge of putting <u>initiatives</u> on the ballot for a citywide vote.

I had no idea how to get a law passed, and neither did my parents. From the commission office I found out I had to file a Citizen's <u>Petition</u> and get 5,000 signatures from registered Denver voters before the initiative could be placed on a ballot. At the time, it seemed so complicated and nearly impossible. Luckily, RMAD took me seriously and they offered to help organize support. In addition, I formed my own organization, Youth Opposed to Animal Acts, to get people interested in the issue. My friends and I spent weekends standing outside grocery stores collecting signatures. We went to the local fair and collected; we went to school sporting events; we went door-to-door. (We always had an adult with us because the law says you have to be eighteen to gather signatures.) Some people were pretty rude, and would say, "What do you want, money?" before practically closing the door in our faces.

A lot of people said, "Wow, you are really young." Or, sometimes, "You can't do this, it's too complicated." But it's not; it's just that most of us don't pay attention to how the system works. It's our right to petition the government, to assemble publicly, to speak freely. We *can* make a difference! It's amazing to me that I've been a part of this, that I stuck to the commitment.

At the end of the summer, after we had collected a little

Vo•cab•u•lary

initiatives (ih NISH uh tivz) proposals for new laws
petition (puh TIH shun) a written demand, with signatures, for legal action

Heather Herman, founder of Youth Opposed to Animal Acts, gets out the vote.

more than 5,000 signatures, the commission dropped the bomb on us: We needed 3,000 more! Only about 2,000 of ours were valid. School was starting and I had marching band practice after class, so there wasn't much time to collect signatures. My friends and I couldn't believe that we'd spent all summer on something that was falling apart. Some wondered if it was worth following through.

But I couldn't give up. Even though I was pretty tired and crabby, I thought about those pictures of elephants with cuts through their skin, and tigers with their claws removed. I decided to send letters to national animal groups requesting donations so that we could hire signature collectors. We got nine national organizations to help out, plus our parents and some of their friends, with our weekend supermarket posts.

On November 5, 2003, we turned in our petition to ban animal acts in circuses performing in Denver, with more than 10,000 signatures! We celebrated at a vegetarian restaurant—

it was an incredible day. Then in January, I spoke at a public hearing before the Denver City Council. I spoke for six minutes—I've never been so nervous—and the story made the front page of the *Rocky Mountain News*. That's when all the TV and radio stations started to call and it turned into a big national story.

The vote comes up this month,[1] and I'm anxious to see the outcome. Maybe someday I will take this a step further and help people in other cities get a similar initiative passed. It would be so amazing if the entire state of Colorado agreed to ban circuses with animals. But that's hundreds of thousands of signatures, which is a lot of hours standing in front of the grocery store! ○

Answer the BIG Question

As you do the following activities, consider the Big Question: **Why do you read?**

WRITE TO LEARN Heather learned how circus animals were treated when she read a brochure on the subject. Think about how you might make a difference in your community. Write a brief entry in your notebook.

LITERATURE GROUPS Join two or three other students who have read "Animal House." Discuss your responses to the article. How do you feel about Heather's campaign? Do you think animal acts should be banned in circuses?

....

[1] Although voters defeated this proposal on August 10, 2004, it did bring great attention to the treatment of circus animals. Animal rights groups were encouraged by the level of awareness the proposal raised. They vow to continue their struggle for humane treatment of circus animals.

SHORT CIRCUIT

THAT WAS AWESOME, MASA!

YEAH, MASA, YOU BEAT YOUR OWN HIGH SCORE!

AS A TEEN GROWING UP IN TOKYO, MASA'S ON THE CUTTING EDGE OF TECHNOLOGY. HE HAS ALL THE LATEST GADGETS, AND EVERY DAY TECHNOLOGY HELPS MAKES HIS LIFE EASIER. OR COULD A VISIT FROM MASA'S COUSIN NAO CHANGE HIS MIND ABOUT JUST HOW HELPFUL TECHNOLOGY REALLY IS?

*IN JAPAN ARCADES ARE CALLED GAME CENTERS.

by Ben Shannon

What do you do when technology fails you?

111

115

119

WRITE TO LEARN
Think about why the author wrote this graphic novel and what you've learned about relying on technology to do everything. Write about it in your notebook.

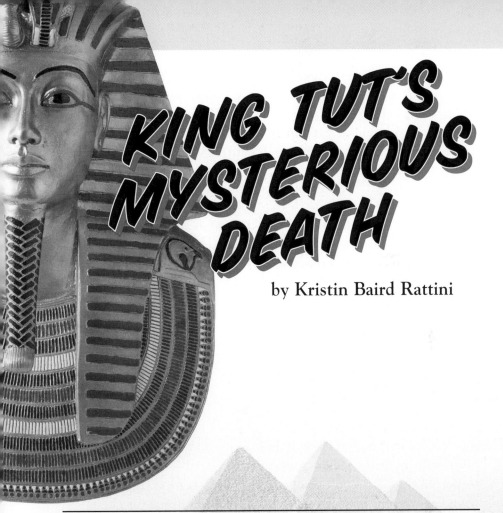

KING TUT'S MYSTERIOUS DEATH

by Kristin Baird Rattini

What caused the sudden and mysterious death of King Tut?

King Tutankhamun's army just lost a major battle. His subjects could be facing a terrible <u>plague</u>. Egypt's king probably has a lot on his mind as he goes to bed for the night. Suddenly someone leaps out of the shadows and strikes the king with a fatal blow to the back of the head. Tut's nine-year reign comes to a quick and mysterious end.

Vo·cab·u·lary

plague (playg) a disease that infects large numbers of people and kills many of those infected

That's one of many theories about how Egypt's most famous king died at age 19. The puzzle has fascinated researchers since 1922, when British <u>archaeologist</u> Howard Carter discovered Tut's 3,300-year-old tomb. Determined to find the answer, National Geographic Explorer-in-Residence Zahi Hawass used modern technology to put this old theory to the test.

The Investigation

"I was almost trembling when I arrived at the tomb," Hawass says. His team of experts carefully removed King Tut's mummy from its royal grave and placed it in a computed tomography (CT) scanner. The machine created detailed images of Tut's mummy, which were reconstructed on a computer. That way scientists could examine Tut from any angle without damaging him. The result? New clues in this ancient mystery! ❶

> ❶ **Understand Text Structure**
> In what order does the writer describe the scientists' procedure?

First Suspect

An old x-ray of King Tut, taken in 1968, showed a bone fragment loose in the back of the mummy's skull and a possible head injury. Many investigators suspected that Tut had been fatally hit from behind. But who would gain from the <u>pharaoh</u>'s death? Perhaps it was his close advisor Aye. Much older and more experienced than the king, Aye had great power. Was he hungry for more? After all, Aye did take over as pharaoh after Tut's death.

Second Suspect

Or maybe Tut's army commander, Horemheb, was the culprit. As Egypt's military leader, Horemheb was supposed to protect his country. But did the king need protection from him? Horemheb became pharaoh after Aye and removed all mentions of Tut from

---

Vo·cab·u·lary

archaeologist (ar kee OL uh jist) a scientist who studies ancient peoples by examining their material remains

pharaoh (FAIR oh) an ancient Egyptian ruler

public monuments. Aye and Horemheb make good suspects, but Hawass's team concludes that Tut wasn't hit from behind after all. The CT scan shows that the bone broke into fragments after Tut's death. The damage probably occurred when Tut's body was mummified or when Carter removed the mummy from its coffin.

More Clues

It's unlikely that a teenage king would have died of natural causes. So what really happened? Could Tut have died as a result of an accident? The mummy's breastbone and many of its ribs were missing. Some think Tut may have fallen in battle, or taken his chariot for a deadly joy ride. "If that were true, the CT scan would have shown damage to Tut's spine," Hawass says. "But it didn't." Could the king have been poisoned or did he catch a deadly disease? CT scans can't tell us everything, but the scientists found no evidence of long-term poisoning or illness.

A Break in the Case

The CT scan did reveal an important clue: a broken left leg. Some experts think the break happened just days before Tut died, which caused a life-threatening infection.

Others think Carter's team accidentally broke the bone. That makes this just one more theory in King Tut's unsolved death. Says Hawass: "The mystery continues." O

Answer the BIG Question

As you do the following activities, consider the Big Question:
Why do you read?

WRITE TO LEARN Think about the author's purpose in writing this article. Then, jot down your reason for reading. What kept you interested? Write a brief entry in your notebook.

PARTNER TALK With a partner who has also read this selection, discuss your responses to the article. Which theory do you think is the most likely explanation for King Tut's untimely death?

What makes life good?

What makes you happy? Knowing what's important to you helps you understand yourself—and others. As you read each selection, ask the question: **What makes life good?**

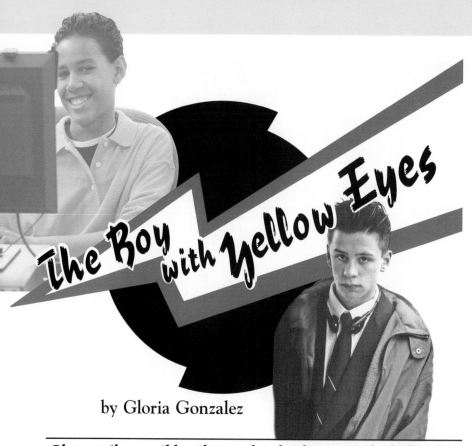

The Boy with Yellow Eyes

by Gloria Gonzalez

Discover the one thing that made a bookworm and a bully join forces.

*O*nly a handful of the residents of Preston Heights recall the actual events. And even then, years and conflicting accounts have clouded the facts.

Still, in some quarters, and especially during the <u>relentless</u> winters unique to the hillside village, the incident is spoken of with pride and awe.

Till today, if you get a couple of old-timers in the same room,

Vo·cab·u·lary

relentless (rih LENT lus) unyielding; never stopping; endless

a heated debate will erupt over the <u>mundane</u> detail of whether Norman was ten or going on thirteen. They'll also argue whether he lost one shoe or both in the scuffle.

What the parties do agree on is that it happened in Preston Heights and it involved Norman and his next-door neighbor Willie, whose age for some reason is never questioned—thirteen.

And of course . . . the stranger.

Opinions are equally divided on whether the stranger's limp was caused by a deformed right or left leg. But everyone, to a man, can tell you exactly what the Vice President of the United States was wearing when he arrived and what he ordered for lunch. (In fact, his discarded <u>gingham</u> cloth napkin, since laundered, is part of the local exhibit, which includes his signature in the hotel's register.)

The only other point of total agreement is that Norman was the least likely of heroes. He had none of the qualities that could have foretold his sudden fame.

Norman was not the kind of kid who would cause you to break out in a grin if you saw him ride your way on a bike.

1. He couldn't ride a bike.

2. He rarely <u>emerged</u> from his house.

3. He was considered . . . well . . . weird.

This last opinion was based on the fact that Norman would be seen heading toward or leaving the library, and always hugging an armful of books. To the townfolk it seemed unhealthy for a young boy to read so much. They predicted a total loss of eyesight by the time he reached nineteen.

Willie, however, was a kid who, had there been a Normal Kid Pageant, would have won first and tied for second and third. A dynamic baseball player, daring bike rider, crackerjack newspaper delivery boy—he was the town's delight. Never mind that he was

Vo•cab•u•lary

mundane (mun DAYN) ordinary; typical or commonplace
gingham (GING um) yarn-dyed cotton
emerged (ih MURJD) came out

flunking all school subjects and had a reputation as a bully; he was, after all, "a real boy."

The differences did not escape the boys themselves. Though neighbors, separated only by splintery bushes, they never as much as shared a "Hi."

To Willie, Norman was simply the kid with the yellow eyes. Not that they were actually yellow—more of a brown-hazel—but often, the way the sunlight bounced off the thick eyeglasses, it seemed to create a yellow haze.

(Years later, in a rare interview, Norman was asked if he had missed having friends while growing up. He replied: "Not at all. I had Huck and Tom Sawyer.")

To Norman, Willie was exhausting. He talked fast, ran fast, walked fast, and, he suspected, even slept fast. (If such a thing could be measured.) It was tiring just to sit behind him in class and listen to his endless chatter.

If Norman was slow motion, Willie was definitely fast forward. ❶ Which brings us to the stranger, who fit somewhere in between.

> ❶ **Connect**
> Do you know anyone like Norman or Willie?

Some say the stranger arrived one early summer day on foot. Others believe he came on the bus from Boulder.

One fact is <u>undisputed</u>: he took a room on the second floor of McCory's hotel. Not that he had much of a choice; it was the only lodging in town. The hotel dated back to the construction of the first railroad. It had been hastily thrown together to house the army of

---

Vo•cab•u•lary

undisputed (un dis PYOOT ed) not in disagreement

laborers that would lay the train tracks. Unfortunately, the hilly terrain stymied the work force and the project was eventually abandoned, leaving behind three passenger and two freight cars.

George McCory, the town's undertaker, purchased the hotel and soon found he could make more money by housing the living.

The hotel parlor soon became the common milling ground. Here you could always get into a game of checkers, buy stamps, mail a letter, or receive news of neighboring towns via the traveling salesmen.

That's why when the stranger first arrived, his presence went almost unnoticed. It was only after he was still visible over a period of weeks that others became aware of him. A tall, muscular man in his thirties with a ready smile, he made a favorable impression. Maybe it was the limp. Many attributed it to the war then raging in Europe. Too polite to inquire, the hotel regulars silently accepted his "wound."

Since the man was never seen during the day and rarely till after supper, his comings and goings drew much speculation. Local gossip had it that he was an artist who'd come to Preston Heights to paint the unusual terrain. This theory was fueled by the sight of the man always carrying a dark satchel. Some held that the man was famous. ❷

Perhaps that legend would have endured except for three insignificant, unrelated events:

1. The library decided to paint its reading room.
2. Willie's baseball coach had a tooth pulled.
3. The stranger overslept.

❷ **Evaluate**
What opinions are you forming about the stranger?

Vo•cab•u•lary

stymied (STY meed) baffled someone or prevented someone from acting
satchel (SAT chul) a small bag
endured (en DYOORD) lasted

On the day of the "incident," Norman headed, as usual, to the library. Mrs. Brenner, the librarian, met him at the entrance and explained that due to the cleanup work the library was temporarily closed.

The thought of studying in his stuffy bedroom (no air could circulate because of all the books he ordered from Chicago and New York publishers) sent him instead to the railroad yards.

The discarded railroad cars—which had been painted a zippy burgundy when new—now bore the scars of merciless winters and oppressive summers. Vandalism and neglect had added to the toll. For too many years, kids had deemed it their own amusement park. In recent times, the decaying cars had even been abandoned by the vandals. Rumor had it that rats and raccoons openly roamed the burgundy cars.

Norman knew it wasn't true. At least once a month, when the weather was nice, he would head for the rail yard, lugging his books, to settle comfortably in a cushioned seat in car #7215, his head pressed against the wooden window frame (now paneless). When the day's shadow hit the bottom of the page, he knew to close the book and head home.

On this day, the high position of the sun assured him of at least four uninterrupted hours of reading.

Across town, in the school yard, Willie stood with friends swinging his baseball bat at the air. He looked forward to practice almost as much as to the games. That's why when the coach appeared to say he had to cancel due to an impacted tooth, the teenager found himself at a loss as to what to do.

It was too early to start his newspaper money collection. Knowing it was best to strike when families were seated for dinner, he wandered aimlessly toward the rail yards with a mind to picking up some chunky rocks and using them as balls to swat about the empty field.

And so it was that he found himself in the <u>proximity</u> of car #7215.

The unusually warm weather had its effect on the stranger who now dozed in the freight car, an iron link away from #7215. The heat had caused him to discard his usual caution in return for a slight breeze. He had lifted the huge steel doors that slid upward, affording him a welcome breeze from the quiet countryside. The cool air had lulled his senses, stretching his customary nap long past its normal half hour.

Perhaps it was his two months of success, his feeling of <u>invincibility</u>, or his unconscious desire for danger that caused him to be careless this day. In any event, when he awoke, he did not bother to lower the steel door. **3**

3 Monitor Comprehension
Why is the stranger careless on this day?

Vo•cab•u•lary

proximity (prok SIM ih tee) closeness; nearness
invincibility (in vin suh BIL ih tee) state of being impossible to harm

He opened his black satchel and removed the network of tubes, cylinders, wires, bolts, and antennas which he expertly positioned in a matter of minutes. It was by now an automatic labor. His mind refreshed by sleep, he thought ahead to the coming week when he would be safely aboard the steamer that would carry him across the ocean. The lightness of his touch, as he twisted the spidery wires, reflected his carefree attitude. **4**

> **4 Interpret**
> Why are the actions of the stranger suspicious?

Norman's first reaction was to ignore Willie's sudden entrance.

"You see my ball go by here?"

Norman didn't even look up from the book he was reading. "No."

"Not exactly a ball, more like a rock," Willie said, sitting on the armrest of a seat, with his legs blocking the aisle.

"No," Norman answered.

Normally, Willie would have stalked out, but it was cooler inside the car, and most appealing of all, Norman looked so relaxed and comfortable that he felt <u>compelled</u> to ruin it.

"What are you doing, anyway?"

"Reading."

"I figured that. That's all you ever do. Aren't you afraid you're going to lose your eyesight?"

Norman's lack of response did not still Willie.

"I think reading is dumb."

"I think hitting a rock with a stick is dumb."

Vo•cab•u•lary

compelled (kum PELD) forced to do something

"Oh, yeah? You ever try it?"

"No. You ever try reading?"

"When the teacher makes me. I'd rather hit a rock. It's fun."

"So is reading."

Willie didn't buy it. "When I hit a ball, I'm *doing* something. Reading is not doing."

Norman removed his glasses and closely regarded Willie with his full attention.

"Do you know what I was *doing* when you barged in here? I was running through a haunted castle being chased by a vampire who was very, very thirsty. If that isn't 'doing,' I don't know what is."

This led to Norman's explaining the plot of Bram Stoker's *Dracula*. Willie, totally engrossed, sat on the floor listening to the tale of horror.

Norman was telling him about Renfield—and his daily diet of spiders and insects—when a distant clicking sound averted his attention.

"Probably a woodpecker," Willie said, urging the other boy to get back to the story.

Norman stretched his neck closer to the sound.

"If it is, it's the smartest woodpecker in history," Norman said, straining to hear.

Something in Norman's expression caused Willie to whisper, "What are you talking about?"

Norman swiftly signaled him to be quiet and silently crept toward the source of the tapping.

Willie, suddenly frightened for reasons he could not explain, followed closely. "What is it?" he asked, gripping his baseball bat.

The tapping was louder now.

"It's coming from the freight car." Norman dropped to the floor, his body hunched against the steel door separating them from the other car. Willie fell alongside him. "What is it?" he half pleaded.

Norman took a pencil from his pocket and began scribbling furiously on the margins of the library book. Willie noticed that he wrote with the rhythm of the clicking sound. Whenever the tapping stopped for a moment, so did Norman's pencil.

Willie glanced at the jottings, but it was difficult to make out the words. He did make out one short phrase. "End is near."

Norman and the clicking stopped at the same time.

"What does it mean?" Willie whispered, his fear growing. He had known fear once before, when a stray dog, foaming at the mouth, had cornered him behind the general store. But this was worse. Here the threat was unknown.

Norman quickly stashed the book under a seat and jumped to his feet. "We have to stop him!" he told Willie.

"Who?"

"The spy," Norman said as he slid open the heavy door and dashed outside.

A startled Willie sat frozen.

The bright sun slammed Norman in the face as he jumped from the train car and rolled underneath the freight compartment. He was silently happy to see Willie join him seconds later.

"What are we doing?" Willie asked, frightened of the answer.

"Waiting."

"For what?" he whispered.

"Him," Norman said, pointing to the underbelly of the rusted car.

Before Willie could reply, the stranger jumped from above their heads, clutching his dark suitcase. They watched as his limping form started to move away.

Norman sprung from under the car, raced after the man, and—to Willie's horror—tackled him from behind. The satchel went flying in the surprise attack.

"Grab it! Grab it!" Norman screamed. **5**

5 Connect
How would you react in a similar situation?

The stranger clawed the ground and struggled to his feet, fighting like a wild man. His eyes were ablaze with hate. His arms, hands, and feet spun like a <u>deranged</u> windmill. His actions were swift but Norman was quicker. Try as he might to grab the boy, the man kept slashing at the air. He managed to clutch the boy's foot, but Norman quickly wiggled out of his shoe. The man grabbed him by his pants leg and pulled him to the ground.

Vo·cab·u·lary

deranged (duh RANJD) insane; crazy

"Do something!" Norman screamed at Willie, who stood paralyzed with fear. The man was now <u>crouched</u> over the boy's body and was gripping his neck.

Willie, seeing Norman's legs thrash helplessly in the air, swung his baseball bat with all his strength and caught the stranger—low and inside.

"About time," Norman coughed, massaging his throbbing neck.

Hours later, sitting in the hotel lobby with the chief of police, the boys watched wearily as swarms of people dashed up and down the stairs. They knew the man's room was being torn apart.

In the hotel kitchen the stranger was surrounded by FBI agents who had been summoned from the state capital, seventy-eight miles away. More were en route from Washington, D.C.

By nightfall the hotel was completely isolated from the public and everyone heard of how Willie and Norman had caught themselves a real-life Nazi spy.

It took weeks for the full story to emerge, and even then the citizens felt that the whole story would never be revealed. (Norman's *Dracula* book, for instance, had been whisked away by agents.) What was learned was that the man had been transmitting information to a colleague in Boulder. That man had managed to slip away and was now believed to be back in Berlin. Two of the stranger's <u>conspirators</u> in New York—one a woman—were arrested and being held in a federal prison outside of Virginia.

Three months later, in a highly publicized visit, the Vice President of the United States came to Preston Heights to thank the boys personally. Film crews shot footage of the unlikely trio that would be shown in movie theaters throughout the country; Preston Heights would never be the same.

Vo•cab•u•lary

crouched (krowchd) stooped, especially with the knees bent
conspirators (kun SPEER uh torz) people who make an agreement to do something wrong or illegal; plotters

The cameras were there when Norman was asked how he had been able to understand the Morse code. "I learned it from a book," he said.

Asked how he had been able to overpower the man, Willie grinned. "Easy. I'm batting .409 on the school team."

Preston Heights blossomed under the glare of national attention. Tourists visiting the state made it a point to spend the night at McCory's hotel and gawk at the corner table in the dining room where the Vice President ate lunch with the boys and their parents.

Willie did not go on to become a major league slugger. Instead, he left Preston Heights to join the navy and rose to the rank of chief petty officer upon retirement.

Norman attended Georgetown University and went on to serve as press secretary for a New Jersey senator.

Every Christmas they exchange cards and a list of books each has read during the previous year. **6**

Norman is still ahead of Willie, two to one. ○

6 Interpret
What turned Willie into a reader?

![Answer the **BIG** Question]

As you do the following activities, consider the Big Question:
What makes life good?

WRITE TO LEARN Write a brief entry in your notebook. Describe a situation in which you joined up with someone who was very different from you. Describe how you got together and how the situation turned out.

LITERATURE GROUPS Join two or three other students who have read this selection. Discuss your responses to the selection and your feelings about how it relates to the Big Question.

Ode to Weight Lifting

by Gary Soto

How can a twelve-year-old build a brand-new body?

Tony eats apples
On Saturday morning,
Two for each arm,
And one for the backs
Of his calves.
He's twelve
And a weight lifter in his garage.
He bites into an apple,
And, chewing,
He <u>curls</u> weights—
One, two, three . . .
His face reddens,

Vo•cab•u•lary

curls (kurlz) lifts weights by using a curling motion

And a blue vein
Deepens on his neck—
Four, five, six . . .
Sweat inches down
His cheek. A curl of
Hair falls in his face—
Seven, eight, nine . . .
He grunts and strains—
Ten, eleven, twelve!
Tony curls his age,
And he would curl his weight
Of 83 pounds, but he
Would pull a muscle
In his arm.

Tony pulls off his T-shirt.
He <u>flexes</u> his <u>biceps</u>,
And apples show up in his arms.
"Pretty good," he says,
His fists clenched.
He takes another
Bite of apple,
And out of happiness
Bites the apples
In his biceps, tenderly

Vo•cab•u•lary

flexes (FLEK ses) bends or stretches
biceps (BY seps) large upper-arm muscles

Of course. The teeth
Marks are pink,
His arms brown,
And his roar red as a lion's
With a paw swiping at air. **❶** ○

❶ Connect
When you exercise, do you feel the same way Tony does?

Answer the
BIG Question

As you do the following activities, consider the Big Question:
What makes life good?

WRITE TO LEARN Imagine you are Tony. In your notebook, rewrite the poem to describe what he is thinking as he counts out his curls. Start by changing the lines that come after "One, two, three . . . " and then do the same for each group of numbers.

LITERATURE GROUPS Join two or three other students who have read this selection. Discuss your feelings about how it relates to the Big Question.

Look Around and See Only Friends

by Samantha Smith

Can one kid really make a difference?

When ten-year-old Samantha Smith of Maine wrote to Soviet Premier Yuri Andropov of her worry over the potential for nuclear war between the United States and the Soviet Union, she received a personal letter and an invitation to visit. Her tour of the Soviet Union in the summer of 1983 endeared her to the Soviet people. That fall, as a young spokesperson for peace, she was invited to address the Children's Symposium on the Year 2001 held in Kobe, Japan. Sadly, Samantha and her father were killed in a plane crash in 1985.

Look Around and See Only Friends

Kobe, Japan
December 26, 1983

I have to begin with an apology. My father helped me with my speech, and look—I discovered that he doesn't know a single word of Japanese!

Luckily, I have learned some of your language. Since I got here, I've been trying to learn as much as possible. So let me begin by saying *Nihon no minasan Konnichiwa* [Hello everybody in Japan] . . .

Until last April, I had never traveled outside the eastern United States. I had never even heard of <u>sushi</u>!

Then, because I had written a letter to Yuri Andropov, I found myself in Moscow, in Leningrad, and at a beautiful camp on the Black Sea near Yalta. I was on airplanes that took me over many foreign countries. After my trip to Russia—which actually should be called the Soviet Union—I came back to the same school and the same teachers and the same kids in Manchester, Maine. I didn't think I had changed at all, but, boy, had they changed! . . . ❶

❶ Interpret
How did Samantha's classmates change?

But today, we're not here to look back on the summer or to look backward at all. We're here to look ahead. I spent the last several weeks picturing myself in the year 2001, and thought of all the things that I would like the world to be eighteen years from today.

First of all, I don't want to have these freckles anymore, and I want this tooth straightened, and I hope I'll like the idea of being almost thirty. Maybe it's because I've traveled a lot and maybe it's because I've met so many wonderful people who look a little different from the way I look—maybe their skin, or their eyes, or their language is not like mine—but I can picture them becoming my best friends . . . Maybe it's because of these things that I think

---

Vo•cab•u•lary

sushi (SOO shee) a food item made of cold cooked rice and raw fish

the year 2001 and the years that follow are going to be just great . . .

What I wish for is something I'll call the International Granddaughter Exchange. I guess if I were a boy, I'd call it the International Grandson Exchange. But, I'm not a boy, so I'll stick with granddaughter. The International Granddaughter Exchange would have the highest political leaders in nations all over the world sending their granddaughters or nieces—(or, okay, grandsons or nephews)—to live with families of opposite nations. Soviet leaders' granddaughters would spend two weeks in America. American leaders' granddaughters would spend two weeks in the Soviet Union. And, wherever possible, granddaughters of other opposing countries would exchange visits, and we would have better understanding all over the world. ❷

And now I will say my wish in Japanese: *Sekaiju ni heiwa ga kimasu yo ni* [I wish for world peace and understanding].

❷ **Connect**
Would you want to participate in an international exchange?

Last summer, I had the amazing chance to visit the beautiful and awesome Soviet Union. I loved making friends with those girls and boys, and I think they enjoyed meeting an American kid. Let's keep doing it! Let's find a way to get some of those girls and boys to visit Japan, and America, and China, and Peru. And let's find a way for you to visit Soviet kids and American kids, kids who can't speak a word of Japanese—even kids who drive in American cars.

If we start with an International Granddaughter Exchange and keep expanding it and expanding it, then the year 2001 can be the year when all of us can look around and see only friends, no opposite nations, no enemies, and no bombs.

My grandparents are not important political leaders. In fact, one grandfather of mine was a doctor and one is a retired minister. But I've had the privilege of being an international granddaughter, and let me tell you that it is one terrific experience . . .

My father, who is back in Maine, didn't help me with the end of my speech, so he'll probably be surprised when I say, Why don't you all come back home with me and meet my friends there!

Thank you for your attention. *Dómo arigato gozai mashita!* ○

Answer the BIG Question

As you do the following activities, consider the Big Question:
What makes life good?

WRITE TO LEARN If you were going to write to a world leader today, whom would you write to? What would you say? Write a brief letter to a world leader in your notebook. You might want to show your letter to your parents and then mail it.

LITERATURE GROUPS Join two or three other students who have read this selection. Discuss the following questions: If you gave a speech to a big group of people, what group would you choose? What would you call your speech? How does this relate to the Big Question?

Roller Coaster Thrills

by Emily Sohn

Why do some people love roller coasters?

We tried to act calm. My friend Greg and I were waiting in line for the Incredible Hulk Coaster—a ride at the Islands of Adventure theme park in Orlando, Florida.

Roller Coaster Thrills

Every few minutes the roller coaster flew by, hurling its passengers upside down, whipping them from side to side, and shaking everything out of their pockets. Screams filled the air.

My insides <u>churned</u>. It had been years since I'd been on a roller coaster. "Why am I doing this to myself," I wondered. "Why, in fact, do people go on roller coasters at all?"

"Where else in the world can you scream at the top of your lungs and throw your arms in the air?" Frank Farley asks. "If you did that in most other places, they'd take you to your parents and probably put you through a <u>psychological</u> evaluation." Farley is a psychologist at Temple University in Philadelphia.

The freedom to act wildly is one reason why millions of people <u>flock</u> to amusement parks every year. ❶ Roller coasters are a major part of this attraction, and the people who run the parks keep looking for ways to make coasters taller, faster, and scarier.

❶ **Evaluate**
Does this explanation sound reasonable to you?

The new Top Thrill Dragster at Cedar Point in Sandusky, Ohio, for example, rises 420 feet into the air and travels at speeds up to 120 miles per hour. It's the tallest and fastest coaster in the world. And there's no shortage of people willing and eager to ride it.

Coaster Appeal

For many people, there's only one good reason to go to an amusement park: the roller coaster. Other people, however, would rather hide behind the closest candy stand than go near a coaster.

What separates these two types of people—those who seek thrills and those who prefer the quiet life?

Roller coasters often appeal to kids whose lives are stressful, structured, or controlled, Farley says.

Vo•cab•u•lary

churned (churnd) moved or stirred up violently
psychological (sy kuh LAW jih kul) of or about the mind or emotions
flock (flok) to gather or move in a group

"The summers of yore where kids could be kids and float down a river in an inner tube are over," he says. "Roller coasters are a way of breaking out of the <u>humdrum</u> and expectations of everyday life. You can let it all go and scream and shout or do whatever you want."

Attendance at amusement parks shows that many adults feel the same way.

Compared with skateboarding, extreme mountain biking, and other adventure sports, riding roller coasters is safe. Parents usually don't mind when kids go on coasters.

Vo•cab•u•lary

humdrum (HUM drum) monotony

Roller coasters also have a way of bringing people together. Riders share the thrill and adventure of surviving what feels like an extreme experience.

A Matter of Personality

Whether you like to ride a roller coaster may depend on your personality.

Farley suggests that, when it comes to thrill-seeking behavior, there's a spectrum of personality types. At one extreme are risk-taking people who always seek out new experiences, whether the adventures involve skydiving, mountain climbing, or even coming up with new mathematical theories. Farley describes such people as having type-T personalities. "T" stands for thrill.

At the other extreme are people who avoid risks and hate new experiences. Farley describes these people as having type-t personalities. ❷

Most people lie somewhere in between, he says.

Some recent research has pinpointed genes that may drive some people to seek out new experiences. A gene is a tiny part of a chromosome, a component of living cells. Traits are passed from parent to offspring through genes. Genes determine, for example, a plant leaf's shape, an animal's mating behavior, or the color of your eyes.

❷ Monitor Comprehension
What is the difference between a type-T personality and a type-t personality?

The tendency to pursue adventure and adapt to new challenges was probably helpful when our ancestors first left Africa and started exploring the globe, Robert Moyzis says. He's a biochemist at the University of California, Irvine.

Vo•cab•u•lary

spectrum (SPEK trum) a range of things or ideas
traits (trayts) a defining characteristic

Research by Moyzis and his coworkers has shown that a certain form of a gene called DRD4 is more common in people descended from ancestors who traveled long distances to settle new areas than in descendants of those who stayed behind.

This gene form is also more common in kids who have been diagnosed with attention deficit hyperactivity disorder (ADHD) than in those who don't have the disorder. Kids who have ADHD find it hard to sit still and pay attention and tend to act without thinking.

Genes, passed on from your parents and ancestors, may contribute to how you feel about riding roller coasters. However, past experiences and even the friends you hang out with also can influence your preference.

Extreme Experiences

For many thrill seekers, roller coasters have a physical appeal, too. You feel things happen to your body that you don't otherwise experience.

New technologies have allowed engineers to design coasters that change speeds quickly, shoot up hundreds of feet into the air, and make all sorts of twists. The forces on your body can be intense.

Amazingly, for some people, even roller coasters aren't thrilling enough.

Last year, Farley traveled to Nepal to interview people who had climbed Mt. Everest. It was the 50th anniversary of the first successful climb up the tallest mountain in the world.

"Climbing Mt. Everest is one of the riskiest things a person can do," Farley says. He didn't climb the mountain himself, but Farley has taken such risks as whitewater rafting in the Andes mountains of South America and racing in hot-air balloons across China and Russia.

Farley interviewed 51 mountaineers, all of whom had reached the summit of Mt. Everest and returned safely, to find out what drives them to take such extreme risks.

"I want to find out what processes they went through to do what they did," Farley says. "Most people can't be Everest climbers, but they can push the envelope in their own lives. There may be clues in what these [mountaineers] do."

You don't have to climb Mt. Everest to benefit from a little bit of risk taking. If you get sick of school, become bored at home, or have a fight with a friend, one good answer may be to hop on a coaster. You'll be screaming your head off in no time and sharing the experience with others! **3** ○

3 Connect
What do you do to relieve boredom or anger?

Answer the BIG Question

As you do the following activities, consider the Big Question:
What makes life good?

WRITE TO LEARN Would you want to climb Mount Everest or travel in outer space? What thrilling activity would you most want to do? In your notebook, write a few sentences to describe what you might feel during the experience.

PARTNER TALK Join with another student who has read this selection. Discuss your experiences with seeking or avoiding thrills and risks and how they relate to the Big Question.

SKATE park

by Alec Zobrame

An unlikely friendship blooms when a brain and a jock help each other out.

Later that day

Hey!

Hey, thanks, Squeak.

My name's David, and you're welcome.

I'm Isabell.

I owe you, Isabell. If there's anything I can ever do...

Maybe you can do something.

You're a brainy kid – can you read this?

Wow – it's for a big skateboard competition. Bet you could win it, too!

The first prize is a place on the interstate team!

But this has to be sent in by today!

155

WRITE TO LEARN
Each scene in a graphic novel is called a "cell." In your notebook, write one or two cells that illustrate what Isabell finds out about herself and her friend. Include dialogue.

Macavity: The Mystery Cat

by T.S. Eliot

Who or what is to blame when things mysteriously disappear?

Macavity's a Mystery Cat: he's called the Hidden Paw—
For he's the master criminal who can <u>defy</u> the Law.
He's the <u>bafflement</u> of Scotland Yard, the Flying Squad's despair:
For when they reach the scene of crime—Macavity's not there!

Macavity, Macavity, there's no one like Macavity,
He's broken every human law, he breaks the law of gravity.
His powers of <u>levitation</u> would make a <u>fakir</u> stare,
And when you reach the scene of crime—
Macavity's not there!
You may seek him in the basement, you may
look up in the air—
But I tell you once and once again,
Macavity's not there! **1**

> **1 Monitor Comprehension**
> Why doesn't Macavity get caught?

Vo·cab·u·lary

defy (dih FY) to refuse to obey
bafflement (BAF ul ment) puzzlement or confusion
levitation (lev ih TAY shun) the act of rising into the air and floating
fakir (fuh KIR) a holy beggar, especially one who does magic

Macavity The Mystery Cat

Macavity's a ginger cat, he's very tall and thin;
You would know him if you saw him, for his eyes are sunken in.
His brow is deeply lined with thought, his head is highly domed;
His coat is dusty from neglect, his whiskers are uncombed.
He sways his head from side to side, with movements like a snake;
And when you think he's half asleep, he's always wide awake.

Macavity, Macavity, there's no one like Macavity,
For he's a <u>fiend</u> in feline shape, a monster of <u>depravity</u>.

You may meet him in a by-street, you may see him in the square—
But when a crime's discovered, then Macavity's not there!

He's outwardly respectable. (They say he cheats at cards.)
And his footprints are not found in any file of Scotland Yard's.
And when the <u>larder</u>'s looted, or the jewel-case is <u>rifled</u>,
Or when the milk is missing, or another Peke's been <u>stifled</u>,
Or the greenhouse glass is broken, and the trellis past repair—
Ay, there's the wonder of the thing! Macavity's not there!

And when the Foreign Office finds a Treaty's gone astray,
Or the Admiralty lose some plans and drawings by the way,
There may be a scrap of paper in the hall or on the stair,
But it's useless to investigate—Macavity's not there!
And when the loss had been <u>disclosed</u>, the Secret Service say:
'It must have been Macavity!'—but he's a mile away.
You'll be sure to find him resting, or a-licking of his thumbs,
Or engaged in doing complicated long division sums.

Vo•cab•u•lary

fiend (feend) an evil or wicked person
depravity (dih PRAV ih tee) a way of life that ignores doing what is right; corruption
larder (LAR dur) a place where food is kept
rifled (RY fuld) searched through with an intention to steal
stifled (STY fuld) smothered
disclosed (dis KLOHZD) made known; revealed

Macavity, Macavity, there's no one like Macavity.

There never was a Cat of such <u>deceitfulness</u> and <u>suavity</u>.

He always has an <u>alibi</u>, and one or two to spare:

At whatever time the deed took place—

Macavity wasn't there! ❷

And they say that all the Cats whose wicked

deeds are widely known—

(I might mention Mungojerrie, I might

mention Griddlebone)[1]

Are nothing more than agents for the Cat who all the time

Just controls their operations: the Napoleon of Crime! ○

❷ **Interpret**
Why might other cats be jealous of Macavity?

Answer the BIG Question

As you do the following activities, consider the Big Question:
What makes life good?

WRITE TO LEARN In your notebook, create a wanted poster for Macavity. Include information on what he looks like, his habits, and the crimes he has been accused of committing.

PARTNER TALK Get together with another student who has read this selection and role-play a police detective asking Macavity about his part in a crime. Include references to the poem in your questions and answers. Be sure to ask Macavity why he does what he does.

. . . .
[1]Mungojerrie and Griddlebone are names for imaginary criminal cats.

Vo•cab•u•lary

deceitfulness (dih SEET ful nes) dishonesty
suavity (SWAW vuh tee) charm and good manners, sometimes insincere
alibi (AL uh by) a claim that a person was somewhere other than the crime scene when the crime was committed

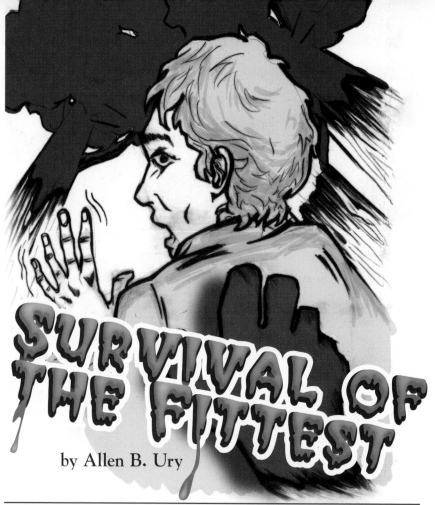

SURVIVAL OF THE FITTEST

by Allen B. Ury

A teen's first hunting trip takes a shockingly unexpected turn.

Dale Chaffin lay tangled in his bed covers. "Up and at 'em!" his Uncle Emory shouted. "Dawn has cracked and it's time for you to get cracking!"

Dale moaned, grabbed his pillow, and slammed it over his head, hoping his uncle would get the message and leave him in peace. Five-thirty in the morning was an ungodly hour for any human being to wake up, let alone a thirteen-year-old boy who'd been up till 11:00 the night before watching a suspense thriller movie on satellite TV. **1**

> **1 Interpret**
> How does Dale feel about being awakened by his uncle?

But Uncle Emory refused to retreat. Instead, he stepped forward and ripped the covers off Dale's bed.

"I said, get up, Dale! Time's a' wasting!" the big man bellowed. "Today's the day you learn what life and living are all about!"

Dale moaned again, then painfully struggled to lift himself into a sitting position. Uncle Emory <u>tousled</u> the boy's shaggy brown hair, then slapped him heartily on the back.

"There ya go, son," he said approvingly. "Now get yourself showered and dressed. Breakfast is already on the stove. I'm making eggs, bacon, biscuits, and hashbrowns. A *man's* breakfast!"

Tugging at the waist of his camouflage-colored pants, Uncle Emory turned and marched from the room like a soldier ready to do battle. And that comparison wasn't far from the truth, Dale realized. For today, he and his uncle were scheduled to go to war. But their fight would not be with human soldiers or others who were threatening their freedom or way of life. There were no causes here to be championed, no rights to be defended, or territory to be conquered. This war wasn't even about honor.

No, today Dale and his uncle would take up arms against some of nature's most beautiful and harmless creations. They would attempt to erase from the face of the planet creatures whose poise and grace had been celebrated by artists and poets throughout the ages, and who truly <u>embodied</u> the virtues of strength, honesty, and innocence. In other words, Dale and his Uncle Emory were going deer hunting.

That, unfortunately, was not what Dale wanted to do. All he really wanted to do was go back to sleep.

Nevertheless, a half-hour later, Dale was showered, dressed, and sitting at the kitchen table. Before him lay enough food to feed a dozen kids his age, and probably enough fat to clog a sewer pipe. At home, Dale's parents were careful to make sure that

---

Vo•cab•u•lary

tousled (TAW suld) messed up or made untidy
embodied (em BAW deed) made concrete; able to be observed

their son ate healthy foods. Here, at his uncle's cabin in northern Minnesota, the idea of "low cholesterol" appeared to be a foreign concept.

"So, Dale, you all set to bag yourself a buck?" Uncle Emory <u>chortled</u>, cheerfully ladling a biscuit with a large portion of gravy. "A set of antlers can look mighty handsome on a young man's wall."

"Actually, I don't feel so good this morning," Dale said weakly. "Maybe you'd better go out alone."

"Nonsense!" Uncle Emory cried. "When your folks dropped you off here for the week, I told 'em I'd make a man out of you, and that's just what I'm going to do. You're going to hunt yourself a deer, and you're going to *like* it!" ❷

"But I don't *want* to be a hunter!" Dale protested. "The whole idea of shooting defenseless animals is so . . . " He searched for the right word. " . . . so *stupid!*"

❷ **Interpret**
What kind of man is Uncle Emory?

"*Stupid?*" Uncle Emory blustered. "You ever eat a hamburger, boy? Ever eat a hot dog? Where do you think that meat comes from? Beef trees?"

"That's different," Dale insisted. "When a butcher kills a cow or a pig, he does it to help feed people, not because he thinks it's fun."

"When I kill deer, I eat the venison," Uncle Emory said defensively, referring to deer meat.

"But would you buy venison in the supermarket?" Dale shot back. "Have you ever ordered a Bambi-burger at a restaurant? Of course not. The real reason you hunt deer is because it gives you pleasure. You like to kill. And that's the part I think is sick."

Uncle Emory's eyes narrowed and he leaned his big, 250-pound body over the table toward his young, nervous nephew.

Vo·cab·u·lary

chortled (CHOR tuld) laughed in a snorting way

"Let me explain something to you, Dale," he said sternly. "The U.S. Constitution gives me an inalienable right to own and use a gun, and I believe it is the duty of all human beings to do so."

Dale looked confused. "Huh?"

"Humans became the <u>dominant</u> species on this planet for no other reason than they were willing to claim that position through force of arms," his uncle explained slowly. "When some animal killed one of ours, we killed ten of theirs. When a creature tried to eat us, we made sure to eat it first. That's how humans came to be number one." Uncle Emory folded his arms across his big barrel chest. "The name of the game is survival of the fittest. Today, it's up to every one of us to make sure we stay on top by demonstrating our dominance over the animal kingdom." **3**

"You're saying that if we don't go deer hunting, all the deer are going to figure we're weak and try to kill us?" Dale asked <u>incredulously</u>. "Like all these forest animals are going to come charging down out of the woods and go rampaging through our cities? Sorry, Uncle Emory, but I don't think so."

> **3 Monitor Comprehension**
> According to Uncle Emory, what makes humans number one?

"I'm saying that hunting is how a man shows he's a man!" Uncle Emory declared. "Otherwise, we're no better than rabbits! Now finish up and get ready to hit the road."

And so, as soon as they'd cleared the kitchen table, Dale and his uncle hopped into his uncle's Land Rover and sped off into the surrounding woods. Uncle Emory drove only about ten minutes before pulling off into a clearing and killing his engine. He then removed his hunting rifle from the gun rack mounted in the rear of the cab, checked his pockets to make sure he had enough ammunition, then climbed out of the vehicle.

Vo•cab•u•lary

dominant (DAW muh nunt) most powerful; controlling
incredulously (in KREJ uh lus lee) with disbelief

"Which rifle would you like?" he asked Dale, who hadn't moved from his seat.

"I'm not going to do it," the boy responded stubbornly. "I'm not going to murder a poor, defenseless forest creature."

"Fine," his uncle replied, his voice tinged with anger. "But you're not going to sit there all day, either. You're coming with me. As far as I'm concerned, you can think of this as a nature hike."

The way his uncle said "nature hike" was sarcastic enough to let Dale know that he felt nothing but <u>contempt</u> for his nephew's <u>pacifist</u> ideals. But Dale refused to let his uncle get the better of him. Struggling to stay calm, he climbed out of the Land Rover and made a show of locking his door before closing it.

"Can't be too careful out in the woods," Dale noted, his voice <u>laden</u> with as much sarcasm as his uncle's. "Leave a car unlocked, and those uppity animals might hot wire the thing and take it for a joyride."

"Let's get moving, smart guy," Uncle Emory grumbled, then started off into the nearby pines.

Once they were well off the road, Uncle Emory slowed his pace and began scanning the woods for signs of movement. Dale stayed close behind him,

Vo•cab•u•lary

contempt (kun TEMPT) scorn; a total lack of respect; a feeling of disgust
pacifist (PA suh fust) peaceful; believing in promoting peace
laden (LAYD un) loaded; weighed down; burdened

hoping against hope that whatever animal they encountered would have the good sense to run for its life before his uncle had a chance to squeeze off a shot.

Dale was actually beginning to enjoy being out in the cool, moist woods when Uncle Emory raised a hand, motioning him to stop. Looking in the same direction as his uncle, he saw a young deer grazing on the far side of some nearby trees.

Uncle Emory motioned for Dale to keep still, then ever-so-slowly raised his rifle into firing position. Unable to watch, Dale closed his eyes and covered his ears. But what he heard next was not a gun blast. It was a terrible growl. His eyes snapped opened and he saw that the deer had heard it, too. Pricking up its ears, the frightened animal turned and sped off into the woods at lightning speed.

"What the heck was *that?*" Uncle Emory asked, clearly upset.

"I think it was my stomach," Dale answered with an embarrassed grin. "I don't think all the bacon and hashbrowns are digesting very well."

"Well, keep it down!" Uncle Emory grumbled. "You're scaring off the deer!"

With that, the big man moved on. Dale stayed close behind him, pleased with the knowledge that even if his uncle's cooking might someday kill them both, at least on this day it had spared the life of an innocent forest creature. **4**

4 Monitor Comprehension
How does Dale's stomach come to the rescue?

The next hour passed without incident. Uncle Emory would walk a hundred yards or so, stand still while he scanned the woods for prey, then press on and repeat the ritual a few minutes later. Dale was beginning to think that the whole expedition would prove to be a bust, which would suit him just fine.

Then, while they were starting to circle back toward the Land Rover, Uncle Emory suddenly stopped short and motioned for Dale to do the same.

"What is it?" Dale asked softly.

"Shhhh," Uncle Emory whispered. "There's something out there."

Dale peered toward the trees ahead, but all he could see were trunks, branches, leaves, and mud.

"I don't see anything," he said quietly.

"Something's out there," his uncle stated coldly. "It's watching us. I can feel it."

For the first time all day, a chill ran through Dale's body. And it wasn't from the dampness. Death was in the air. He could smell it. His uncle had come out here to <u>snuff</u> out a life, and one way or another, he was going to have his way.

With aching slowness, Uncle Emory raised his rifle to his shoulder. Gripping the barrel guard with his left hand, he wrapped his right index finger around the trigger, then carefully put his eye to the rifle's telescopic scope.

"I still don't see anything," Dale croaked, his heart pounding like a bass drum. Not knowing what kind of animal his uncle was about to destroy made the suspense even more painful.

"It's there," his uncle insisted. "I can see it moving through the trees."

Dale watched with rising terror as Uncle Emory, moving with the practiced care of a trained marksman, lined up his shot, then squeezed the trigger.

Bang! The shot exploded through the still forest air like a thunderclap. It was so loud that Dale was nearly knocked off his feet. Uncle Emory apparently was equally startled, for he suddenly lost his balance and—*Bang!*—sent another shot flying off wildly into the trees off to his left.

But then a third blast sounded, and instantly it occurred to Dale that the first shot hadn't come from Uncle Emory's rifle. Instead, someone was actually shooting at *them!*

Vo•cab•u•lary

snuff (snuf) to put an end to

Ka-boom! Another thunderous blast ripped through the air. At virtually the same moment, a chunk of the tree directly to Dale's right exploded into tiny splinters.

"What the—?" Dale exclaimed, but he was unable to finish his thought before another blast <u>ricocheted</u> off a rock close to Uncle Emory's feet, creating a shower of blinding sparks.

"Seek cover!" his uncle shouted.

On the verge of panic, Dale turned and ran like the wind, finally diving behind the wide trunk of a giant oak tree. Uncle Emory joined him a few seconds later.

"What's going on?" Dale cried in terror. **5**

> **5 Evaluate**
> How does the author help you feel Dale's fear?

"I don't know," Uncle Emory confessed through breathless gasps. "Some nut is taking pot shots at us!"

"Who?" Dale demanded.

"I don't know! I didn't get a look at him," said Uncle Emory as he dug through his pockets for fresh ammo.

Bam! Another shot came screaming through the woods. It glanced off the trunk just a few inches from Uncle Emory's head, taking out a chunk of wood the size of a watermelon.

"That's no rifle he's using," the big man noted. "It's more like a cannon!"

"What are we going to do?" Dale asked, tears now welling up in his eyes.

"We gotta get the heck out of here!" Uncle Emory blubbered. Then he turned,

Vo·cab·u·lary

ricocheted (RI koh shayd) bounced off

fired off one wild shot, grabbed Dale by the hand, and sped off into the forest.

Leaves and branches whizzed by Dale's face as he and his uncle <u>vaulted</u> through the woods like Olympic sprinters. Behind them, powerful gunshots continued to blast through the air, their impacts often coming dangerously close to bringing down the pair.

Then suddenly, about a half-mile from the Land Rover, Uncle Emory lost his footing. Stumbling weakly, the big man wheezed and groaned as his lungs struggled for air.

"Uncle Emory, what's wrong?" Dale asked fearfully.

"I can't go on," the big man gasped hoarsely. He grabbed the car keys from his pocket and handed them to Dale. "Keep running. Save yourself!"

"No, Uncle Emory!" Dale protested. "I can't leave you here. You *have* to run!"

"I—I can't do it," Uncle Emory said, clearly having trouble getting the words out. "I shouldn't have had that third helping of—"

Just then, Dale heard the sound of something pounding through the woods toward them. The gunman, whoever he was, was approaching fast. Another shot blasted through the air, and Dale instinctively ducked as the bush beside him was blown to twigs.

"I said leave me, Dale!" Uncle Emory screamed. "Save yourself!" **6**

This time, Dale did as he was told. Pumping his arms like twin <u>pistons</u>, he ran across the muddy earth, leapt over <u>gnarled</u> roots, and zigzagged his way around towering pines.

6 Connect
How would you react if you were in Dale's situation?

Vo•cab•u•lary

vaulted (VAWL ted) took a running leap over something
pistons (PIS tunz) sliding plugs that fit closely inside a cylinder
gnarled (narld) rough, twisted, and knotty, as a tree trunk
or branches

Finally, he burst out of the forest into the clear-cut path around the road where they had parked. There, just a hundred yards away, was the Land Rover. Hope rising in his heart, Dale was sprinting at full speed for the safety of the car when—*BAM!* Instantly, the ground at his feet exploded in a shower of dirt and debris and Dale was sailing through the air. About twenty feet later, he slammed shoulder first into the ground.

Too stunned to feel any pain, Dale gasped for air and tried to focus his eyes. What he saw nearly caused his heart to stop.

Two beings were walking toward him. Both appeared to be at least seven feet tall, had thin, muscular bodies covered with reptilian scales, and sported oversized heads topped with eyes that hung from stalks like a snail. Both of the nightmarish monsters were dressed in leather-like clothes decorated with dozens of tiny metallic plates, and each carried a long-stemmed object Dale imagined was some sort of alien weapon.

As they approached, each of the creatures raised its firearm and trained it on Dale's helpless body.

I'm going to die, Dale thought, steeling himself. And then one of the beings—the smaller of the pair—addressed the other, its voice echoing directly into Dale's mind.

"I don't want to kill this one, Father," the small creature said in a tone suggesting its confusion. "It looks so young and helpless."

"You're right," the tall one replied, its mouth never moving. "This one is a child. We'll let it go. Better to wait till it grows up . . . and kill it then."

The creatures turned as two more of their kind stepped from the woods carrying Uncle Emory's body trussed up on a pole like some wild game killed on an African safari.

"I still don't understand the point of killing these humans," Dale heard the young one say to its father.

"It's the natural order of things," the older one replied. "It's how a Grezzemblik proves he's a Grezzemblik! Survival of the fittest!"

A moment later, a large, glowing, orange disc appeared above the four creatures. The aliens gathered themselves in a group below it, carrying Uncle Emory's body between them, and the next second, they dissolved in a sparkle of dancing lights.

Back on the ground, Dale just lay there, slack-jawed, unable to believe the scene he just witnessed. And then, vowing never to even come near a hunting rifle again, he closed his eyes and was instantly enveloped by the thick, warm blanket of dreamless peaceful sleep. **7** ○

7 Evaluate
How do you think the author feels about hunting?

Answer the
BIG Question

As you do the following activities, consider the Big Question:
What makes life good?

WRITE TO LEARN Think about the author's main purpose in writing this story. Then write a short paragraph in your notebook describing how the author influenced your way of thinking about how humans hunt animals.

PARTNER TALK Join with a partner and brainstorm examples of strong-weak pairs, such as a bully and a person who often gets picked on. Discuss how these pairs would think about the statement: The name of this game is survival of the fittest.

Learning English

by Luis Alberto Ambroggio
translated from the Spanish by Lori M. Carlson

Can you express the deepest truth about yourself in a different language?

Life
to understand me
you have to know Spanish
feel it in the blood of your soul.

If I speak another language
and use different words
for feelings that will always stay the same
I don't know
if I'll continue being
the same person. ○

Answer the BIG Question

As you do the following activities, consider the Big Question:
What makes life good?

WRITE TO LEARN What would it be like to learn a new language? Write a brief paragraph in your notebook describing some of the challenges you might face and how you would deal with them.

LITERATURE GROUPS Join two or three other students who have read this selection. Imagine you learned a new language. In what ways might you be a different person when you spoke your second language?

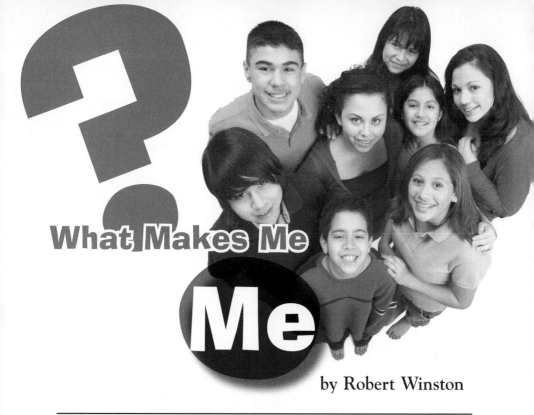

What Makes Me Me

by Robert Winston

What makes LIFE GOOD? Take this test to discover your likes and dislikes—and what they mean.

Test Your Personality

Take this test in your notebook to find out more about your personality. For each question, write down your answer as "yes," "no," or "not sure." There are no correct answers in this test—just try to be as honest as possible. Follow the instructions beginning on page 202 to add up your scores. Continue reading to find out what your results mean.

1. Do you like doing things that are a little dangerous?
2. If you don't like someone, are you afraid to tell them what you think of them?
3. Do you like having long conversations on the phone?
4. Are you good at remembering people's birthdays?
5. Would you rather hang around with a large gang than just one or two friends?

6. Are you very sensitive to criticism?

7. Do you get bored with hobbies easily and keep trying new ones?

8. Do you enjoy talking to new people and getting to know them?

9. Do you usually do your homework on time?

10. Do you feel sorry for people who are unhappy?

11. Are you good at staying calm under pressure?

12. If someone upsets you, do you usually forgive and forget?

13. Would other people describe you as shy?

14. Do you usually plan what you're going to do over the weekend?

15. Do you keep your room neat and clean?

16. Is it rare for you to get into arguments with people?

17. Do you like exploring strange places?

18. Are you scared of what other people might think about you?

19. Do you ever offer to help with the dishes?

20. Would you consider yourself a bit of a rebel?

21. Do you usually do things to the best of your ability?

22. Would you like to try bungee jumping, skydiving, or white-water rafting?

23. Do you often get angry about small things?

24. Does your taste in music and clothes keep changing?

25. Do you find it easy to trust people?

26. Do you like artistic or creative hobbies?

27. If you disagree with someone, would you keep quiet about it?

28. Would you describe yourself as carefree and relaxed?

29. Do you finish most books you start reading?

30. Are you someone who gets anxious easily?

Remember, you can answer "not sure" if you want.

What Makes Me Me?

Add Up Your Scores Below

Openness
Score 2 for a "yes" to questions 7, 17, 20, 24, 26.
Score 2 for a "no" to question 14.
Score 1 for a "not sure" to 7, 14, 17, 20, 24, 26.
Add your scores.
3 or less = low; 4–8 = medium; 9 or more = high.

Conscientiousness
Score 2 for a "yes" to questions 4, 9, 15, 19, 21, 29.
Score 1 for a "not sure" to 4, 9, 15, 19, 21, 29.
Add your scores.
3 or less = low; 4–8 = medium; 9 or more = high.

Extroversion
Score 2 for a "yes" to questions 1, 3, 5, 8, 22.
Score 2 for a "no" to question 13.
Score 1 for a "not sure" to 1, 3, 5, 8, 13, 22.
Add your scores.
3 or less = low; 4–8 = medium; 9 or more = high.

Agreeableness
Score 2 for a "yes" to questions 2, 10, 12, 16, 25, 27.
Score 1 for a "not sure" to 2, 10, 12, 16, 25, 27.
Add your scores.
3 or less = low; 4–8 = medium; 9 or more = high.

Neuroticism
Score 2 for a "yes" to questions 6, 18, 23, 30.
Score 2 for a "no" to 11 and 28.
Score 1 for a "not sure" to 6, 11, 18, 23, 28, 30.

Vo•cab•u•lary

conscientiousness (kon shee EN shus nes) showing careful attention to what is right and wrong
extroversion (EX truh vur zhun) the quality of being outgoing and happier among other people
neuroticism (nuh RAH ti sizm) the quality of being sensitive or easily upset

Add your scores. 3 or less = low; 4–8 = medium; 9 or more = high.

What's My Personality?

Some people are loud and popular, others are quiet and shy. Some people fly off the handle easily, others never get worked up. Personality is something we judge <u>intuitively</u>, warming to some people but not others, so how can you study it scientifically? Psychologists tackle this problem by breaking down personality into different <u>dimensions</u>.

The Big Five

One of the most common tests psychologists use to study personality is the Big Five test, which breaks down personality into the five dimensions on page 202. These dimensions are independent, which means that your score in one dimension has no bearing on the others.

You might be very extroverted, for instance, but quite disagreeable. To do the Big Five test properly, you need to work through questionnaires designed by psychologists. The test on the previous pages can only give you a hint at your true scores, so don't worry if the results seem disappointing.

Is Personality in the Genes?

Studies of identical twins suggest that genes do have a big influence on everyone's personality. In one major study, genes accounted for about 40 percent of the variation in people's Big Five scores, and the environment accounted for about 35 percent of the variation. (The remaining 25 percent was due to

---

Vo•cab•u•lary

intuitively (in TOO ih tiv lee) by feeling or knowing something that cannot be explained logically
dimensions (duh MEN shunz) elements or aspects

sampling error.)

You need a bit of all these personality traits.

Conscientiousness

If you scored highly for conscientiousness, you're probably sensible, reliable, and hard working. Conscientious people strive to do their best at everything and are usually very neat and tidy, though sometimes a little fussy. If you got a low score, you're probably a bit disorganized and find things like homework and washing dishes very <u>tedious</u>.

Extroversion

Extroverts love excitement and fun. If you scored highly here, you're probably very confident, talkative, and like mixing with people. You may also be a thrill seeker with a taste for danger. If you got a low score, you're more likely to be an introvert. Introverts tend to be shy and wary. They prefer being with friends they know well to being in a crowd.

Neuroticism

Neuroticism is a measure of how highly strung and emotionally sensitive you are. A neurotic person gets upset, worried, or excited more easily than other people. The opposite of a neurotic person is someone who's very calm and relaxed, seldom gets emotional, and may sometimes seem to be indifferent to the world.

Agreeableness

Agreeableness is a measure of how easy you are to get along with. If you scored highly, people probably find you cooperative and good-natured. If you got a low score, you might be too outspoken or argumentative sometimes. People tend to become more agreeable as they get older.

Vo•cab•u•lary

tedious (TEE dee us) boring; tiresome

Openness

If you're very open, you like new experiences and change. You make decisions on the spur of the moment rather than by following plans, and you tend to dip into things rather than <u>immersing</u> yourself in one hobby. People who score low on openness prefer familiar surroundings and routines, and they may become highly absorbed in one hobby. **❶**

❶ Evaluate
How useful is the information you gained about your personality?

One way of thinking about your personality is to decide whether you're an extrovert or an introvert. Do you devote your attention to the outer world of people and activities or the inner world of ideas and experiences? Do you crave excitement and company, or do you prefer spending time on your own, away from the crowd?

Vo•cab•u•lary

immersing (ih MURS ing) involving oneself completely

Introvert

If you're an introvert, you are

- Quiet and reserved
- Serious and cautious
- Sensitive and reflective
- Happy on your own

Introverts tend to think things through before talking and acting, and are good at listening to others. They are shy and quiet, which sometimes makes them seem aloof or unfriendly. Introverts do well in jobs that involve working independently, thinking carefully, and analyzing information.

Extrovert

If you're an extrovert, you are

- Outgoing and communicative
- Adventurous and risk-taking
- Confident and assertive
- Easily bored

Extroverts are energized by others. They are confident and make friends easily, and they can be great fun. Sometimes, however, extroverts can come across as shallow or loud. Extroverts do well in active jobs that involve meeting lots of people, and they make great leaders. ○

Answer the BIG Question

As you do the following activities, consider the Big Question:
What makes life good?

WRITE TO LEARN Do you agree or disagree with what the test said about your personality? Did anything about the results surprise you? In your notebook, write a few sentences about your reaction to your test results.

LITERATURE GROUPS Join two or three other students who have read this selection. Discuss your responses to the selection and your feelings about how it relates to the Big Question.

WORRY SEEMS TO SHORTEN A TIMID RAT'S LIFE

by Emily Sohn

Doctors have discovered that being a bit adventurous may be good for you.

Afraid to try new things? You might want to think about swallowing your fear and getting over it, if a study of rats is any indication.

Rats that prefer to surround themselves with familiar things tend to die at an earlier age than more adventurous rats do, a recent study found. If the same is true for people, being open to certain kinds of new experiences might help you live longer.

As babies, some rats climb all over new objects, and they tend to be just as adventurous and curious as adults. Other rats are more <u>timid</u> throughout their lives. In <u>neutral</u> situations, both curious

---

Vo•cab•u•lary

timid (TIM id) lacking courage; shy
neutral (NOO tral) between two extremes; neither good nor bad

and <u>cautious</u> rats have the same amount of a chemical called corticosterone in their blood. Levels of corticosterone, a <u>hormone</u>, rise when an animal is under lots of stress.

In one study, two <u>psychologists</u> from the University of Chicago looked at 14 pairs of rat brothers who were 15 months old. One brother was bold, the other timid. When restrained in a tube, the timid rats had much higher levels of corticosterone than their brothers had, the researchers found. The response lasted for more than 2 hours.

On top of that, timid rats in the study lived only about 600 days. Adventurous rats survived around 700 days. **1**

1 Interpret
Is stress good or bad for you?

Adventurous people might produce fewer stress hormones, too, which could help them live longer. But researchers aren't ready to recommend that you let go of all your fears. Risky behavior can end lives before stress hormones even have a chance to make a difference. ○

Answer the BIG Question

As you do the following activities, consider the Big Question:
What makes life good?

WRITE TO LEARN Do you think people can choose whether to be adventurous or cautious? Why or why not? Write a paragraph in your notebook.

LITERATURE GROUPS Join two or three other students who have read this selection. Discuss your responses to the selection and your feelings about how it relates to the Big Question.

Vo•cab•u•lary

cautious (KAW shus) likely to avoid danger or trouble; careful
hormone (HOR mohn) a chemical made by glands in the body
psychologists (sy KAWL uh jists) people who study the ways people act, think, and feel

LAUGH

by **Mark Rafenstein**

What makes *you* laugh?

Walking home from school, Melissa and her girlfriend saw Chad—a boy Melissa had a crush on—and a group of his friends up ahead. In a couple of minutes, Melissa and her friend would pass them. "Try to act cool," she thought. But as she attempted to do so, Melissa forgot one *minor* thing—to watch where she was walking—and promptly tripped on a crack in the sidewalk. The result was a world-class stumble that landed her on the ground right in front of Chad. ❶

How did Melissa react to this potentially

> ❶ **Connect**
> What would you do in a situation like this one?

embarrassing situation? At first she wanted to crawl under the nearest rock. "What a geek they must think I am!" she thought. But then, almost as suddenly as she had tripped, Melissa's "inner clown" came to life and she started laughing.

She turned to the boys and said, "What a trip! That sidewalk really cracks me up." Appreciating the puns, everyone was soon laughing—not *at* Melissa—but *with* her.

Had Melissa chosen to deal with her situation by getting angry at herself or by running away, the results of the incident probably would have been totally different. For example, perhaps Chad might not have asked Melissa to the school dance, which he did the next day after telling her how much he liked her sense of humor. Or perhaps she might have gotten herself upset to the point of becoming physically ill or to the point of avoiding Chad in the future.

It's Good for You

Having a fun sense of humor and being able to laugh at yourself are signs of good mental health. Steven M. Sultanoff, a psychologist, says that people who are able to laugh at themselves show a "solid level of self-esteem and self-concept." Such people are much better equipped to deal with all the downs life has to offer.

Laughter is also good for our bodies, according to Dr. William Frye, one of the nation's leading experts on humor and health. He says that a good laugh can speed up the heart rate, increase blood circulation, and exercise muscles all over the body. In other words, we can get aerobic exercise by laughing! "And after the laughing is over," says Dr. Frye, "you feel relaxed."

New medical studies reveal even more positives about laughing. Research says that laughter may help do the following:

Vo•cab•u•lary

puns (punz) jokes based on a play on words
self-esteem (self uh STEEM) a feeling of pride in oneself; self-respect
self-concept (self KON sept) one's image of oneself
equipped (ee KWIPT) prepared

- Prevent heart attacks by easing tension, stress, and anger. All three of these have been linked with heart attacks.

- Prevent strokes by helping to improve circulation.

- Prevent cancer by relieving depression. Some experts believe people are more susceptible to cancer when they are depressed.

- Lessen the discomfort cancer victims sometimes feel.

- Give a boost to our immune system's ability to fight off infections by producing white blood cells that attack and kill cells infected by viruses.

- Increase the <u>generation</u> and activity of natural killer cells that fight tumors.

It is clear that laughter and a good sense of humor can benefit our minds and bodies in many ways. But not all humor is healthful.

Vo•cab•u•lary

generation (jen uh RAY shun) the act of creating or bringing something into being

Laugh

That Hurts

According to Dr. Sultanoff, "Humor that is directed at others is the most dangerous and potentially harmful type of humor." Humor that insults, puts down, or mocks someone falls into this category. So do sarcasm, sneering, and cutting remarks. **2**

Another type of humor involves directing a joke or funny story at an incident or situation. Although this type of humor is usually OK because it is directed away from others, a bit of caution is in order. Sometimes jokes can unintentionally hurt someone. For example, a joke about natural disasters probably would not be appropriate to tell a person who has just lost his home in a terrible flood.

2 Monitor Comprehension
When is laughter bad for you or others?

How to Laugh at Yourself

You don't have to "study" laughter in order to learn how to laugh. Laughter is a natural reaction requiring no formal lesson plans and no rules. There are some things you can do, however, to expand your humor <u>horizons</u>.

One way to do this is to come to the realization that no one is perfect. Everyone goofs up once in a while. Instead of getting angry every time you mess up, learn how to find something humorous about the situation and laugh it off. Don't take yourself too seriously.

Another thing you can do is to learn as much as you can about what makes you laugh. Then, suggests Dr. Frye, try building a "humor library of funny books, videotapes, and props. If you're having a bad day, just go to your humor library and find the things that make you laugh."

Once you discover what makes you laugh, by all means share. Humor is more contagious than the most powerful disease. Spread it around a bit! ○

Answer the
BIG Question

As you do the following activities, consider the Big Question:
What makes life good?

WRITE TO LEARN Think of a time when you embarrassed yourself big time. How would laughing at yourself have changed the situation? Write a paragraph in your notebook.

PARTNER TALK Join another student who has read this selection. Discuss your responses to the selection and your feelings about how it relates to the Big Question. Is humor a part of what makes life good?

Vo•cab•u•lary

horizons (huh RYE zunz) the outer limits of one's experience, knowledge, or opportunities

What influences you?

Why do you make the choices you do? Sometimes your friends or what you see on TV influences you. Other times you may strive to be like the people you admire. The selections in this unit will ask you to think about the question: **What influences you?**

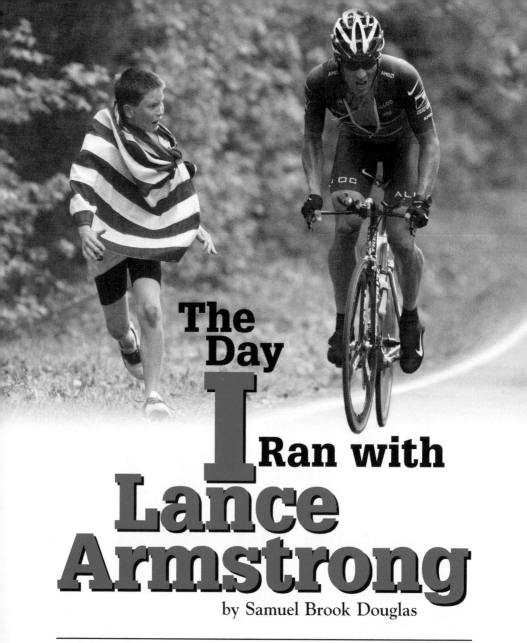

The Day I Ran with Lance Armstrong

by Samuel Brook Douglas

How does it feel to meet your hero?

My journey with cycling started very early. When I was two years old, I rode my first two miles on a bike. When I was five, I rode my first ten miles and learned how to ride without training wheels.

I wanted a real cycling outfit so badly that I chose to be Lance Armstrong for Halloween when I was eight years old.

I loved cycling so much that I even had a Tour de France birthday party. My friends and I biked all around the Berry College campus. My mom added flag stickers to our helmets when we pretended to be riding in European countries.

When I was nine, my dad, Uncle Dean, and I rode on bicycles on part of the Bike Ride Across Georgia.

When I was in fourth grade, I wrote this poem:

Samuel
Smart, handsome
I'm as fast as a cheetah
Love of Lance Armstrong and God
Who feels fearless
Who needs parents
Who would like to see the next Tour de France
Part of a big family Douglas ❶

When my parents read my poem, they decided we should all see the next Tour de France. They kept our trip a secret and told me only two weeks before leaving for Europe. I was very excited.

❶ **Identify Author's Perspective**
How does Samuel feel about Lance Armstrong?

We hiked three miles up the rocky Pyrenees Mountains to get our first glimpse of the Tour de France. We were very excited when the cyclists rode swiftly up the steep mountain.

We then followed the tour to Sabres, a small village. My brothers and I saw helicopters land, bringing officials to view the race. My brothers and I were yelling loudly at the cyclists: "Lance, Lance, Lance." Lance looked up at us to see if he recognized us and smiled. We enjoyed seeing many beautiful sights, especially the fields of sunflowers.

During the time trials in Nantes, we waited six long hours in the pouring rain to see Lance again.

We went to Paris to watch the final stage of the 2003 Tour

de France. The cyclists raced through the cobblestone streets of Champs-Elysees.

I thought that this was the end of my dream. Then in February 2004, it was announced that Lance Armstrong would be participating in the 2004 Tour de Georgia. My whole family starting chanting, "We went to France to see Lance, and now he is following us home to Rome!"

Stage three of the 2004 Tour de Georgia took the cyclists up the very steep Clock Tower Hill in downtown Rome, Georgia.

Lance won stage three, but not the Yellow Jersey.

Stage four of the Tour de Georgia was a steep climb up Mt. Alto. This was a time trial race where racers go one-by-one against the clock. We positioned ourselves on a steep incline to get a good view of each rider.

It was then that I decided to wear the American flag as a cape and run beside each and every rider to encourage him up the mountain.

As Lance cycled up the mountain, I cheered, "Lance, I saw you in France," and he answered, "Thanks!" I had spoken to my hero. I thought this was the end of my dream.

The next morning the whole world would see Lance and me on the front page of their newspapers. I thought this was the end of my dream. ❷

I was determined to get Lance Armstrong's autograph on our photo. I waited outside his team bus. Soon, a man emerged from the bus and said, "Aren't you the kid in the newspaper with Lance?"

❷ **Compare and Contrast**
How was Samuel's experience in Georgia like or different from the one in France?

I was allowed to walk beyond the barrier with a VIP pass and was given VIP treatment. I was presented with a U.S. Postal hat.

After the conclusion of stage seven of the Tour de Georgia, Lance Armstrong returned to his team bus. It was then that he autographed the newspaper with our photo inside and gave me his

water bottle. I thought this was the end of my dream.

Four days later, I learned the photo of Lance Armstrong and me would be featured in the May 2004 edition of *Sports Illustrated*.

Is this truly the end of my story, or is there more to be written? Only time will tell! Maybe one day, I will be a cyclist in a race and a little boy will be encouraging me up a steep hill. **3** ○

—*Samuel Brook Douglas, 11, Georgia*

3 Identify Author's Purpose
Why did Samuel write the article?

Answer the BIG Question

When you do the following activities, consider the Big Question:
What influences you?

WRITE TO LEARN Samuel ran up the hill to encourage the riders going up the steep hill in the Tour de Georgia. How did Lance Armstrong encourage Samuel? How do you think this event influenced his life? Write your answers in your notebook.

PARTNER TALK Whom do you admire most? Why? Discuss your answers with a classmate.

ACTOR MUSICIAN

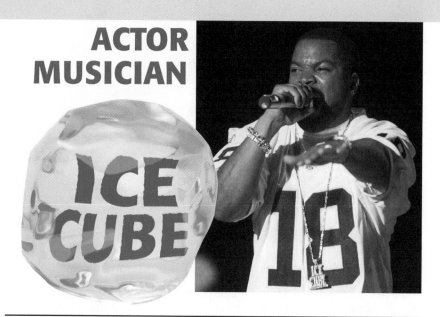

He's a rapper, writer, actor, and major celebrity. But whom does Ice Cube look up to?

by McClain J., Kansas City, MO,
and Angela R., Gibson, AZ

"**A**re We There Yet?" is his latest movie, but it's a _rhetorical_ question because the man known as Ice Cube is most definitely there—at the top. ❶

Ice Cube is an appropriate nickname for a man as multifaceted as O'Shea Jackson. From shaping gangster rap in the '90s to writing and starring in movies, this 35-year-old native of South Central Los Angeles has become a force in Hollywood. Whether you have his CDs or plan to see his latest movie, Ice Cube demands attention.

> ❶ **Identify Author's Perspective**
> What does the author think about Ice Cube?

Vo•cab•u•lary

rhetorical (ruh TOR ik uhl) a question asked for effect, not for a reply

Famous for his words and opinions, Ice Cube had this to say about writing in our pre-interview chat:

Teen Ink sounds like a great thing because people really underestimate the voice of kids, of youngsters. That's one of the reasons we got into hip-hop music: to be able to have some kind of voice, to be able to state our opinions to whomever would listen. And you have a magazine just dedicated to that, which is very smart. You know, it'd be smart if adults picked it up and actually read it. They'd learn a lot about themselves and their kids.

You know, everything starts with the writing—I don't care if you are doing a song or a movie or an article, instructions— everything starts with writing.

I have four kids, a son who just turned 18, a 13-year-old son, a 10-year-old daughter, and a four-year-old son. A lot of parents forget how it was to be their children's ages. Never forget how it was to be their age—that is the key, and remember what you went through. Remember what you thought of the world and don't forget, don't get caught up in your own age.

Angela: I'd like to know whom you admired most growing up and who had the greatest influence on you?

I was fortunate to have my father and brother with me. My brother is nine years older than myself. I looked up to both of them because they were always available, always there with anything I needed to help me get through the day, you know, living in South Central Los Angeles and trying not to get caught in all the traps it had. So I have to say my father and my brother had the biggest influence on me.

You know, I love people like entertainers and athletes but, my pops always told me, those famous people don't put no food on your table. ❷

Keep everything in perspective. You know, they get paid for what they are doing, you kind of give up your emotions for free so, you know, that always put

> ❷ **Compare and Contrast**
> How does Ice Cube compare celebrities' impact on him with the influence of his father and brother?

everything in perspective about who is really having an influence on my life.

McClain: What is the biggest obstacle you've had to face?

That's hard to sum up, but it's kind of always trying to show people that you can do it.

A lot of people love to doubt everybody but themselves, or you have to come in with <u>accolades</u> before they respect what you can do. So, growing up being in the business is always "give me a chance to show you I can do what I say I can do." That's been the biggest obstacle.

A: Do you think music (or any creative works for that matter) should be censored?

No, I think censorship is dangerous. Because it pulls out questions—who are the censors? What do they know? You know what I mean, that's really what it boils down to.

I think all art should have age limits, you know? There is nothing wrong with putting age limits on things. Categories, a rating system for movies—there is nothing wrong with that.

Vo•cab•u•lary

accolades (AK koh laydz) awards

Yeah, you know, kids do see bad things when it comes to art and media, but that don't necessarily make them bad people in the end.

Censorship is bad because you have people censoring people, and what do they know?

M: What is the biggest <u>misconception</u> about being Ice Cube and who are some of the big influences on your film career?

The biggest misconception is that I am just Ice Cube. Ice Cube is my ego. Ice Cube's my nickname. People real close to me don't call me Ice Cube, you know what I mean?

So, always the misconception is, you know, I am what I put out only. I am not saying that's not a part of me. It is, but it's not the only part of me. It's the part that I have to put out, you know. So, that's the biggest misconception.

Influences as far as my film career, people like John Singleton, he directed *Boyz in the Hood, Shaft,* and *2 Fast 2 Furious.* He put me in my first movie. He told me to write movies. He said, "You can write a rap, you can write a movie." That kind of opened up a door in my head; I never even thought about it like that, you know. So, he is a big influence on me. He is the one who planted the seed in me that's kind of grown into what it is now. He is the one that I give all the credit to when it comes to my film career. That's where it started. **3**

3 Distinguish Fact from Opinion
Which part of Ice Cube's response contains facts?

A: All right. So, growing up, was there any one experience that really shaped or influenced your life?

I had a half-sister who got killed in 1981. And I was just 12, so that was my wake-up call in life, and what it is really about, you know.

Gotta prevent stuff from happening to you. You know, that's

Vo•cab•u•lary

misconception (mis kuhn SEP shun) a misunderstanding

what youngsters and adults have to think about. Not "Oh, if this happens I'm going to do this," but preventing it from happening to you. So, you have to be alert about your life and which way it is going.

A: I'm a real bookaholic and read all the time. My favorite book so far is *The Human Stain* by Philip Roth or perhaps *Crime and Punishment*. What are a couple of books you think every teenager should read?

You know, I'm more of a pick-up-the-newspaper kind of guy. You know, a *Newsweek*, *Time* magazine type of guy. I think reading is important in any form. I think a person who's trying to learn to like reading should start off reading about a topic they are interested in, or a person they are interested in.

One of the first books I ever read was *The Autobiography of Malcolm X*. I read it because I had heard about him so much, and I wanted to know who this dude was. So, it was something I was interested in, and it kept me reading.

The key is to find something that clicks in you and makes you love to read. So start off with the thing you are interested in. I mean if you like sports, go get the sports pages and read up on what happened last night. Read about it instead of letting the ESPN man tell you what happened. That's going to get you used to liking reading. ○

Answer the BIG Question

When you do the following activities, consider the Big Question:
What influences you?

WRITE TO LEARN List the influences in Ice Cube's life and their impact on him in your notebook.

PARTNER TALK Join with a classmate who has read this selection. Take turns playing the role of reporter and celebrity. Interview each other about the people who have had the strongest influence on you.

third down and forever

☆ ☆ ☆ ☆ ☆ ☆ ☆ ☆ ☆ ☆ ☆

When your future's at stake, can you find the courage to speak up for yourself?

by Douglas Holgate

"HEY KIDDO, YOU PLAYED A GREAT GAME TODAY."

"NOTHING LIKE A FOURTH-QUARTER COMEBACK HUH? SIGN OF A TRUE CHAMPION!"

"ESPECIALLY IN A BIG CONFERENCE GAME LIKE THAT."

"THANKS DAD. YEAH IT WAS OKAY... THOUGH WE WOULDN'T HAVE BEEN IN THAT SITUATION IF I WAS CONCENTRATING."

"I SHOULD HAVE LOOKED OFF PAT MORE ON THAT THIRD-QUARTER INTERCEPTION."

"...AND I HADN'T COUNTED ON THE BLITZ COMING AT ME FROM THE LEFT SIDE SO IT HURRIED MY THROW A LITTLE."

...IT WAS PRETTY BASIC STUFF.

YEAH, BUT YOU PULLED IT OUT IN THE END. AND THAT'S WHAT COUNTS, RIGHT?

"*SIGH*...QUARTERBACK OF THE HIGH SCHOOL FOOTBALL TEAM...EVERYONE EXPECTS YOU TO BE THIS BIG SUPERSTAR WHO'S GOING PLACES, BUT YOU CAN'T EVEN COME STRAIGHT WITH YOUR PARENTS."

"GOING TO COLLEGE TO PLAY FOOTBALL IS TOO EASY AND GOING TO COLLEGE TO STUDY ART WOULD BE COMPLETELY OUT OF THE QUESTION."

"BUT I'VE GOT BIGGER PLANS THAN GOING TO BUSINESS SCHOOL AND BEING STUCK IN THE SAME TINY HARDWARE STORE I'VE BEEN IN THE LAST 17 YEARS!"

"GEEZ. HOW HARD CAN IT BE TO TELL THEM THAT? IT'S NOT THAT BIG A DEAL, IS IT?"

"HAH! OF COURSE IT IS! DAD'S ALREADY MADE HIS MIND UP AND ART AND FOOTBALL ARE CERTAINLY NOT IN MY NEAR FUTURE."

"MAYBE THE FLYER DESIGNS I'VE DONE WILL CHANGE HIS MIND. I DON'T THINK HE EVEN REALIZES THE REASON IT'S BEEN SO BUSY LATELY."

"YES! BRILLIANT!... WAY TO PROVE A POINT, SHAUN. YOU'RE A GENIUS!"

SIGH

"I'M PROBABLY NOT EVEN THAT GOOD...SO I DON'T KNOW WHY I'M EVEN BOTHERING."

"EXACTLY!"

HEY! SHAUN!!

SO HAVE YOU TOLD THEM YET?

I'M PROBABLY NOT EVEN THAT GOOD...

...SO LET'S STOP TALKING ABOUT IT!!!

HE GAVE YOU THE "GRAB THE BULL BY THE HORNS," "OPPORTUNITY ONLY COMES ALONG ONCE," TALK AGAIN, DIDN'T HE?

OH BOY. DID YOU TELL HIM ABOUT THE FLYERS?

...NOT YET.

MAN...WHAT IS WRONG WITH YOU?! YOU'RE BIGGER AND BETTER THAN "HARDWARE GUY"...

YOU KNOW IT. I KNOW IT.

I KNOW I KNOW! I JUST FEEL BAD, OKAY? HE'S GOT ALL THESE PLANS THAT HE'S BEEN LOOKING FORWARD TO FOR YEARS!

...AND TELLING HIM "BAD LUCK DAD, I DON'T WANT TO FOLLOW YOUR DREAM BECAUSE I WANT TO GO STUDY SOMETHING YOU FIND COMPLETELY POINTLESS," ISN'T EXACTLY GOING TO CUT IT!

I DON'T THINK HE'D EVEN GO FOR ME PLAYING FOOTBALL IN COLLEGE, LET ALONE STUDYING ART!

HMM, THIS CERTAINLY IS ONE OF LIFE'S GREAT BRAIN-TEASERS.

COME ON. LETS GO GET A SODA OR SOMETHING...I HAVE TO GET HOME SOON FOR DINNER.

HEY! CAN I LOOK AT YOUR SKETCHBOOK AGAIN WHEN WE GET THERE?

1993...

WOW! YOU'RE A GREAT DRAWER. YOU COULD BE FAMOUS ONE DAY!

THANKS!

1996...

I RECKON YOU'LL EVEN BE GOOD ENOUGH TO DRAW HULK ONE DAY!

I'D PREFER BATMAN!

1998...

DANG! HOW DO YOU MAKE IT SO LIFELIKE?!

1999...

I CAN SEE YOUR WORK HANGING HERE ONE DAY, MAN!

TRUST ME.

2001...

DUDE, HOW CRAZY WAS JACKSON POLLOCK?

MENTAL. BUT BRILLIANT!

2003...

IF I BEAT YOU, YOU TALK TO MR. PARKS!

NEVER!

TODAY...

SO YOU SEE. I'M LIKE SOME KIND OF UNCEASING MOTIVATIONAL DOOM ROBOT! YOU JUST CAN'T WIN.

AH HECK. IT'S ALMOST 6:30. I BETTER HEAD HOME. I'LL SEE YOU TOMORROW, MAN!

CHANGING THE SUBJECT WILL GET YOU NOWHERE, HUMAN! BEGONE FROM MY SIGHT!

209

THE NEXT DAY...

OKAY – HIT THE CHANGE ROOM BOYS! GREAT PRACTICE!

DON'T FORGET. WE HAVE ANOTHER BIG GAME THIS WEEKEND.

AND I'VE ALSO BEEN TOLD THERE WILL BE SOME SCOUTS IN THE CROWD, SO SOME BIG INCENTIVES TO REALLY PLAY WELL.

JUST DO IT SHAUN!!!

HEH. YOU'RE CRAZY MAN.

HEY!

WHAT ARE YA? CHICKEN?!

WHATS THAT GUY'S PROBLEM!? HE'S LUCKY WE DON'T GO UP THERE. DISRESPECT MAN. I CAN'T STAND IT!

GEEZ PAT, LEAVE HIM ALONE. HE'S JUST KIDDING AROUND.

DUDE, WHY ARE YOU EVEN FRIENDS WITH THAT GUY?

EXACTLY! LISTEN TO KANOA! YOU'RE POPULAR, MAN, YOU CAN HANG OUT WITH ANYONE!

BUT YOU CHOOSE TO HANG OUT WITH HIM!?

DOOMBOT COMMANDS IT!

BACK OFF PAT! YOU DON'T EVEN KNOW HIM!

YEAH? WELL I KNOW HE'S A LOSER. AND ONLY LOSERS HANG OUT WITH LOSERS. SO ENJOY!

YEAH... WHATEVER.

AND I WONDER WHY I QUESTION DOING THIS INSTEAD OF HELPING OUT MY DAD?

HOLA SEÑOR!! WHAT DO YOU THINK OF MY POSTERS??

YOU LIKE THAT THING AT THE BOTTOM? IT'S A FIGHTING MUDCAT!!!

I LOVE THEM. THE OTHER GUYS? NOT SO MUCH.

BAH! THEY WOULDN'T KNOW ART IF IT KICKED THEM IN THE FACE.

YOU DO REALIZE THOUGH THAT A 'FIGHTING MUDCAT' IS A CATFISH. NOT A CAT WITH BOXING GLOVES COVERED IN DIRT?

WHAT?! NO! YOU'RE KIDDING, RIGHT?

DO YOU THINK THAT'S WHY THEY DIDN'T LIKE MY POSTER?

HAH! YEAH, MAN – I WOULDN'T BE SURPRISED.

ANYWAY! YOU GOT YOUR STUFF? LET'S GO CHECK OUT WHAT'S ON AT THE MOVIES.

COOL! I GOTTA GO CHANGE. MEET YOU BACK HERE IN ABOUT TEN MINUTES?

WORD!

WHAT KIND OF MASCOT IS A CATFISH ANYWAY?!

BANG!

HOME 10 GUESTS 2

ALL ON 2 DOWN 4 YDS TO GO 2 QTR 4

TWEET!

THAT'S THE GAME, BOYS!

13

"WELL THAT'S THAT THEN. I GUESS DAD WAS RIGHT. JUST A HOBBY. NO WAY I'M GETTING ANYWHERE WITH A LOSS..."

"...SO NOW I DON'T EVEN HAVE FOOTBALL TO FALL BACK ON. LOOKS LIKE IT'S BUSINESS SCHOOL AND HARDWARE FROM NOW ON, BUDDY!"

"CONGRATULATIONS!"

MR. THOMAS?

HI... MY NAME IS JOHN FRANKS, I'M WITH MIDWAY U.

YOU PLAYED A GREAT GAME OUT THERE TODAY. YOU SHOULD BE PROUD. YOU REALLY HELD THE TEAM TOGETHER.

OH...THANKS. SORRY I COULDN'T HOLD THEM TOGETHER FOR A WIN.

OH, I'M NOT REALLY CONCERNED WITH THE RESULT, SON.

WHAT I **AM** IMPRESSED WITH IS YOUR COMPOSURE AND ATTITUDE UNDER THAT PRESSURE.

SO MUCH SO THAT I'D LIKE TO GIVE YOU SOME INFORMATION ON WHAT MIDWAY HAS TO OFFER YOU.

OH!

"I THINK YOU COULD HAVE A REALLY GREAT FUTURE WITH US."

MIDWAY U
The finest arts curriculum in the country

Education
Excellence
Experience

"...AND IF YOU WOULDN'T MIND, I'D LIKE TO COME AROUND AND ALSO HAVE A CHAT WITH YOUR PARENTS ABOUT EVERYTHING THAT'S INVOLVED."

S...SURE!

12

END.

WRITE TO LEARN
Who has a stronger influence in your life: your friends or your parents? In your notebook, write about which group influences you more and why.

DEALING WITH
PEER
PRESSURE

by Kevin J. Took, M.D.

Peer pressure: Can you turn it around?

Dealing with Peer Pressure

"**C**ome on! ALL of us are cutting math. Who wants to go take that quiz? We're going to take a walk and get lunch instead. Let's go!" says the coolest kid in your class. Do you do what you know is right and go to math class, quiz and all? Or do you give in and go with them?

As you grow older, you'll be faced with some challenging decisions. Some don't have a clear right or wrong answer—like should you play soccer or field hockey? Other decisions involve serious moral questions, like whether to cut class, try cigarettes, or lie to your parents.

Making decisions on your own is hard enough, but when other people get involved and try to pressure you one way or another it can be even harder. People who are your age, like your classmates, are called peers. When they try to influence how you act, to get you to do something, it's called peer pressure. It's something everyone has to deal with—even adults. Let's talk about how to handle it. ❶

Defining Peer Pressure

Peers influence your life, even if you don't realize it, just by spending time with you. You learn from them, and they learn from you. It's only human nature to listen to and learn from other people in your age group.

> ❶ **Identify Author's Purpose**
> Why did the author write this article?

Peers can have a positive influence on each other. Maybe another student in your science class taught you an easy way to remember the planets in the solar system, or someone on the soccer team taught you a cool trick with the ball. You might admire a friend who is always a good sport and try to be more like him or her. Maybe you got others excited about your new favorite book, and now everyone's reading it. These are examples of how peers positively influence each other every day.

Sometimes peers influence each other in negative ways. For example, a few kids in school might try to get you to cut class with them, your soccer friend might try to convince you to be mean to another player and never pass her the ball, or a kid in

the neighborhood might want you to shoplift with him.

Why Do People Give In to Peer Pressure?

Some kids give in to peer pressure because they want to be liked, to fit in, or because they worry that other kids may make fun of them if they don't go along with the group. Others may go along because they are curious to try something new that others are doing. The idea that "everyone's doing it" may influence some kids to leave their better judgment, or their common sense, behind.

How to Walk Away from Peer Pressure

It is tough to be the only one who says "no" to peer pressure, but you can do it. Paying attention to your own feelings and beliefs about what is right and wrong can help you know the right thing to do. Inner strength and self-confidence can help you stand firm, walk away, and resist doing something when you know better.

It can really help to have at least one other peer, or friend, who is willing to say "no," too. This takes a lot of the power out of peer pressure and makes it much easier to resist. It's great to have friends with values similar to yours who will back you up when you don't want to do something. ❷

❷ **Distinguish Fact from Opinion** Is most of this article based on fact or opinion?

You've probably had a parent or teacher advise you to "choose your friends wisely." Peer pressure is a big reason why they say this. If you choose friends who don't use drugs, cut class, smoke cigarettes, or lie to their parents, then you probably won't do these things either, even if other kids do. ❸ Try to help a friend who's having trouble resisting peer pressure. It can be powerful for one kid to join another by simply saying, "I'm with you—let's go."

> ❸ **Analyze Persuasive Techniques**
> How does the writer try to convince you to resist peer pressure?

Even if you're faced with peer pressure while you're alone, there are still things you can do. You can simply stay away from peers who pressure you to do stuff you know is wrong. You can tell them "no" and walk away. Better yet, find other friends and classmates to pal around with.

If you continue to face peer pressure and you're finding it difficult to handle, talk to someone you trust. Don't feel guilty if you've made a mistake or two. Talking to a parent, teacher, or school counselor can help you feel much better and prepare you for the next time you face peer pressure.

Powerful, Positive Peer Pressure

Peer pressure is not always a bad thing. For example, positive peer pressure can be used to pressure bullies into acting better toward other kids. If enough kids get together, peers can pressure each other into doing what's right! ○

Answer the BIG Question

When you do the following activities, consider the Big Question:
What influences you?

WRITE TO LEARN Think of a time you were positively influenced by a peer. Think of a time someone tried to pressure you into doing something you shouldn't. Write a paragraph in your notebook explaining each situation and how you handled it.

PARTNER TALK Meet with a classmate who has read this selection. Share your ideas of how peer pressure can be a positive thing.

Thanking the Birds

by Joseph Bruchac

Share an Apache man's wisdom about the gifts of the earth.

One day 30 years ago, Swift Eagle, an <u>Apache</u> man, visited some friends on the Onondaga Indian Reservation in central New York. While he was out walking, he heard sounds of boys playing in the bushes.

"There's another one. Shoot it!" said one of the boys.

When he pushed through the brush to see what was happening, he found that they had been shooting small birds with a BB gun. They had already killed a chickadee, a robin, and several blackbirds. The boys looked up at him, uncertain what he was going to do or say.

There are several things that a non-Indian bird lover might have done: given a stern lecture on the evil of killing birds; threatened to tell the boys' parents on them for doing something they had been told not to do; or even spanked them. Swift Eagle, however, did something else.

"Ah," he said, "I see you have been hunting. Pick up your game and come with me."

Vo•cab•u•lary

Apache (uh PA chee) a member of a group of Native American peoples of the Southwestern United States

He led the boys to a place where they could make a fire and cook the birds. He made sure they said a "thank you" to the spirits of the birds before eating them, and as they ate he told stories. It was important, he said, to be thankful to the birds for the gifts of their songs, their feathers, and their bodies as food. The last thing he said to them they never forgot—for it was one of those boys who told me this story many years later: "You know, our Creator gave the gift of life to everything that is alive. Life is a very sacred thing. But our Creator knows that we have to eat to stay alive. That is why it is permitted to hunt to feed ourselves and our people. So I understand that you boys must have been very, very hungry to kill those little birds." ❶

I have always liked that story, for it illustrates several things. Although there was a wide range of customs, life-ways, and languages—in pre-Columbian times more than 400 different languages were spoken on the North American continent—many close similarities existed between virtually all of the Native American peoples. Thus ideas held by an Apache from the Southwest fitted into the lives and traditions of Onondagas in the Northeast.

> ❶ **Analyze Persuasive Techniques**
> How does Swift Eagle persuade the boys to change their ways?

Vo·cab·u·lary

pre-Columbian (pree cuh LUHM bee uhn) before Columbus arrived in America

One of these ideas, expressed in Swift Eagle's words to the boys, was the continent-wide belief that mankind depended on the natural world for survival, on the one hand, and had to respect it and remain in right relationship with it, on the other...

As the <u>anecdote</u> about Swift Eagle also shows, the children were taught the values of their culture through example and stories. Instead of scolding or lecturing them, Swift Eagle showed the boys how to build a fire and cook the game they had shot, giving the songbirds the same respect he would have given a rabbit or deer. He told stories that pointed out the value of those birds as living beings. The <u>ritual</u> activity of making the fire, thanking the spirit of the birds, hearing the stories, and then eating the game they had killed taught the boys more than a hundred stern lectures would have done, and the lesson stayed with them all their lives. **2** ○

> **2 Distinguish Fact from Opinion**
> Is this statement about the boys a fact, or is it the author's opinion?

Answer the BIG Question

When you do the following activities, consider the Big Question:
What influences you?

WRITE TO LEARN How did Swift Eagle try to change the boys' minds about hunting birds? Do you think they learned their lesson? Write down your answers in your notebook.

LITERATURE GROUPS Join with two or three classmates who have read the selection. Talk about a time when an adult influenced your behavior and how he or she did it.

Vo·cab·u·lary

anecdote (AN eck doht) a short, amusing story
ritual (RICH oo uhl) according to religious law or social custom

JIMMY JET AND HIS TV SET

by Shel Silverstein

Poor Jimmy Jet is so influenced by TV that the unthinkable happens.

I'll tell you the story of Jimmy Jet—
And you know what I tell you is true.
He loved to watch his TV set
Almost as much as you.

He watched all day, he watched all night
Till he grew pale and lean,
From "The Early Show" to "The Late Late Show"
And all the shows between.

He watched till his eyes were frozen wide,
And his bottom grew into his chair.
And his chin turned into a tuning dial,
And antennae grew out of his hair.

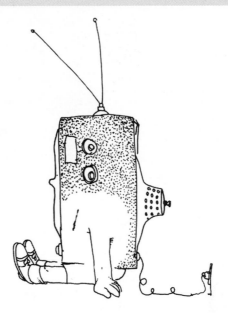

And his brains turned into TV tubes,
And his face to a TV screen.
And two knobs saying "VERT." and "HORIZ."
Grew where his ears had been. ❶

And he grew a plug that looked like a tail
So we plugged in little Jim.
And now instead of him watching TV
We all sit around and watch him. ○

❶ **Identify Author's Purpose**
Why do you think this poet wrote this poem?

Answer the **BIG** Question

When you do the following activities, consider the Big Question:
What influences you?

WRITE TO LEARN Watching too much TV can affect a person's health. Write a brief entry in your notebook answering the question: How can watching TV negatively affect your health?

PARTNER TALK Meet with a classmate who has read the selection. Discuss your entries and the ways in which TV affects your lives.

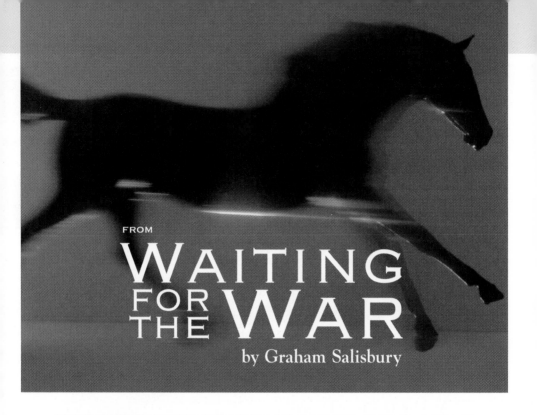

FROM

WAITING
FOR
THE WAR

by Graham Salisbury

Two young men reach out across cultures, but one of them may soon be facing his own death.

A young Hawaiian boy named Henry has just bought a horse. He can't ride the horse, and now he begins to wonder why he bought it. In addition, Henry must pay for the horse's upkeep. To earn money, Henry and his friend Sammy hop on a bus to Hotel Street in downtown Honolulu where they shine shoes. On the bus, Henry and Sammy meet an American soldier.

Every bus at every stop on every day was always sweaty full. But they squeezed onto it anyway, rode standing up, packing in like Vienna sausages. Mostly local people were on it, but there were also some war workers and a few military guys, who all looked young, some almost as young as Henry and Sammy.

One guy on the bus was crammed up close to Henry. He was snappy clean in his khaki uniform. Army guy, probably from Schofield. Henry liked his hat, tilted to the side like it was. The guy caught Henry looking and dipped his chin, Hello.

Henry turned away.

Later Henry glanced at him again. He guessed the guy was probably about nineteen. He had dark hair, almost black. And blue eyes. Henry hadn't seen that very often, black hair and blue eyes.

"Howdy," the army guy said to Henry. The guy was just trying to be friendly.

Henry didn't know what to do.

"My name's Mike," the guy said.

Sammy, who was standing right behind Henry, let out a small scoffing sound that said, *Can you believe this joker is talking to us?*

Henry looked down at his feet.

They rode for thirty minutes more in silence. Once the driver stopped the bus and got out and smoked a cigarette. The drivers did things like that because they had so many customers they didn't care anymore how they treated them, and everyone waited on the bus, afraid to get off and lose their place. When he was done, the driver got back on and continued on toward Honolulu.

Half the people on the bus got off on Hotel Street, Henry and Sammy among them. And Mike, who went off by himself. Funny he was by himself, Henry thought. Mostly those guys went around in packs.

"He likes you," Sammy whispered.

"Shuddup. You're sick, you know? You need help."

"Yeah, yeah."

They walked around. It was hot, the street sending up as much heat as the sun. Every place you looked was jammed with uniforms, white for navy, khaki for army, everywhere.

"Let's go check out the tattoo shops," Sammy said.

"Which ones? There must be fifty of them."

"All of them got Filipino artists," Sammy said. "You know,

Vo•cab•u•lary
scoffing (SKAWF ing) mocking

sometimes they do five hundred tattoos a day. You know what's the most popular? *Remember Pearl Harbor.*"

"How do you know that?"

"I know."

"Shh. You so full of it, Sammy."

"No. It's true. My uncle told me that."

He was probably right, since Sammy had Filipino blood. ❶

"Hey," Henry said, "how about Savage?"

"What?"

"The horse. Call him Savage."

"Junk," Sammy said. "How 'bout <u>Spats</u>?"

"Spats?"

"He got a white foot."

"But he only has one."

"So?"

"So you gotta call him Spat, then. Not Spats."

Sammy frowned. "Sound like somebody spit something."

"The no-name horse."

Sammy said, "What did Wong call it?"

"The horse."

Sammy shook his head. "I still like Bucky."

A fight broke out in front of a bar. Men yelling and shoving. Henry and Sammy ran over to see. A war worker and a navy guy were going at it, but two navy SPs broke it up before it got any farther. The war worker guy went off looking back and swearing at the navy guy, telling him he better watch his back.

> ❶ **Distinguish Fact from Opinion**
> Does Sammy's Filipino blood make his statement about tattoos a fact?

Vo·cab·u·lary

spats (spats) cloth or leather covers for the upper part of a shoe and ankle

"Look," Henry said.

Sammy turned around.

Mike.

Mike smiled when he saw them and came over, saying, "Not much of a fight, huh?"

Henry still didn't know what to do around Mike, or any service guy who was by himself. He sure didn't want to talk to him. But he did wonder where he was from. Ohio, probably. Or maybe Iowa. They were all from places like that—at least that's what his father told him. "From Ohio to the grave," he'd said. "So sad. They're just kids. Farmers and grocery-store stock boys. Come way out here to fight and die."

But Henry never thought about that. He didn't care where they were from. He just knew he didn't like them. Like the rest of his friends.

"Uh . . . yeah," Henry said. "The SPs broke it up."

"So," Mike said, then said no more.

Sammy turned to walk away.

Henry wanted to go, too, but the guy was just trying to be friendly and, well, he wasn't so bad. Henry grabbed Sammy's arm. "Wait."

Sammy stopped and turned back quickly, like maybe Henry was going to fight the guy.

Henry searched for something to say. Nothing came.

"I hate this street," Mike said. "Nothing's real, you know? Don't it seem that way to you?"

Sammy tugged at Henry's arm, like, *Come on, let's get out of here already. We got shoes to shine.*

"Yeah," Henry said to the army guy. "But it's kind of fun to watch all you guys stand around waiting."

Mike shook his head. "That's what we do, ain't it? Wait. Wait for everything. Wait for a cup of coffee. Wait for a shoeshine. Wait for the war."

Henry hadn't ever thought of that before, wait for the war. Strange.

Sammy turned his back to them.

"What's your name?" the army guy, Mike, asked.

"Henry. And this is Sammy," he added, pointing a thumb back over his shoulder.

Finally Sammy turned around. He nodded, but coldly, like maybe he'd rather spit than talk. ❷

"He's not as bad as he looks," Henry said, grinning.

Mike put out his hand to shake.

Henry hesitated but shook. The guy's grip was strong. That was good.

> ❷ **Compare and Contrast**
> How are Henry's and Sammy's reactions to Mike different?

Sammy shook, too, <u>reluctantly</u>, and Henry prayed to heaven that his father wasn't watching from some secret hole in the wall.

"Where you from?" Henry asked, and Sammy threw his head back as if to say, *Jeez, you gotta be kidding, come on, let's go.*

"Tyler, Texas. Ever heard of it?"

"No. But I heard of Texas."

Mike nodded, then dipped his head toward the rope hanging out of Henry's pocket. "What's the rope for?"

Henry turned to look. He'd forgotten all about it. "Uh . . . oh, that. I got a horse. Me and Sammy was riding it today."

Sammy <u>stifled</u> a laugh.

"No kidding," Mike said. "What kind of horse is it?"

"A brown one."

"A brown one?"

Vo·cab·u·lary

reluctantly (rih LUK tunt lee) unwillingly
stifled (STY fuld) held back

"Yeah, brown."

Mike scratched the back of his head and thought a moment. "You think . . ." He paused, thought some more. "You . . . you think I could ride your horse? I ain't seen mine in six months."

That woke Sammy up. He grinned. "Sure, you can ride it," he said.

Henry said, "He's kind of . . . well, he don't let nobody ride him but me." The last thing he wanted was to have this _haole_ messing up his horse. And if his father ever heard of it, he'd—

"Got him trained, huh?" Mike said.

Sammy laughed.

"What?" Mike asked. "You boys pulling my leg?"

"No-no," Henry said. "I really got a horse. It's just . . . hard to ride, that's all."

"Yeah, hard to ride," Sammy added. "We can't even catch it."

Henry thought, _We?_

"Bet he'd let me on him," Mike said.

"How much?" Sammy asked.

"What do you mean?" Mike said.

"You said you bet. How much?"

Mike grinned. "Okay. How much you got?"

That stopped Sammy, who was broke as a lizard. He waved Mike off, as if to say, _Forget it already._

"Tell you what," Mike said. "If I can't ride the horse, I'll give each of you five bucks. But if I _can_ ride him, then you let me visit him once in a while. How's that?"

"You got a deal," Sammy said, sticking out his hand to shake.

"Hey," Henry said. "It's not your horse to bet."

Vo•cab•u•lary

haole (HOW lee) a Hawaiian word for foreigner; here it means a white person

"Sure it is," Sammy said. "I'm the trainer."

Okay, Henry thought. *Fine*. What did he have to lose, anyway? If he got five bucks from Mike, the horse would be free. He shook hands with Mike. "Let's go, then."

Mike grinned. "Now you're talkin'."

The horse was way over on the far side of the field, standing in the blue shade of a <u>mango</u> tree. The air was still, no breeze, no cars or people around. Henry, Sammy, and Mike leaned against the rotting wood fence, batting flies away from their faces, studying the horse.

"He ain't a purebred or anything," Mike said. "But he don't look bad. Nice lines, nice head. He got a name?" **3**

"Bucky."

"Not Bucky," Henry said, shoving Sammy. "He don't have a name yet. I'm still thinking about it."

"How long you had the horse?" Mike asked.

"A week."

Mike nodded. "Let's go take a look."

Mike stepped up and over the fence. Henry and Sammy followed him into the pasture, single file.

On the other side, the horse stood staring at them, head up, ears cocked forward. When they got about halfway across, the horse bolted and trotted down to the lower corner.

Mike stopped and looked around. About two acres of grass and weeds. A few trees. He turned to the pond near the lower end where the horse was now. "How deep is the water?"

Henry shrugged. "I don't know. Five or six feet. In the middle.

3 Distinguish Fact from Opinion

Are Mike's comments about the horse a fact or an opinion?

Vo•cab•u•lary

mango (MAYN goh) a tropical Asian evergreen tree grown for its sweet fruit

I don't think it's any deeper than that."

Sammy said, "You got two five buckses on you?"

Mike pulled out a small folded wad of bills, and Sammy's eyes grew into plates. "Don't you worry, I got it. But the thing is, I'm keeping it, because me and that horse down there are going to get along just fine."

Sammy grinned. "That's what you think."

Mike said, "Stay close behind me, and walk slow."

The horse raised its head and trotted off a ways. Mike stopped and the horse stopped, looking back at them. With his eyes still on the horse, Mike reached back, saying, "Let me have that rope."

Henry handed him the rope from his back pocket.

Mike let one end of it drop, then looped it back into his hand. "You boys go stand over by the fence."

Henry and Sammy went down to the fence, walking backward. "What are you going do?" Sammy asked.

"Make friends. Talk a little."

"*Talk?*" Sammy snickered, then mumbled to Henry, "You heard that? He going to talk to the horse." He half laughed then glanced back at Mike. "This I gotta see."

"Me too," Henry said. "The guy strange, yeah?"

Mike walked over to the pond. He studied it a moment, then looked up. The horse was on the other side of it now, watching him.

Sammy said, "Pretty soon he going see why we call him Bucky."

Vo•cab•u•lary

snickered (SNIK urd) partly held back a laugh

Mike walked around the pond.

The horse headed away, not running, just keeping a certain distance with one ear cocked back toward Mike. It snorted once and threw its head.

Mike stopped again. This time he looked to the side, not directly at the horse.

The horse stood waiting.

Mike walked away from it. Just kind of strolled off. And the horse took a few steps toward him. Amazing.

Mike stopped.

The horse stopped.

Mike walked, and the horse followed.

This went on for a few minutes until the horse finally walked all the way up to Mike's back. But Mike didn't try to put the rope over his neck. In fact, he didn't even turn around. He just stood with his back to the horse. When the horse was only a couple of feet away, Mike finally turned and faced it. He said something softly. **4**

"What he's saying?" Sammy asked.

"Who knows. Weird, man."

"You telling me."

Mike reached up to put his hand on the horse's nose. And the horse didn't throw his head like he always did when Henry got near him. Mike said something again, and reached into his pocket.

"What's he got? Sammy asked.

Henry didn't answer, too interested in how Mike was taming the horse.

The horse ate whatever it was Mike has in his pocket, and Mike ran his hand along its neck. Then, slowly, he looped the rope around the horse's nose, making a kind of rope bridle. There

4 Compare and Contrast
What are some similarities between the way Mike makes friends with the horse and the way he approaches the boys?

was a name for it, but Henry couldn't remember what it was. *Hack* something. Anyway, the horse let Mike do it, just let him.

"Look at that," Henry whispered.

"He still ain't riding it."

Mike led the horse over to the pond, then let the end of the rope fall to the ground. The horse stood still.

Mike took off his shoes and socks. He took off his hat and set it on the shoes. Then his watch.

"What he going do now?" Sammy said. "Go swimming?"

"Shhh. Quiet."

Mike unbuttoned his shirt, took it off. Then his pants and olive-green undershirt. He looked back at Henry and Sammy and grinned.

"Look at that dingdong, standing there in his boxers."

"I think you're right. He's going swimming."

"Man, that guy is white."

"Look like a squid."

Mike led the horse into the pond, talking to it and easing it in slowly. The horse went willingly. No problem. Right in, up to its chest. Mike dipped his hand in the water and scooped up a handful, then let it fall over the horse's back.

"He's giving it a bath," Sammy said.

Henry frowned. What was the guy *doing*?

Then Mike leaned against the horse. Just leaned.

A minute or two later, he threw himself up over its back, so that he lay over it on his stomach, like a blanket. The horse moved but settled down quickly.

"Ahhh," Henry whispered. "The guy is smart, very, very smart. He going get on him in the water, where the horse can't run, or throw him off, or if he does throw him off, going be an easy fall. Smart."

When the horse was settled, Mike eased up on its back and sat, bareback. For a long moment he just sat.

Henry grinned. He liked what he was seeing. Someone could at least get on the horse, even if it was a mainland army guy. Mike was okay. He didn't call anyone "boy" or "native" or complain about where he was. **5**

> **5 Compare and Contrast**
> How is Mike different from other *haoles* Henry has met?

Mike took up the rope bridle and nudged the horse with his heels. The horse jumped, then walked out of the pond. Mike rode around the pond. Rode up to the top of the pasture, then back.

Henry thought Mike looked pretty good on him.

Mike clucked his tongue, and the horse broke into an easy run. Mike rode smoothly on its back, and Henry could hardly believe that someone could ride a horse like that with no saddle and not bounce off.

"I don't believe it," Sammy said.

"The guy knows what he's doing."

"Unlike us."

"Yeah, unlike us."

A few minutes later, Mike rode up. Stopped, sat looking down at them. "This is still a fine horse, Henry. He's a little old, and he hasn't been ridden in a while, but he's been ridden in the past."

"He wouldn't even let me near him."

"You just have to know how to talk to him, that's all."

"Stupid to talk to a horse," Sammy said.

"No, it ain't. It's part of gaining his trust. After that he'll let you ride him."

Sammy frowned.

Henry said, "Well, I guess you won the bet."

"You want to try riding him?"

"Nah."

"Come on. He's your horse."

"It won't let me on it."

"Sure he will." Mike slid off. "Come, stand here by him, let him smell you, let him look at you."

"Uh . . . I don't know," Henry said.

The horse twisted an ear toward him.

"Go ahead," Mike said. "Rub his nose, tell him he's a good horse."

Henry inched closer and rubbed the horse's nose. It was soft, soft as feathers. The eye was big and shiny. Brown. "Nice horse," he said, like you'd say to a dog.

"Good," Mike said, "Here, take the rope. Walk around, let him follow you."

Henry led the horse around the pond.

Mike and Sammy stood silently watching.

Out on the ocean two destroyers and a transport ship were heading away from Pearl Harbor. In the distance you could hear the faint cracking of rifle shots, men maneuvering in the hills. A plane droned by, silver in the clear blue sky. **6**

> **6 Identify Author's Purpose**
> Why does the author mention the war preparations at this point?

When Henry got back Mike said, "Okay, see if you can get on him. If he gets jumpy, you can take him into the water like I did. He likes the water. Come up and lean on his side, let him get used to you. Then try to get up on him."

Henry put his arms over the horse's back and leaned on him. The horse's ears turned back, then forward again.

"See?" Mike said. "Now go on, get on him."

Henry took the rope bridle, grabbed a hank of mane, and jumped up on its back. The horse took a few sidesteps, then settled down. Henry grinned.

Vo•cab•u•lary

maneuvering (muh NOO vur ing) moving as part of a planned military exercise
droned (drohnd) made a low humming sound

"See?" Sammy said. "I told you you could ride it if you were nice to it."

Henry rode the horse to the top of the field, then back down again. "He's really *not* a bad horse," he said when he got back.

"No, he sure ain't," Mike said.

Henry rode around the pond two times, then came back and slid off. He took the rope bridle off and set the horse free. But the horse just stood there.

Mike went down to the pond to get his clothes. He was dry now, from the sun. He got dressed and the three of them walked back over to the road.

Mike said, "So it's okay, then, if I come see the horse?"

"Yeah-yeah," Henry said. "Anytime. Just come see 'um, ride 'um, whatever you want."

Mike grinned and shook hands with Henry and Sammy. "Thanks. I hope I can get up here a couple more times before I ship out."

"Yeah, couple times," Henry said. "Hey, what you had in your pocket, that you gave the horse?"

"Jelly beans."

"Hah," Henry said.

"When he does something right, reward him. Always reward good work, good behavior."

Sammy said, "Like when you guys get a medal, yeah?"

Mike looked down and said, "Yeah, like that. Well . . ." **7**

"Yeah," Henry said.

Mike nodded and waited a moment, then nodded again and started down the road to the bus stop.

"He's not a bad guy," Sammy said. "For a *haole* army guy."

"He sure knows horses."

"Yeah."

> **7 Compare and Contrast**
> How is a medal awarded in wartime similar to and different from the reward the horse gets for good behavior?

Henry and Sammy were silent a moment. Henry kept thinking of what Mike had said about waiting for the war. Waiting for the war. He'd never thought of it like that before, all of those guys just waiting to go fight. They'd always just been guys causing trouble around town. But, Henry thought, that was nothing next to the trouble they were waiting for.

"He might die soon, you know, Sammy."

Sammy shook his head. "A lot of them don't come back."

For the first time since the bombing of Pearl Harbor, for the first time since the three-day ship fires and massive clouds of dirty smoke and mass burials, for the first time since the arrest of his Japanese friends and neighbors, for the first time since then, Henry thought about how even now, right now, today, guys like Mike were out there somewhere dying in the war, going out on a transport ship and not coming back. Young guys, like him and Sammy. Just kids from Texas.

"I hope he makes it," Henry said.

"Yeah."

"But probably . . ."

In that moment, with those words, Henry changed. He could feel it in his guts, a weird, dark feeling—all those young guys just like him, those guys from the mainland, from farms and towns and cities, coming way out here to wait for the war, to wait, to wait, to wait—then to go. And die. All of them would die, he thought.

Henry winced, then shook his head. He rubbed the back of his neck.

"You know what I going name my horse, Sammy?"

"What."

"Mike."

"Mike?"

"After the guy."

"Yeah," Sammy said. He was quiet a moment, then he said, "Because why?"

"Because that guy . . . he going ship out . . . and he ain't coming back."

"You don't know that."

"One way or the other, Sammy, he ain't coming back."

"What you mean?"

"I mean he going get shot and die. Or he going live through things that going make him feel like he was dead. That's what I think, and it ain't right, you know? It ain't supposed to be that way." **8**

They were both silent for a long while.

Finally Sammy looked back at the horse and said, "Mike."

"Yeah . . . Mike."

The horse took a step forward, grazing. And above the mountains, white clouds slept. ○

8 Identify Author's Perspective
How does the author feel about war?

Answer the BIG Question

When you do the following activities, consider the Big Question: **What influences you?**

WRITE TO LEARN Think about a time when you may have misjudged someone based on how the person looked or the social group he or she belonged to. Write a brief entry in your notebook describing your experience.

LITERATURE GROUPS Mike helps Henry grow. He teaches him how to tame a horse and makes Henry think about what will happen to the young soldiers. Meet with two other students who have read this story. Discuss a time when someone helped you grow in some way. How did you feel about that person?

The Struggle to Be an All-American Girl

by Elizabeth Wong

How far would you go to avoid being different?

*I*t's still there, the Chinese school on Yale Street where my brother and I used to go. Despite the new coat of paint and the high wire fence, the school I knew 10 years ago remains remarkably <u>stoically</u> the same.

Every day at 5 p.m., instead of playing with our fourth- and fifth-grade friends or sneaking out to the empty lot to hunt ghosts and animal bones, my brother and I had to go to Chinese school. No amount of kicking, screaming, or pleading could <u>dissuade</u> my

---

Vo•cab•u•lary

stoically (STOH ih klee) without showing feeling; in a calm way
dissuade (dih SWAYD) to change someone's mind

239

mother, who was solidly determined to have us learn the language of our heritage.

<u>Forcibly</u> she walked us the seven long, hilly blocks from our home to school, depositing our defiant tearful faces before the stern principal. My only memory of him is that he swayed on his heels like a palm tree, and he always clasped his impatient twitching hands behind his back. I recognized him as a repressed <u>maniacal</u> child killer, and knew that if we ever saw his hands we'd be in big trouble. ❶ We all sat in little chairs in an empty auditorium. The room smelled like Chinese medicine, an imported faraway mustiness. Like ancient mothballs or dusty closets. I hated that smell. I favored crisp new scents. Like the soft French perfume that my American teacher wore in public school. There was a stage far to the right, flanked by an American flag and the flag of the Nationalist Republic of China, which was also red, white, and blue, but not as pretty.

> ❶ **Distinguish Fact from Opinion**
> Is the writer stating a fact or voicing an opinion?

Although the emphasis at the school was mainly language—speaking, reading, writing—the lessons always began with an exercise in politeness. With the entrance of the teacher, the best student would tap a bell and everyone would get up, <u>kowtow</u>, and chant, "Sing san ho," the <u>phonetic</u> for "How are you, teacher?" Being 10 years old, I had better things to learn than <u>ideographs</u> copied painstakingly in lines that ran right to left from the tip of a moc but, a real ink pen that had to be held in an awkward way if blotches were to be avoided. After all, I could do the multiplication tables, name the satellites of Mars, and write reports on *Little Women* and *Black Beauty*. Nancy Drew, my

Vo•cab•u•lary

forcibly (FOR sih blee) with force
maniacal (muh NY ih kul) mad, crazy
kowtow (KOW tow) to kneel and touch the forehead to the ground in respect
phonetic (foh NET ick) spoken language or speech sounds
ideographs (ID ee oh grafs) symbols for words

favorite book heroine, never spoke Chinese.

The language was a source of embarrassment. More times than not, I had tried to <u>dissociate</u> myself from the nagging loud voice that followed me wherever I wandered in the nearby American supermarket outside Chinatown. The voice belonged to my grandmother, a fragile woman in her 70s who could outshout the best of the street vendors. Her humor was <u>raunchy</u>, her Chinese rhythmless, patternless. It was quick, it was loud, it was unbeautiful. It was not like the quiet, lilting romance of French or the gentle refinement of the American South. Chinese sounded <u>pedestrian</u>. Public.

In Chinatown, the comings and goings of hundreds of Chinese on their daily tasks sounded <u>chaotic</u> and frenzied. I did not want to be thought of as mad, as talking gibberish. When I spoke English, people nodded at me, smiled sweetly, said encouraging words. Even the people in my culture would cluck and say that I'd do well in life. "My, doesn't she move her lips fast," they'd say, meaning that I'd be able to keep up with the world outside Chinatown.

My brother was even more <u>fanatical</u> than I about speaking English. He was especially hard on my mother, criticizing her, often cruelly, for her <u>pidgin</u> speech—smatterings of Chinese scattered like chop suey in her conversation. "It's not 'What it is,' Mom," he'd

Vo•cab•u•lary

dissociate (dis SOH shee ayt) to separate oneself from something
raunchy (RAWN chee) vulgar
pedestrian (puh DES tree en) commonplace, average
chaotic (kay AW tik) confused, unpredictable
fanatical (fuh NAT uh kuhl) excessively devoted
pidgin (PIH jin) simplified, usually mixing words of more than one language

say in <u>exasperation</u>. "It's 'What *is*, what *is*, what *is*!'" Sometimes, Mom might leave out an occasional "the" or "a," or perhaps a verb of being. He would stop her in mid-sentence. "Say it again, Mom. Say it right." When he tripped over his own tongue, he'd blame it on her: "See, Mom, it's all your fault. You set a bad example."

What infuriated my mother most was when my brother cornered her on her consonants, especially "r." My father had played a cruel joke on Mom by assigning her an American name that her tongue wouldn't allow her to say. No matter how hard she tried, "Ruth" always ended up "Luth" or "Roof."

After two years of writing with a *moc but* and reciting words with multiples of meanings, I finally was granted a cultural divorce. I was permitted to stop Chinese school. I thought of myself as multicultural. I preferred tacos to egg rolls; I enjoyed Cinco de Mayo more than Chinese New Year. At last, I was one of you; I wasn't one of them.

Sadly, I still am. **2** ○

> **2 Identify Author's Perspective**
> How does the author feel about her heritage?

Answer the BIG Question

When you do the following activities, consider the Big Question: **What influences you?**

WRITE TO LEARN Write a paragraph in your notebook to answer the following question: What influences in the author's life made her embrace the American culture and deny her Chinese heritage?

PARTNER TALK Share your paragraph with a partner who has read the selection. Discuss how you might feel in Elizabeth's situation.

Vo•cab•u•lary

exasperation (eg zas pur AY shun) annoyance, aggravation

A Crush

by Cynthia Rylant

A secret love causes more than just flowers to blossom.

*W*hen the windows of Stan's Hardware started filling up with flowers, everyone in town knew something had happened. <u>Excess</u> flowers usually mean death, but since these were all real flowers bearing the aroma of nature instead of floral preservative, and since they stood bunched in clear mason jars instead of impaled on Styrofoam crosses, everyone knew nobody had died. So they all figured somebody had a crush and kept quiet.

There wasn't really a Stan of Stan's Hardware. Dick Wilcox was the owner, and since he'd never liked his own name, he gave

Vo•cab•u•lary

excess (EK ses) extra; more than needed

243

his store half the name of his childhood hero, Stan Laurel in the movies. Dick had been married for twenty-seven years. Once, his wife Helen had dropped a German chocolate cake on his head at a Lion's Club dance, so Dick and Helen were not likely candidates for the honest expression of the flowers in those clear mason jars lining the windows of Stan's Hardware, and <u>speculation</u> had to move on to Dolores. **❶**

❶ Compare and Contrast
How are Dolores and Dick alike? How are they different?

Dolores was the assistant manager at Stan's and had worked there for twenty years, since high school. She knew the store like a mother knows her baby, so Dick—who had trouble keeping up with things like prices and new brands of <u>drywall compound</u>—tried to keep himself busy in the back and give Dolores the run of the floor. This worked fine because the carpenters and plumbers and painters in town trusted Dolores and took her advice to heart. They also liked her tattoo.

Dolores was the only woman in town with a tattoo. On the days she went sleeveless, one could see it on the <u>taut</u> brown skin of her upper arm: "Howl at the Moon." The picture was of a baying coyote which must have been a dark gray in its early days but which had faded to the color of the <u>spackling paste</u> Dolores stocked in the third aisle. Nobody had gotten out of Dolores the true story behind the tattoo. Some of the men who came in liked to show off their own, and they'd roll up their sleeves or pull open their shirts, <u>exhibiting</u> bald eagles and rattlesnakes, and they'd try to coax out of Dolores the history of her coyote. All of the men

---

Vo•cab•u•lary

speculation (spek yoo LAY shun) contemplation or consideration of a subject

drywall compound (DRY wahl KAWM pownd) a paste used to patch holes in walls

taut (tawt) pulled or drawn tight; not slack

spackling paste (SPAK ling payst) a substance used to repair walls before painting

exhibiting (ek SIH bih ting) to show outwardly; display

had gotten their tattoos when they were in the service, drunk on weekend leave and full of the spitfire of young soldiers. Dolores had never been in the service and she'd never seen weekend leave and there wasn't a tattoo parlor anywhere near. They couldn't figure why or where any half-sober woman would have a howling coyote ground into the soft skin of her upper arm. But Dolores wasn't telling. ❷

> ❷ **Identify Author's Perspective**
> How do you think the author feels about tattoos?

That the flowers in Stan's front window had anything to do with Dolores seemed completely improbable. As far as anyone knew, Dolores had never been in love nor had anyone ever been in love with her. Some believed it was the tattoo, of course, or the fine dark hair coating Dolores's upper lip which kept suitors away. Some felt it was because Dolores was just more of a man than most of the men in town, and fellows couldn't figure out how to court someone who knew more about the carburetor of a car or the back side of a washing machine than they did. Others thought Dolores simply didn't want love. This was a popular theory among the women in town who sold Avon and Mary Kay cosmetics. Whenever one of them ran into the hardware for a package of light bulbs or some batteries, she would mentally pluck every one of the black hairs above Dolores's lip. Then she'd wash that grease out of Dolores's hair, give her a good blunt cut, dress her in a decent silk-blend blouse with a nice Liz Claiborne skirt from the Sports line, and, finally, tone down that swarthy, longshoreman look of Dolores's with a concealing beige foundation, some frosted peach lipstick, and a good gray liner for the eyes.

Vo•cab•u•lary

spitfire (SPIT fyr) a quick-tempered or highly excitable person
improbable (im PRAW buh bul) unlikely to take place or be true
carburetor (CAR bur ay tur) a device used in internal-combustion engines to produce an explosive mixture of vaporized fuel and air
swarthy (SWAHR thee) having a dark complexion or color
longshoreman (lawng SHOR muhn) a dock worker who loads and unloads ships

A Crush

Dolores simply didn't want love, the Avon lady would think as she walked back to her car carrying her little bag of batteries. If she did, she'd fix herself up.

The man who was in love with Dolores and who brought her zinnias and cornflowers and <u>nasturtiums</u> and marigolds and asters and four-o'clocks in clear mason jars did not know any of this. He did not know that men showed Dolores their tattoos. He did not know that Dolores understood how to use and to sell a belt sander. He did not know that Dolores needed some concealing beige foundation so she could get someone to love her. The man who brought flowers to Dolores on Wednesdays when the hardware opened its doors at 7:00 a.m. didn't care who Dolores had ever been or what anyone had ever thought of her. He loved her and he wanted to bring her flowers.

Ernie had lived in this town all of his life and had never before met Dolores. He was thirty-three years old, and for thirty-one of those years he had lived at home with his mother in a small, dark house on the edge of town near Beckwith's Orchards. Ernie had been a beautiful baby, with a shock of shining black hair and large blue eyes and a round, wise face. But as he had grown, it had become clearer and clearer that though he was indeed a perfectly beautiful child, his mind had not developed with the same perfection. Ernie would not be able to speak in sentences until he was six years old. He would not be able to count the apples in a bowl until he was eight. By the time he was ten, he could sing a simple song. At age twelve, he understood what a joke was. And when he was twenty, something he saw on television made him cry.

Ernie's mother kept him in the house with her because it was easier, so Ernie knew nothing of the world except this house. They lived, the two of them, in tiny dark rooms always

---

Vo·cab·u·lary

nasturtiums (nah STUR shumz) herbs with brightly colored flowers illuminated by the glow of a television set, Ernie's bags of Oreos and Nutter Butters littering the floor, his baseball cards scattered across the sofa, his heavy winter coat thrown over the arm of a chair so he could wear it whenever he wanted, and his box of Burpee seed packages sitting in the middle of the kitchen table.

These Ernie cherished. The seeds had been delivered to his home by mistake. One day a woman wearing a brown uniform had pulled up in a brown truck, walked quickly to the front porch of Ernie's house, set a box down, and with a couple of toots of her horn, driven off again. Ernie had watched her through the curtains, and when she was gone, had ventured onto the porch and shyly, cautiously, picked up the box. His mother checked it when he carried it inside. The box didn't have their name on it but the brown truck was gone, so whatever was in the box was theirs to keep. Ernie pulled off the heavy tape, his fingers trembling, and found inside the box more little packages of seeds than he could count. He lifted them out, one by one, and examined the beautiful photographs of flowers on each. His mother was not interested, had returned to the television, but Ernie sat down at the kitchen table and quietly looked at each package for a long time, his fingers running across the slick paper and outlining the shapes of zinnias and cornflowers and nasturtiums and marigolds and asters and four-o'clocks, his eyes drawing up their colors.

Two months later Ernie's mother died. A neighbor found her at the mailbox beside the road. People from the county courthouse came out to get Ernie, and as they ushered him from the home he would never see again, he picked up the box of seed packages from his kitchen table and passed through the doorway.

Eventually Ernie was moved to a large white house near the main street of town. This house was called a group home, because in it lived a group of people who, like Ernie, could not live on their own. There were six of them. Each had his own

---

Vo•cab•u•lary

illuminated (il LOO muh nay ted) provided or brightened with light
ventured (VEN churd) proceeded despite possible danger or risk

room. When Ernie was shown the room that would be his, he put the box of Burpee seeds—which he had kept with him since his mother's death—on the little table beside the bed and then he sat down on the bed and cried.

Ernie cried every day for nearly a month. And then he stopped. He dried his tears and he learned how to bake refrigerator biscuits and how to dust mop and what to do if the indoor plants looked brown.

Ernie loved watering the indoor plants and it was this pleasure which finally drew him outside. One of the young men who worked at the group home—a college student named Jack—grew a large garden in the back of the house. It was full of tomato vines and the large yellow blossoms of healthy squash. During his first summer at the house, Ernie would stand at the kitchen window, watching Jack and sometimes a resident of the home move among the vegetables. Ernie was curious, but too afraid to go into the garden.

Then one day when Ernie was watching through the window, he noticed that Jack was ripping open several slick little packages and emptying them into the ground. Ernie panicked and ran to his room. But the box of Burpee seeds was still there on his table, untouched. He grabbed it, slid it under his bed, then went back through the house and out into the garden as if he had done this every day of his life.

He stood beside Jack, watching him empty seed packages into the soft black soil, and as the packages were emptied, Ernie asked for them, holding out his hand, his eyes on the photographs of red radishes and purple eggplant. Jack handed the empty packages over with a smile and with that gesture became Ernie's first friend. **3**

3 Compare and Contrast
Compare Ernie's life at the home with his life with his mother.

Jack tried to explain to Ernie that the seeds would grow into vegetables but Ernie could not believe this until he saw it come true. And when it did, he looked all the more <u>intently</u> at the packages of zinnias and cornflowers and the rest hidden beneath his bed. He thought more deeply about them but he could not carry them to the garden. He could not let the garden have his seeds.

That was the first year in the large white house.

The second year, Ernie saw Dolores, and after that he thought of nothing else but her and of the photographs of flowers beneath his bed.

Jack had decided to take Ernie downtown for breakfast every Wednesday morning to ease him into the world outside that of the group home. They left very early, at 5:45 a.m., so there would be few people and almost no traffic to frighten Ernie and make him beg for his room. Jack and Ernie drove to the Big Boy restaurant which sat across the street from Stan's Hardware. There they ate eggs and bacon and French toast among those whose work demanded rising before the sun: bus drivers, policemen, nurses, mill workers. Their first time in the Big Boy, Ernie was too nervous to eat. The second time, he could eat but he couldn't look up. The third time, he not only ate everything on his plate, but he lifted his head and he looked out the window of the Big Boy restaurant toward Stan's Hardware across the street. There he saw a dark-haired woman in jeans and a black

---

Vo·cab·u·lar·y

intently (in TENT lee) firmly fixed; concentrated

A Crush

T-shirt unlocking the front door of the building, and that was the moment Ernie started loving Dolores and thinking about giving up his seeds to the soft black soil of Jack's garden.

Love is such a mystery, and when it strikes the heart of one as mysterious as Ernie himself, it can hardly be spoken of. Ernie could not explain to Jack why he went directly to his room later that morning, pulled the box of Burpee seeds from under his bed, then grabbed Jack's hand in the kitchen and walked with him to the garden where Ernie had come to believe things would grow. Ernie handed the packets of seeds one by one to Jack, who stood in silent admiration of the lovely photographs before asking Ernie several times, "Are you sure you want to plant these?" Ernie was sure. It didn't take him very long, and when the seeds all lay under the moist black earth, Ernie carried his empty packages inside the house and spent the rest of the day spreading them across his bed in different arrangements.

That was in June. For the next several Wednesdays at 7:00 a.m., Ernie watched every movement of the dark-haired woman behind the lighted windows of Stan's Hardware. Jack watched Ernie watch Dolores, and <u>discreetly</u> said nothing.

When Ernie's flowers began growing in July, Ernie spent most of his time in the garden. He would watch the garden for hours, as if he expected it suddenly to move or to impress him with a quick trick. The fragile green stems of his flowers stood uncertainly in the soil, like baby colts on their first legs, but the young plants performed no magic for Ernie's eyes. They saved their shows for the middle of the night and the next day surprised Ernie with tender small blooms in all the colors the photographs had promised.

The flowers grew fast and <u>hardy</u>, and one early Wednesday morning when they looked as big and bright as their pictures on the empty packages, Ernie pulled a glass canning jar off a dusty

---

Vo•cab•u•lary

discreetly (dih SKREET lee) with discretion; prudently and with wise self-restraint
hardy (HAR dee) capable of surviving unfavorable conditions

shelf in the basement of his house. He washed the jar, half filled it with water, then carried it to the garden where he placed in it one of every kind of flower he had grown. He met Jack at the car and rode off to the Big Boy with the jar of flowers held tight between his small hands. Jack told him it was a beautiful bouquet.

When they reached the door of the Big Boy, Ernie stopped and pulled at Jack's arm, pointing to the building across the street. "OK," Jack said, and he led Ernie to the front door of Stan's Hardware. It was 6:00 a.m. and the building was still dark. Ernie set the clear mason jar full of flowers under the sign that read "Closed," then he smiled at Jack and followed him back across the street to get breakfast.

When Dolores arrived at seven and picked up the jar of zinnias and cornflowers and nasturtiums and marigolds and asters and four-o'clocks, Ernie and Jack were watching her from a booth in the Big Boy. Each had a wide smile on his face as Dolores put her nose to the flowers. Ernie giggled. They watched the lights of the hardware store come up and saw Dolores place the clear mason jar on the ledge of the front window. They drove home still smiling.

All the rest of that summer Ernie left a jar of flowers every Wednesday morning at the front door of Stan's Hardware. Neither Dick Wilcox nor Dolores could figure out why the flowers kept coming, and each of them assumed somebody had a crush on the other. But the flowers had an effect on them anyway. **4** Dick started spending more time out on the floor making conversation with the customers, while Dolores stopped wearing T-shirts to work and instead wore crisp white blouses with the sleeves rolled back off her wrists. Occasionally she put on a bracelet.

4 Compare and Contrast Compare the effect the flowers had on Dick and Dolores.

By summer's end Jack and Ernie had become very good friends, and when the flowers in the garden behind their house began to wither, and Ernie's face began to grow gray as he watched them, Jack brought home one bright day in late September a great long box. Ernie followed Jack as he carried it down to the basement and watched as Jack pulled a long glass tube from the box and attached this tube to the wall above a table. When Jack plugged in the tube's electric cord, a soft lavender light washed the room.

"Sunshine," said Jack.

Then he went back to his car for a smaller box. He carried this down to the basement where Ernie still stood staring at the strange light. Jack handed Ernie the small box, and when Ernie opened it he found more little packages of seeds than he could count, with new kinds of photographs on the slick paper.

"Violets," Jack said, pointing to one of them.

Then he and Ernie went outside to get some dirt. ○

Answer the BIG Question

When you do the following activities, consider the Big Question: **What influences you?**

WRITE TO LEARN What or who influenced the characters in the story to change? Make a chart like the following to record your answers in your notebook.

PARTNER TALK Discuss your thoughts about the characters with a classmate who has read this selection.

Character	Change	What caused the change?
Dolores		
Dick		
Ernie		

A Gold Miner's Tale

by Bobbi Katz

Water and sand—could that really be all it takes to get fabulously rich?

Frank Wexler
Dawson City, Yukon Territory, 1898

> I was twenty-one years old.
> Fired up by dreams of gold.
> Rushing West in '49
> To stake a claim to my own mine!
> What did I find when I got there?
> Thousands of "<u>rushers</u>" everywhere!
> Water and sand. That's ALL it takes.
> Swish your pan. Pick out the <u>flakes</u>!
>
> A meal?
> A horse?
> A place to stay?
> Who'd believe what we had to pay!
> Bought a shovel. Bought a pan.

Vo•cab•u•lary

rushers (RUH sherz) people who traveled to California in pursuit of gold
flakes (flayks) gold flakes

Soon I'd be a rich young man.
Water and sand. That's ALL it takes.
Swish your pan. Pick out the flakes!
Pan after pan. I'd swish and wish
For a glint of pay dirt in my dish.
Asleep at night, what did I see?
Nuggets the daylight hid from me.
It takes more than a flash in the pan
To make a rusher a rich young man.

The gold I found? Just enough to get by.
I gave up when my claim went dry.
Water and sand. That's ALL it takes.
Swish your pan. Pick out the flakes!
Got a job in a hydraulic mine.
Hated the work, but the pay was fine.
So when I heard about Pikes Peak,
I was in the Rockies within a week!

Vo•cab•u•lary

hydraulic (hy DRAW lik) **mine** a process of mining using water
Pikes Peak (PYKS peek) mountain located near Colorado Springs, Colorado

Water and sand. That's ALL it takes.
Swish your pan. Pick out the flakes!
I should have known better.
With a grubstake so small,
I left Colorado with nothing at all.
No job. No gold. Just a shovel and a pan.
But I walked away a wiser man. ❶

"Gold in the Klondike!"
Wouldn't you think
I'd be up there in a wink?
But with my new plan to pan gold flakes,
I didn't make the same mistakes.
Before I joined the great stampede,
I thought: What will stampeders need?
Now I'm a Dawson millionaire!
I sell them ALL long underwear. ○

> ❶ **Compare and Contrast**
> How did the miner's experience contrast with his expectation?

Answer the BIG Question

When you do the following activities, consider the Big Question:
What influences you?

WRITE TO LEARN How is the speaker in the poem influenced by others? Why does he follow them west and to Pikes Peak? What does he learn from his experiences? Write a brief paragraph in your notebook that answers these questions.

PARTNER TALK The speaker in the poem turned a disappointment into an opportunity. Discuss with a partner a real or imaginary situation in which you could do the same thing.

Vo•cab•u•lary

grubstake (GRUHB stayk) money given to a miner to fund his trip in exchange for sharing the profits of his discoveries

How can you become who you want to be?

In this unit, you will read the stories of real people and fictional characters. These stories may inspire you to give your own answer to the question: **How can you become who you want to be?**

THE NO-GUITAR BLUES

by Gary Soto

What happens when an honest person wants something so badly he'll lie to get it?

The moment Fausto saw the group Los Lobos on "American Bandstand," he knew exactly what he wanted to do with his life—play guitar. His eyes grew large with excitement as Los Lobos ground out a song while teenagers bounced off each other on the crowded dance floor.

He had watched "American Bandstand" for years and had heard Ray Camacho and the Teardrops at Romain Playground, but it had never occurred to him that he too might become a musician. That afternoon Fausto knew his mission in life: to play guitar in his own band; to sweat out his songs and prance around the stage; to make money and dress weird.

Fausto turned off the television set and walked outside, wondering how he could get enough money to buy a guitar. He couldn't ask his parents because they would just say, "Money doesn't grow on trees" or "What do you think we are, bankers?" And besides, they hated rock music. They were into the *conjunto* music of Lydia Mendoza, Flaco Jimenez, and Little Joe and La Familia. And, as Fausto recalled, the last <u>album</u> they bought was *The Chipmunks Sing Christmas Favorites*. ❶

But what the heck, he'd give it a try. He returned inside and watched his mother make tortillas. He leaned against the kitchen counter, trying to work up the nerve to ask her for a guitar. Finally, he couldn't hold back any longer.

❶ **Connect**
When has an adult responded to a request you made in words like those Fausto's parents used?

"Mom," he said, "I want a guitar for Christmas."

She looked up from rolling tortillas. "Honey, a guitar costs a lot of money."

"How 'bout for my birthday next year," he tried again.

"I can't promise," she said, turning back to her tortillas, "but we'll see."

Fausto walked back outside with a buttered tortilla. He knew his mother was right. His father was a warehouseman at Berven Rugs, where he made good money but not enough to buy everything his children wanted. Fausto decided to mow lawns to earn money, and was pushing the mower down the street before he realized it was winter and no one would hire him. He returned the mower and picked up a rake. He hopped onto his sister's bike (his had two flat tires) and rode north to the nicer section of Fresno in search of work. He went door-to-door, but after three hours he managed to get only one job, and not to rake leaves. He was asked to hurry down to the store to buy a loaf of bread, for which he received a grimy, dirt-caked quarter.

Vo·cab·u·lary

album (AL bum) music recording on a 12-inch vinyl disc

The No-Guitar Blues

He also got an orange, which he ate sitting at the curb. While he was eating, a dog walked up and sniffed his leg. Fausto pushed him away and threw an orange peel skyward. The dog caught it and ate it in one gulp. The dog looked at Fausto and wagged his tail for more. Fausto tossed him a slice of orange, and the dog snapped it up and licked his lips.

"How come you like oranges, dog?"

The dog blinked a pair of sad eyes and whined.

"What's the matter? Cat got your tongue?" Fausto laughed at his joke and offered the dog another slice.

At that moment a dim light came on inside Fausto's head. He saw that it was sort of a fancy dog, a terrier or something, with dog tags and a shiny collar. And it looked well fed and healthy. In his neighborhood, the dogs were never licensed, and if they got sick they were placed near the water heater until they got well.

This dog looked like he belonged to rich people. Fausto cleaned his juice-sticky hands on his pants and got to his feet. The light in his head grew brighter. It just might work. He called the dog, patted its muscular back, and bent down to check the license.

"Great," he said. "There's an address."

The dog's name was Roger, which struck Fausto as weird because he'd never heard of a dog with a human name. Dogs should have names like Bomber, Freckles, Queenie, Killer, and Zero.

Fausto planned to take the dog home and collect a reward. He would say he had found Roger near the freeway. That would scare the daylights out of the owners, who would be so happy that they would probably give him a reward. He felt bad about lying, but the dog *was* loose. And it might even really be lost, because the address was six blocks away.

Fausto stashed the rake and his sister's bike behind a bush, and, tossing an orange peel every time Roger became distracted, walked the dog to his house. He hesitated on the porch until Roger began to scratch the door with a muddy paw. Fausto had come this far, so he figured he might as well go through with it. He knocked softly. When no one answered, he rang the doorbell. A man in a silky bathrobe and slippers opened the door and seemed confused by the sight of his dog and the boy.

"Sir," Fausto said, gripping Roger by the collar. "I found your dog by the freeway. His dog license says he lives here." Fausto looked down at the dog, then up to the man. "He does, doesn't he?"

The man stared at Fausto a long time before saying in a pleasant voice, "That's right." He pulled his robe tighter around him because of the cold and asked Fausto to come in. "So he was by the freeway?"

"Uh-huh."

"You bad, snoopy dog," said the man, wagging his finger. "You probably knocked over some trash cans, too, didn't you?"

Fausto didn't say anything. He looked around, amazed by this house with its shiny furniture and a television as large as the front window at home. Warm bread smells filled the air and music full of soft tinkling floated in from another room.

"Helen," the man called to the kitchen. "We have a visitor." His wife came into the living room wiping her hands on a dish towel and smiling. "And who have we here?" she asked in one of the softest voices Fausto had ever heard.

"This young man said he found Roger near the freeway." Fausto repeated his story to her while staring at a <u>perpetual</u> clock with a bell-shaped glass, the kind his aunt got when she celebrated her twenty-fifth anniversary. The lady frowned and said, wagging a finger at Roger, "Oh, you're a bad boy."

"It was very nice of you to bring Roger home," the man said. "Where do you live?"

"By that vacant lot on Olive," he said. "You know, by Brownie's Flower Place."

The wife looked at her husband, then Fausto. Her eyes twinkled triangles of light as she said, "Well, young man, you're probably hungry. How about a turnover?"

Vo·cab·u·lary

perpetual (pur PECH oo ul) continuing forever

"What do I have to turn over?" Fausto asked, thinking she was talking about yard work or something like turning trays of dried raisins.

"No, no, dear, it's a pastry." She took him by the elbow and guided him to a kitchen that sparkled with copper pans and bright yellow wallpaper. She guided him to the kitchen table and gave him a tall glass of milk and something that looked like an *empanada*. Steamy waves of heat escaped when he tore it in two. He ate with both eyes on the man and woman who stood arm-in-arm smiling at him. They were strange, he thought. But nice.

"That was good," he said after he finished the turnover. "Did you make it, ma'am?"

"Yes, I did. Would you like another?"

"No, thank you. I have to go home now."

As Fausto walked to the door, the man opened his wallet and took out a bill. "This is for you," he said. "Roger is special to us, almost like a son."

Fausto looked at the bill and knew he was in trouble. Not with these nice folks or with his parents but with himself. How could he have been so <u>deceitful</u>? The dog wasn't lost. It was just having a fun Saturday walking around.

"I can't take that."

"You have to. You deserve it, believe me," the man said.

"No, I don't." **2**

"Now don't be silly," said the lady. She took the bill from her husband and stuffed it into Fausto's shirt pocket. "You're a lovely child. Your parents are lucky to have you. Be good. And come see us again, please."

> **2 Infer**
> Why does Fausto try to refuse the reward that Roger's family offered him?

Vo•cab•u•lary

deceitful (dee SEET ful) not honest

Fausto went out, and the lady closed the door. Fausto clutched the bill through his shirt pocket. He felt like ringing the doorbell and begging them to please take the money back, but he knew they would refuse. He hurried away, and at the end of the block, pulled the bill from his shirt pocket: it was a crisp twenty-dollar bill.

"Oh, man, I shouldn't have lied," he said under his breath as he started up the street like a zombie. He wanted to run to church for Saturday confession, but it was past four-thirty, when confession stopped.

He returned to the bush where he had hidden the rake and his sister's bike and rode home slowly, not daring to touch the money in his pocket. At home, in the privacy of his room, he examined the twenty-dollar bill. He had never had so much money. It was probably enough to buy a secondhand guitar. But he felt bad, like the time he stole a dollar from the secret fold inside his older brother's wallet.

Fausto went outside and sat on the fence. "Yeah," he said. "I can probably get a guitar for twenty. Maybe at a yard sale—things are cheaper."

His mother called him to dinner.

The next day he dressed for church without anyone telling him. He was going to go to eight o'clock mass.

"I'm going to church, Mom," he said. His mother was in the kitchen cooking _papas_ and _chorizo con huevos_. A pile of tortillas lay warm under a dish towel.

"Oh, I'm so proud of you, Son." She beamed, turning over the crackling _papas_.

His older brother, Lawrence, who was at the table reading the funnies, mimicked, "Oh, I'm so proud of you, my son," under his breath.

At Saint Theresa's he sat near the front. When Father Jerry began by saying that we are all sinners, Fausto thought he looked right at him. Could he know? Fausto fidgeted with guilt. No, he thought. I only did it yesterday.

Fausto knelt, prayed, and sang. But he couldn't forget the man and the lady, whose names he didn't even know, and the _empanada_ they had given him. It had a strange name but tasted really good. He wondered how they got rich. And how that dome clock worked. He had asked his mother once how his aunt's clock worked. She said it just worked, the way the refrigerator works. It just did.

Fausto caught his mind wandering and tried to concentrate on his sins. He said a Hail Mary and sang, and when the wicker basket came his way, he stuck a hand reluctantly in his pocket and pulled out the twenty-dollar bill. He ironed it between his palms,

---

Vo·cab·u·lary

papas (PAH pahs) Spanish for potatoes
chorizo con huevos (choh REE soh kohn WAY vohs) Spanish for sausage with eggs
mimicked (MIM ikt) imitated closely

and dropped it into the basket. The grown-ups stared. Here was a kid dropping twenty dollars in the basket while they gave just three or four dollars. ❸

❸ Connect
In what ways have you tried to relieve a guilty conscience?

There would be a second collection for Saint Vincent de Paul, the lector announced. The wicker baskets again floated in the pews, and this time the adults around him, given a second chance to show their charity, dug deep into their wallets and purses and dropped in fives and tens. This time Fausto tossed in the grimy quarter.

Fausto felt better after church. He went home and played football in the front yard with his brother and some neighbor kids. He felt cleared of wrongdoing and was so happy that he played one of his best games of football ever. On one play, he tore his good pants, which he knew he shouldn't have been wearing. For a second, while he examined the hole, he wished he hadn't given the twenty dollars away.

Man, I coulda bought me some Levi's, he thought. He pictured his twenty dollars being spent to buy church candles. He pictured a priest buying an armful of flowers with his money.

Fausto had to forget about getting a guitar. He spent the next day playing soccer in his good pants, which were now his old pants. But that night during dinner, his mother said she remembered seeing an old bass <u>guitarron</u> the last time she cleaned out her father's garage.

"It's a little dusty," his mom said, serving his favorite enchiladas, "but I think it works. Grandpa says it works."

Fausto's ears perked up. That was the same kind the guy in Los Lobos played. Instead of asking for the guitar, he waited for his mother to offer it to him. And she did, while gathering the dishes from the table.

"No, Mom, I'll do it," he said, hugging her. "I'll do the dishes forever if you want."

Vo·cab·u·lary

guitarron (gee tah ROHN) a type of guitar

It was the happiest day of his life. No, it was the second-happiest day of his life. The happiest was when his grandfather Lupe placed the guitarron, which was nearly as huge as a washtub, in his arms. Fausto ran a thumb down the strings, which vibrated in his throat and chest. It sounded beautiful, deep and eerie. A pumpkin smile widened on his face.

"OK, *hijo*, now you put your fingers like this," said his grandfather, smelling of tobacco and aftershave. He took Fausto's fingers and placed them on the strings. Fausto strummed a chord on the guitarron, and the bass resounded in their chests.

The guitarron was more complicated than Fausto imagined. But he was confident that after a few more lessons he could start a band that would someday play on "American Bandstand" for the dancing crowds. ○

Answer the BIG Question

As you do the following activities, consider the Big Question:
How can you become who you want to be?

WRITE TO LEARN Write a brief entry in your notebook about how Fausto handled the guilt he felt after lying. How else could he have solved his problem?

PARTNER TALK Get together with another student who has read this selection. Discuss some situations in which a person's honesty might be tested.

Merrick Johnston, Mountain Climber

by Merrick Johnston

What is it like to climb the highest mountain in North America when you're only eleven years old?

Because my entire state (Alaska) is one big playground, anytime I want an adventure, all I have to do is look in my own backyard. I've taken all of my friends on hikes, giving many of them their first true taste of Alaska. I think that many people who live here haven't learned to appreciate what this place has to offer; they seem to spend most of their time inside their houses or driving in their cars. If you get to know Alaska's <u>terrain</u>, life here can be extraordinary.

Hiking and spending time in the mountains are my favorite things to do. My mom runs her own company, Great Alaskan Gourmet Adventures, organizing adventures for people who want

Vo·cab·u·lary

terrain (tur RAYN) the type of land

Merrick Johnston, Mountain Climber

to explore the outdoors. I work with her as a guide. Together, we teach clients hiking and technical skills for rock and ice climbing, and we take them on all kinds of trips to places like Prospect Heights, Wolverine Peak, and Little Switzerland. I've always loved hanging out with the mountaineers I've met through my mom's business. When I hear about their experiences, I think about the things I may be able to accomplish someday. Best of all, working as a guide has exposed me to the joy of mountain climbing at an early age.

When I was nine, I heard one of the more experienced climbers describe what it was like to scale Mount McKinley—the unpredictable climate; the challenging, icy terrain; the awesome feeling of reaching the summit. My interest was sparked right away.

Denali (Mt. McKinley's Indian name) is the highest peak in North America. At 20,320 feet, its arctic conditions make climbing Mt. McKinley a major test of personal strength, technical skill, and teamwork. I dreamed of climbing that icy peak—all I had to do was convince my mom I could!

Two years later, I finally won her over. My mom realized that I was serious about attempting "The High One," as Mt. McKinley is called. I was determined to become the youngest person to accomplish this feat (beating the boy who set the record before me).

I grew up with two older brothers, and most of my friends were boys. You might say I was just "one of the guys." I did everything they did, and more. By the time I was eight, I realized many girls were interested in different activities than boys. I also learned that the boys I hung out with thought they were naturally better athletes than the girls they knew. Well, this fired up my competitive spirit. I wanted to prove girls can do anything, and this helped fuel my desire to climb Mt. McKinley.

Although my mom had given in to my pleas to make the

Vo•cab•u•lary

pleas (pleez) appeals or requests

climb, she said I couldn't go on the expedition alone. We decided to attempt the ascent together, along with an experienced group of climbers. I knew I needed to be strong and fit to take on such a huge challenge.

I was already physically active, spending as much time as I could enjoying outdoor activities like skiing, snowboarding, canoeing, hiking, and rafting. I also played soccer, ran track, and did gymnastics. But it's not just fitness that counts when climbing: You must also have excellent mountaineering skills. On a mountain like Denali, I'd be facing life-threatening situations. If I didn't know what I was doing, I'd pose a threat to myself and to everyone else participating in the climb. ❶

To help prepare for the expedition, my mom and I practiced our glacier-travel techniques, winter camping skills, and climbing with *crampons* (metal spikes clamped onto our boots). We also climbed Alaska's Mount Goode—a 10,900 foot peak in the Chugach Mountains—to test my high-altitude and cold-weather endurance. My mom trained with me daily on the Chugach Range, where I climbed with a 50-pound pack on my back. This helped build my strength and stamina, both of which are important for high-altitude climbing in cold conditions. Because the altitude can zap your strength, it's essential to develop deep reserves of energy to draw from.

We also became familiar with "crevasse rescue" (a crevasse is basically a deep crevice, often found in a glacier). Because glaciers are like large rivers that flow, ebb, and shift, deep crevasses form as the glaciers travel downward. The crevasses can be hundreds of feet deep, and if you fall in and are knocked unconscious, your climbing team must have the skills to haul you up safely with ropes. Scaling mountains has always been a fun way for me to

❶ Connect
In what situations might other people depend on your strength and skill?

Vo•cab•u•lary

stamina (STA min uh) staying power; endurance

spend time. I enjoy the struggles and obstacles I face on the way up, and I like making decisions about the routes.

Mountain climbing gives me a whole different perspective on the world. When I'm on a mountain, I don't worry about any of the things that I worry about at home. I block out the rest of the world and just focus on the next step. I concentrate on my basic needs—having enough food and water, how the weather will affect the climb, planning the next step, obstacles that may lie ahead. It's all about survival, self-reliance, and instinct.

My hiking and climbing experiences have taught me the importance of enjoying the moment. If your only concern is getting to the end of the hike or the top of the mountain, you miss out on all of the wonderful things that happen along the way. Whenever I reach the peak of a mountain, I make a point of enjoying the view and the beauty of my natural surroundings. This means a lot more than just congratulating myself on getting to the top.

After I started preparing for the climb of my dreams, I discovered that my source of motivation had totally changed. Suddenly breaking a record no longer mattered to me. My new goal was simply to enjoy the climb. I also decided the climb shouldn't just be about me, so I collected pledges to raise money

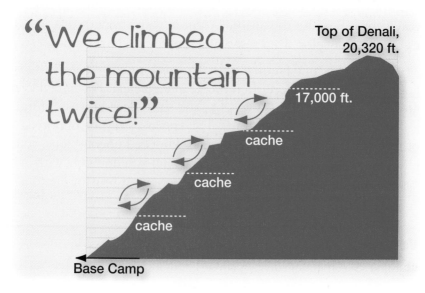

"We climbed the mountain twice!"

Top of Denali, 20,320 ft.

17,000 ft.

cache

cache

cache

Base Camp

for a wellness and child-abuse-prevention center in Anchorage. The higher I climbed, the more money I'd raise for a good cause.

On June 1, 1995, we began our ascent to Denali's summit. Our group consisted of eight people, and we divided into two teams of four.

We carried enough food and fuel to weather any storms. Because hauling a lot of extra gear on our backs was difficult, we regularly loaded up sleds that held our extra food and fuel, then towed the sleds up about 1,000 feet, so we could bury the supplies. Then we returned to our starting point to spend the night.

The next day, if the weather was good, we'd climb to the place where our supplies were buried and begin the entire process again. (So, in a sense, we climbed the mountain twice!) This process took longer, but it gave our bodies a chance to become <u>acclimated</u> to the higher altitude, which meant a better night's sleep. Plus, if we were to get stuck on the mountain due to bad weather, we'd have enough supplies to last for a while.

I discovered that the worst thing to do while hiking up the mountain was to count my footsteps; once I started, it seemed I couldn't stop. Quite frequently on our ascent, I found myself counting my footsteps for hours. I'd try to occupy my mind by singing songs with my friend J.T., who hiked close to me. This helped me stop the endless counting, and I enjoyed the journey more. ❷

❷ Infer
What effect did counting steps have on the climbers?

As we made our way up the mountain, the weather was so bad that we had to stop for days at a time. Although it was June, the temperature hovered around 10 to 15 degrees during the day, and when the wind was blowing, the temperature dropped well below zero. Of the twenty-six days it took to complete the climb, we spent a total of thirteen unable to move.

We dug snow caves for shelter against dangerous blizzards.

Vo•cab•u•lary

acclimated (AK lih may tud) adjusted

Inside the caves, we waited for the storms to end. At 17,200 feet, we had to stay in one spot for seven days in a row. We passed the time playing cards, reading, and singing songs.

We encountered some scary *whiteouts* on the trip. Whiteouts are usually caused by blizzards or extreme snowfall (sometimes by fog). When you're caught in a whiteout, you can't tell where the sky stops and the snow on the mountainside begins.

If I'm familiar with the area in which I'm climbing, whiteouts don't bother me (it's actually kind of fun to make a game out of looking for my friends). But one of the whiteouts we encountered on Denali was so intense that I could barely see my own feet.

When the whiteout hit, we were walking on a high ridge. The snow was coming down hard, and the temperature had plummeted to about 20 degrees below zero. I told myself to keep moving. I wasn't afraid, perhaps because I focused on walking instead of thinking about the danger I was in. Looking back, I remember the whiteout as a fun and <u>exhilarating</u> experience, although most of the team was scared.

The climb proved to be eventful in other ways, too. One day, we were on a ridge 3,000 feet above a crevasse. Everyone was in a bad mood because we were tired and cold (so cold that our eyelashes had frozen). Suddenly I lost my footing and slipped, falling toward the crevasse. As I slid, I reached out and by sheer luck, grabbed my mom's ax, which was stuck in the ice. I was extremely fortunate and fell only a short distance. Who knows how far I could have dropped!

As we approached 11,000 feet on our ascent, I had an even worse scare. Some of my gear was hanging on cords around my neck, including my lip balm, a Swiss army knife, and my sunscreen. The cords somehow got tangled up in the rope that was attached to my chest harness. Before I knew what was happening, the cords were strangling me. I started choking, and I

Vo·cab·u·lary

exhilarating (ek ZIL uh ray ting) refreshing; exciting

tried to yell for help. The wind howled so loudly that no one could hear my cries.

I got scared and began hyperventilating, which frightened me more. Fortunately, the other team caught up to ours, saw what was happening, and helped me get untangled. It took a few minutes for me to calm down and breathe normally again, but I was ready to continue the climb.

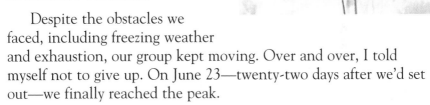

Despite the obstacles we faced, including freezing weather and exhaustion, our group kept moving. Over and over, I told myself not to give up. On June 23—twenty-two days after we'd set out—we finally reached the peak.

What an amazing sight! We stood speechless, staring at the incredible view and the sunset that colored the clouds pink. I'll never forget how pure everything looked from Denali's summit. I huddled next to my mom, feeling awed and, most of all, proud. I had become the youngest person to climb Mt. McKinley, setting a new record.

Later, as we made our way down, I cried. Denali was so extraordinary, and I didn't want to leave it behind. For me, mountains are like a <u>sanctuary</u>, a place where I get to know myself. It's hard to explain how I feel in the mountains. All I know is I feel wonderful.

How I got started:

A famous climber who visited my mom described the experience of climbing Mt. McKinley: This gave me the fever

---

Vo•cab•u•lary

sanctuary (SANG chu ary) a sacred or special place

to climb it myself. Plus, I've always loved outdoor challenges.

Accomplishments:

I raised $3,800 for the Anchorage Center for Families, as a result of my climb. I'm a snowboarder, too—I won second overall in combined slalom and giant slalom in the 1997 National Snowboard Race (a slalom race is a course that tests precision, speed, and flexibility; the giant slalom is designed to test speed, strength, and tenacity). I recently qualified as a member of the USASA Junior National Snowboard Team.

How I stay motivated:

What motivates me is a desire to have fun, and I want to share this enthusiasm with other people. I give talks at schools to inspire other kids to take advantage of the natural world that surrounds them and not take for granted what's right outside their back door.

My future:

I love to stay busy while having fun. My goals are to go to Dartmouth College, go hang gliding off Mount Logan (in Canada's Yukon Territory), be the youngest person to climb Vinson Massif in Antarctica, go parasailing with my snowboard, and enjoy my life. ○

Answer the BIG Question

As you do the following activities, consider the Big Question:
How can you become who you want to be?

WRITE TO LEARN Merrick decided on her goal when she heard other climbers talking about Mount McKinley. What are some other ways people discover their dream? How can you take steps to pursue a goal? Write a response in your notebook.

LITERATURE GROUPS Join two or three other students who have read this selection. Discuss the character traits needed to become a successful mountain climber. Use examples from the selection to back up your answer.

Krumping

IF YOU LOOK LIKE BOZO HAVING SPASMS, YOU'RE DOING IT RIGHT

by Shaheem Reid,
with additional reporting by Mark Bella

Find out why it's cool to be a dancing clown.

We've been deprived all these years. We've never seen Krusty the Clown popping his booty, Ronald McDonald never C-walked, and Bozo . . . forget about it. He could probably barely do a jig, let alone shake his whole body like an enraged zombie from *28 Days Later*. ❶

Well, the dark ages are over. There's a group of California clowns doing the thang.

> **❶ Activate Prior Knowledge**
> What do you know about krumping?

275

Krumping

We've gotten a <u>potent</u> <u>dosage</u> of clown dancing—or krumping, as it's called—in videos such as Missy Elliott's "I'm Really Hot" and the Black Eyed Peas, "Hey Mama." Now the ringleader of the crunk circus act says the mainstream had better look out, because he's bringing more than balloons and giant shoes. The krumping era just may be upon us.

"The clowning and the krumping dance movement, it is a very positive thing because it really does keep kids off the streets," krumping originator Thomas Johnson, a.k.a. Tommy the Clown, explained in Los Angeles recently. "Kids really don't have too much to do around here. This is something exciting for them. To Missy and everybody that has grabbed this whole clowning, krumping, hip-hop style of clown dancing, I want to say thank you for putting it on the national scale. You're doing it."

"I heard about it through ['I'm Really Hot' director] Bryan Barber," Missy Elliott said. "I knew about—we call it clown dancing—but the krumping already. We was already familiar with the dance, but he told me about the painting [of the faces], 'cause he has cousins that do it. I see people doing the dance, but I'd never seen them painted with it. I thought it would be hot for my video."

Painting is almost as important to krumping as the dance moves themselves.

"I like to do either a fade or a scenery," said one of Tommy's dancers, Rocko, as he made himself up in the mirror. "This would be like a scenery or a picture of a whale jumping outta the water into the sun. A fade would be . . . different colors just fading into each other. But there's all types of face paints you could do."

"It just comes to your head and you try to put it together," Tommy said. "Basically we try to mix it up. Different faces, different styles. It's something you gotta do."

Vo•cab•u•lary

potent (POH tent) strong
dosage (DOH sij) an exposure to some experience in a measured amount

Larry Berry, left and Marquisa Gardner—stars of David LaChappelle's latest documentary film—demonstrate a Krump dance move.

Tommy started clown dancing in Compton in 1992 as a way to entertain at birthday parties he performed at. Tommy eventually started getting his pied piper on, enlisting people from the neighborhood to come perform with him at the functions, <u>dubbing</u> themselves the Hip-Hop Clowns. The dance form eventually evolved into what he calls krumping.

"Krumping is when you're dancing and your body is doing a lot of different moves," Tommy explained. "It's really like you're fighting on the dance floor. It's more of an intensity. It can be fast-paced, it can be a lot of moves that are really sharp."

Word of mouth spread over the years, giving Tommy a chance to build his organization and set up local competitions with the kids, the most <u>prevalent</u> being Tommy the Clown's Battle Zone, where

Vo•cab•u•lary

dubbing (DUB bing) naming
prevalent (PREV uh lent) widely known

the kids square off for belts like they do in wrestling. The battling didn't just stay contained to Tommy-sanctioned events as different painted-face crews started popping up around Cali and facing off.

Many of the inner-city kids who have participated say the dancing has kept them away from some potential pitfalls.

"Me, personally, I like to be around [little] kids, I like to make them happy," said Rocko, 19, who's been clown dancing for over three years. "Besides that, it keeps me busy. It gives me something to do. It's positive. That's why I do it, pretty much."

Milk, 17, who appears in Missy's "I'm Really Hot" video and has been krumping for a year and half, agrees. "It just keeps us from doing everything negative—staying outta trouble, keeping yourself busy."

Director/photographer David LaChappelle (*NSYNC, *No Doubt*) directed and produced a documentary on the dance craze last year called *Clowns in the Hood,* which was renamed *Krumped* and premiered at this year's Sundance Film Festival.

"Man, it feels really good to be a part of this hip-hop culture movement," Tommy, the self-appointed "King of Clowns," beamed. "You would never imagine black hip-hop clowns really doing nothing until I brought it to this world. God allowed me to bring it to this world to where it has become a major movement." ○

Answer the BIG Question

As you do the following activities, consider the Big Question:
How can you become who you want to be?

WRITE TO LEARN Imagine you could put two totally unrelated things together to create a movement of your own. What would you choose? Write a brief entry in your notebook about this new combination.

LITERATURE GROUPS Join two or three other students who have read this selection on krumping. Discuss the positive aspects of this new fad and the effect it is having on teens.

Chicago Kids Sink Their Teeth into

DINO CAMP

by Sarah Ives

Imagine traveling across the country to dig up dinosaur remains.

What are you doing this summer? For 14 kids from Chicago, the answer is digging for dinosaurs.

The Junior Paleontologist program run by Project Exploration is much more than your typical summer camp. The program gives kids a taste of what it's like to be a paleontologist. A paleontologist (pail-ee-on-TAWL-o-gist) is a scientist who studies fossils for clues about life in the distant past.

"It's a program about finding your passion," Conor Barnes, a youth-programs manager, said. "It's the biggest challenge of your life."

The program begins with two weeks of training in Chicago, where students learn some of the basics behind studying dinosaurs. That way when students begin fieldwork, "they really understand what they're seeing," Barnes explained.

Then students take the train to Montana, where the real fun begins.

Students begin each day at 6 a.m. By 9 a.m. they head out to a field <u>site</u>, where they do everything from fossil collecting to digging for dinosaurs.

Gabrielle Lyon (left) and Susan, a Junior Paleontologist, apply a coating of plaster to a fossil found during fieldwork.

Students get right into the action. One of Barnes's favorite memories is the time a student found a dinosaur tooth that was 65 million years old.

"He was the first person to hold that particular tooth," Barnes said.

"I could not believe what I found," wrote one student, Marco, in his journal. "It was a tooth from a meat-eater . . . I yelled in happiness."

According to Barnes, "The <u>expedition</u> is just the beginning." Project Exploration continues to support the Junior

---

Vo•cab•u•lary

site (syt) the location of a dig
expedition (ek spi DISH un) a journey made for a specific purpose

Paleontologists when the program is over. Barnes said, "We want to spark and support the students' curiosity. We want them to be lifelong learners."

More about the Junior Paleontologist Program

The Junior Paleontologist program selects kids from Chicago's public schools who show curiosity but don't necessarily have

This fossil was discovered by a Junior Paleontologist at the program's field site in Montana.

good grades. The program is not open to the public. It's free of charge, so any student can participate, regardless of ability to pay. Students must be in 7th through 11th grade.

Project Exploration was co-founded by Paul Sereno, paleontologist and National Geographic explorer-in-residence. To learn more about the program, go to Project Exploration (on the National Geographic website). ○

Answer the BIG Question

As you do the following activities, consider the Big Question:
How can you become who you want to be?

WRITE TO LEARN Write a brief entry in your notebook about how this selection influenced your ideas about careers. What type of career would you like to explore?

LITERATURE GROUPS Join two or three other students who have read this selection. Discuss what you know about fossil collecting and digging for dinosaurs. Would you be interested in participating in a program like the Junior Paleontologists? What would you hope to gain from the experience?

Later...

Wow! I can't believe it! Roger Darzzan!

Yeah! I've seen so many of his movies!

I've seen ALL his movies, TWICE! He's, like, my hero!

And tomorrow I'll show him all my moves when I go for my Level Six belt! He's going to be so impressed when I whup my opponent!!

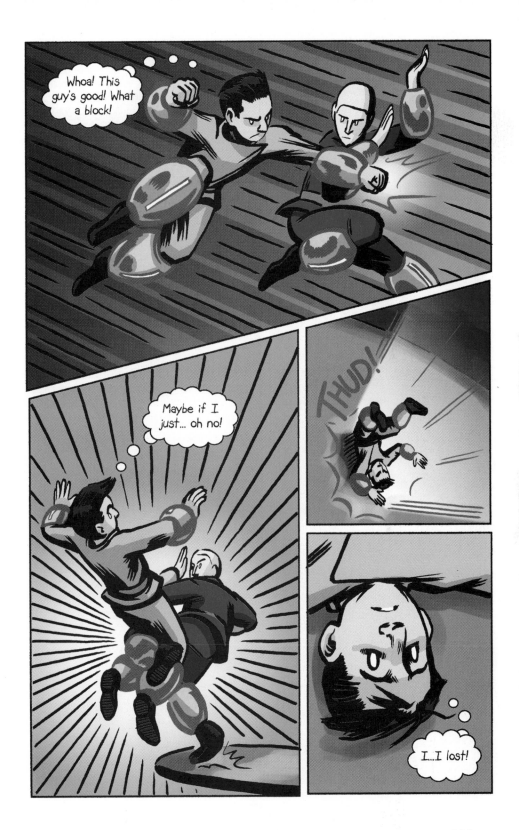

Later...

SEE YOU IN 2235!

That was so embarrassing! I'm such a loser.

I'll never get to the Asteroid Belt level!

Staying here overnight won't change the outcome, you know!

..Wha?... ROGER DARZZAN! WOW!

Awww....it figures. I've always wanted to meet you, and it had to finally happen on the day I failed to get my Level Six belt.

Ha! There's no shame in that. There's always next time, right?

But I want that now! I want an Asteroid Belt!

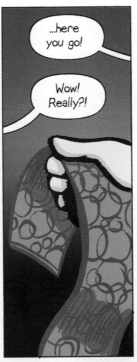

...all a belt is really good for...

...is holding up your pants!

It's okay, kid. You see, it's not about the belts. In the end it's all about what you've learned. The belt might represent that for some, but it doesn't instantly equal knowledge and ability.

Here you go, sir. I'm definitely not ready for this yet.

You need to practice and enjoy what you do first and foremost. The rest will come naturally.

And don't be so hard on yourself! Having a goal is good, but you shouldn't let it take over your life.

WRITE TO LEARN
Think of a goal you have that is important to you. In your notebook, write about how you think the goal will help you become the person you want to be.

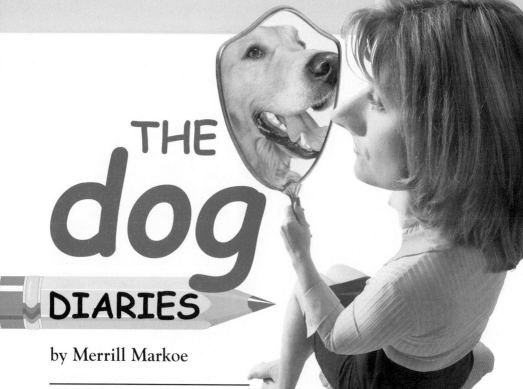

THE dog DIARIES

by Merrill Markoe

"It's a dog's life" takes on new meaning for this author.

I pick dogs that remind me of myself—scrappy, mutt-faced, with a hint of mange. People look for a reflection of their own personalities or the person they dream of being in the eyes of an animal companion. That is the reason I sometimes look into the face of my dog Stan and see <u>wistful</u> sadness and <u>existential angst</u>, when all he is actually doing is slowly scanning the ceiling for flies.

We pet owners demand a great deal from our pets. When we give them the job, it's a career position. Pets are required to listen to us <u>blithely</u>, even if we talk to them in infantile and goofy tones

---

Vo•cab•u•lary

wistful (WIST ful) full of longing
existential angst (eg zis TEN shul ayngkst) worry about the meaning of one's life
blithely (BLYTH lee) in a happy, lighthearted way

of voice that we'd never dare use around another human being for fear of being forced into psychiatric observation. On top of that, we make them wear little sweaters or jackets, and not just the cool kind with the push-up sleeves, either, but weird little felt ones that say, *It's raining cats and dogs*.

We are pretty sure that we and our pets share the same reality, until one day we come home to find that our wistful, intelligent friend who reminds us of our better self has decided a good way to spend the day is to open a box of Brillo pads, unravel a few, distribute some throughout the house, and eat or wear all the rest. And we shake our heads in an inability to comprehend what went wrong here.

Is he bored or is he just out for revenge? He certainly can't be as stupid as this would indicate. In order to answer these questions more fully, I felt I needed some kind of new perspective, a perspective that comes from really knowing both sides of the story.

Thus, I made up my mind to live with my pets as one of them: to share their hopes, their fears, their squeaking vinyl lamb chops, their drinking space at the toilet.

What follows is the revealing, sometimes shocking, sometimes terrifying, sometimes really stupid diary that resulted. **1**

8:45 A.M. We have been lying on our sides in the kitchen for almost an hour now. We started out in the bedroom with just our heads under the bed. But then one of us heard something, and we all ran to the back door. I think our quick response was rather effective because, although I never <u>ascertained</u> exactly what we heard to begin with, I also can't say I recall ever hearing it again.

9:00 A.M. We carefully inspected the molding in the hallway, which led us straight to the heating duct by the bedroom. Just a coincidence? None of us was really sure. So we watched it

> **1 Infer**
> Does the narrator really want to become a dog?

Vo·cab·u·lary

ascertained (as ur TAYND) made certain; found out

suspiciously for a while. Then we watched it for a little while longer.

Then, never letting it out of our sight, we all took a nap. ❷

10:00 A.M. I don't really know whose idea it was to yank back the edge of the carpet and pull apart the carpet pad, but talk about a rousing good time! How strange that I could have lived in this house for all these years, and never before felt the fur of a carpet between my teeth. Or actually bit into a moist, chewy chunk of carpet padding. I will never again think of the carpet as simply a covering for the floor.

> ❷ **Understand Sequence**
> What clues help you keep track of the order of events?

11:15 A.M. When we all wound up in the kitchen, the other two began to stare at me eagerly. Their meaning was clear. The pressure was on for me to produce snacks. They remembered the old me—the one with the prehensile thumb, the one who could open refrigerators and cabinets. I saw they didn't yet realize that today, I intended to live as their equal. But as they continued their staring, I soon became caught up in their obsession. That is the only explanation I have as to why I helped them topple over the garbage. At first I was nervous, watching the murky fluids soak into the floor. But the heady sense of acceptance I felt when we all dove headfirst into the can more than made up for my compromised sense of right and wrong. Pack etiquette demanded that I be the last in line. By the time I really got my head in there, the really good stuff was gone. But wait! I spied a tiny piece of tinfoil hidden in a giant clump of hair, and inside, a wad of previously chewed gum, lightly coated with sugar or salt. I was settling down to my treasure when I had the sense that I was being watched. Raising my head just slightly, I looked into the noses of my companions. Their eyes were glued to that hard rubber mass. Their drools were long and elastic, and so, succumbing to peer pressure, I split up my gum wad three ways.

Vo•cab•u•lary

prehensile (pree HEN sil) adapted for grasping

But I am not sure that I did the right thing. As is so often the case with wanting popularity, I may have gained their short-term acceptance. But I think that in the long run, I lost their real respect. No dog of reasonable intelligence would ever divide up something that could still be chewed.

11:50 A.M. Someone spotted a fly, and all three of us decided to catch him in our teeth. I was greatly relieved when one of the others got to him first.

12:20 P.M. Someone heard something, and in a flash, we were all in the backyard, running back and forth by the fence, periodically hooting. Then one of us spotted a larger-than-usual space between two of the fence boards, and using both teeth and nails, began to make the space larger. Pretty soon, all three of us were doing everything in our power to help. This was a case where the old prehensile thumb really came in handy. Grabbing hold of one of the splinters, I was able to enlarge the hole immediately. Ironically, I alone was unable to squeeze through to freedom, and so I watched with envy as the others ran in pointless circles in the lot next door. What was I going to do? All of my choices were difficult. Sure, I could go back into the house and get a hacksaw, or I could simply let myself out the back gate, but if I did that, did I not betray my companions? And would I not then be obligated to round us all up and punish us? No, I was a collaborator, and I had the lip splinters to prove it. So I went back to the hole and continued chewing. Only a few hundred dollars' worth of fence damage later, I was able to squeeze through that darn hole myself.

1:30 P.M. The extra time I took was just enough for me to lose sight of my two companions. And so, for the first time, I had to rely on my keen, new animal instincts. Like the wild creature I had become, I was able to spot their tracks immediately. They led me in a series of ever-widening circles, then across the lot at a forty-five-degree angle, then into a series of zigzags, then back to the hole again. Finally, I decided to abandon the tracking and head out to the sidewalk. Seconds later, I spotted them both across the street, where they were racing up and back in front of the neighbor's house. They seemed glad to see me, and so I eagerly joined them in their project. The three of us had only been running and hooting for less than an hour when the apparent owner of the house came to the front door. And while I admit this may not have been the best of circumstances for a first introduction, nevertheless I still feel the manner in which he threatened to turn the hose on us was both excessively violent and unnecessarily vulgar.

Clearly, it was up to me to encourage our group to relocate, and I was shocked at how easily I could still take command of our unit. A simple "Let's go, boys," and everyone was willing to follow me home. (It's such a power-packed phrase. That's how I met my last boyfriend!)

3:00 P.M. By the time we had moved our running and hooting activities into our own front yard, we were all getting a little tired. So we lay down on our sides on the porch.

4:10 P.M. We all changed sides.

4:45 P.M. We all changed sides again.

5:20 P.M. We all lay on our backs. (What a nice change of pace!)

6:00 P.M. Everyone was starting to grow restless. Occasionally, one of us would get up, scratch the front door, and moan. I wrestled silently with the temptation simply to let us all in. But then I realized I didn't have any keys on me. Of course, it occurred to me that we could all go back through the new hole in the fence, but everyone else seemed to have forgotten about the entire fence incident by this time. As they say, "a word to the wise." And so, taking a hint from my friends, I began to forget about the whole thing myself.

6:30 P.M. The sound of an approaching car as it pulls into the driveway. The man who shares this house with us is coming home. He is both surprised and perplexed to see us all out in the front yard running in circles. He is also quickly irritated by the fact that no one offers any explanations. And once he opens the front door, he unleashes a furious string of harsh words as he confronts the mounds of garbage someone has strewn all over the house. We have nothing but sympathy for him in his tragic misfortune. But since none of us knows anything about it, we all retire to the coat closet until the whole thing blows over. And later, as he eats his dinner, I sit quietly under the table. As I watch him, a pleasant feeling of calm overtakes me as I realize just how much I have grown as a person. Perhaps that is why the cruel things he says to me seem to have no effect. And so, when he gets up to pour himself another beverage, I raise my head up to his plate, and, with my teeth, I lift off his sandwich. **3** ○

3 Infer
Who do you think this man is?

Answer the
BIG Question

As you do the following activities, consider the Big Question:
How can you become who you want to be?

WRITE TO LEARN If dogs could provide answers, what questions would you have for them? Write a few questions for your pet or some other animal in your notebook.

LITERATURE GROUPS Get together with two or three others who have read "The Dog Diaries." Discuss what the narrator learns about her dogs when she looks at life from their perspective.

IT'S NOT A CRIME TO LOVE SCIENCE

by Juliann F. Willey

Not enough girls taking science? It's a crime! Find out why.

"**C**hemistry class led me to a life of crime." This has become something of a personal <u>slogan</u>. I could also honestly, and perhaps more accurately, say that "Science class led me to a life of crime," because it was my interest in science as a child that planted the seeds for the job I have today: Director of the Delaware State Police Crime Lab, which means I supervise a team made up of a <u>forensic</u> microscopist (me), a questioned-document examiner, two chemists, and a photographer.

When I was a little girl, my love for animals made me think I would one day become a veterinarian. When I got the chance to participate in hands-on science classes and labs in junior high school, I knew for sure that I wanted to grow up to work in science.

Vo·cab·u·lary

slogan (SLOH gun) a brief, attention-getting phrase
forensic (fuh REN sik) relating to science and legal problems

I can remember dissecting earthworms, frogs, and starfish—and not thinking, Yuck!, but rather how cool it was to find out how these creatures functioned. I can remember learning about the planets and the stars so far up above and about minerals and fossils beneath the earth's surface and thinking, Wow! What a world!

My excitement over science did nothing but grow during high school and during my college days, too—only by then I had discovered that I didn't want to be a veterinarian. My courses in analytical and organic chemistry and biochemistry helped me understand how and why things worked the way they do—from how the chemicals in perms make your hair curly to why your blood clots when you get a cut or bruise. Eventually my focus became forensics—the application of science to matters of the law. My interest in forensics had actually been sparked a few years earlier by the television series *Quincy, M.E.*, which starred Jack Klugman as a feisty medical examiner who helped the Los Angeles County police department solve crimes.

Eventually I became a forensic microscopist, and with my three trusty Olympus microscopes I assist in crime-busting by analyzing what we call "known" items (like head hairs or clothing fibers from a victim) and "questioned" items (things collected at the scene of a crime, such as vacuum sweepings and suspects' clothing). The results of my examination are then handed over to the investigating officer—to be used in tracking down a criminal or proving the innocence of a suspect. **❶**

❶ Understand Sequence
What words and phrases help you to follow the order of events in the selection so far?

Given what I do for a living, when I spot something harmful, hurtful, and just plain wrong, I tend to view it as a crime. One of the crimes I've been scoping out for a while is the discouragement of girls from studying the sciences—a surefire method of scaring many away from ever at least considering a career in the field.

And it's a serial crime, taking place all across the nation, affecting girl after girl, day after day. When I contemplate what can be done about it, I can't help but fall back on the procedures I use in my work.

It's Not a Crime to Love Science

So I've looked at the "known" items—information found in various studies—which include:

- Girls are not being encouraged to take science class.

- Boys and girls are not being treated equally in many classrooms.

- Different expectations are placed on boys than on girls. ❷

As for the "questioned" items, traces of strange ideas have been found again and again at the scenes of the crime. Among them:

1. A person who loves science class is definitely uncool.

2. Having a passion for science will have you doing nothing but homework, with no time for fun.

3. The worst thing a girl can do is show her "mental muscles"—especially in front of boys.

4. Anyone who pursues a career in the sciences will end up in some boring job in some boring lab in some boring company somewhere.

My analysis strongly suggests that the prime suspects are Stereotypes and Ignorance, repeat offenders that have been around for a very long time, clogging girls' heads with a lot of nonsense, a lot of lies. They've even got some parents, teachers, and guidance counselors serving as their <u>accomplices</u>—sometimes willingly and often unwittingly—when, for example, they discourage girls from adventures in something like carpentry or auto mechanics. What's more, the culprits have operatives in the entertainment and advertising industries who put out the vile message that a female's sole purpose in life is to be beautiful.

What's to be done? I can't think of anything more necessary than a big dose of truth.

> ❷ **Connect**
> Do these items agree with what you have observed?

Vo•cab•u•lary

accomplices (uh KAWM plus ez) those associated with others in wrongdoing

1. There's nothing more uncool than letting other people keep you from the positive things you enjoy.

2. If you run across a science maniac who's all work and no play, trust me, it's a personality thing. It's not biology or chemistry class that has made this person antisocial and one-dimensional. I am living proof that you can be serious about science and have fun. In high school I ran varsity cross-country, played varsity basketball, participated in various clubs, and went out with friends.

3. The *worst* thing a girl can do is hide her mental muscles—in front of anyone! Not that you should show off your smarts, but it's foolish to camouflage it, because the kinds of people who are worth your while are the kinds of people who respect, admire, and rejoice at intelligence. Those who are intimidated by a smart girl are *definitely* bad news. In the long run, their insecurity will only pull you down and hold you back.

4. The range of jobs in the world of science is awesome. There is something in the field for all kinds of personalities and interests. Science class could lead to a life of healing (a doctor), a life of improving our eating (nutritionist), a life of <u>probing</u> and protecting our world (astronomer, geologist, zoologist, marine biologist, environmental scientist), and so many other careers. When it comes to a job in which a lab is the primary work site, the fact of the matter is that fascinating things go on in labs, and there's really little room for boredom. Think of the challenges facing our world today, such as finding cures for cancer, AIDS, and other diseases; creating vegetable plants that generate high-yield, robust produce; developing materials and

Vo·cab·u·lary

probing (PROH bing) searching and exploring thoroughly

products that are functional yet biodegradable. This is the kind of work that goes on in labs. Of course, if you're into justice and a safer nation, you could always become a forensic scientist like me.

Surely more teachers, parents, and other adults need to step up and join the science awareness patrol by, for example, buying a chemistry set as well as a tea set for a girl who's shown an interest and aptitude for science; by not making a girl feel that a life in the sciences is off-limits to her merely because she is female. **3**

3 Infer How should society's attitude toward girls change?

Such tactics have tremendous value, but it's also <u>vital</u> for girls to take preventive measures to avoid becoming a victim of the crime, by saying no to Stereotypes and Ignorance, by holding up the truth.

And the world will become a more welcoming place for girls who want to say yes to the sciences. ○

Answer the BIG Question

As you do the following activities, consider the Big Question:
How can you become who you want to be?

WRITE TO LEARN Have you encountered stereotypes about brainy girls or girls who like science? If you are a girl, how did they make you feel? If you are a boy, do you believe any of them? Write a response in your notebook.

LITERATURE GROUPS Join two or three other students who have read this selection. Discuss one career in which you can foresee obstacles to success. What positive steps can be taken to overcome these obstacles?

Vo•cab•u•lary

vital (VY tul) very important

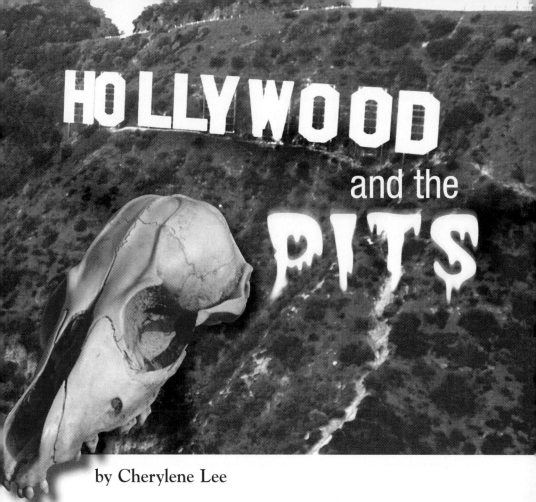

HOLLYWOOD and the PITS

by Cherylene Lee

Find out how a child actress made her way from the stage to the sticky brown La Brea Tar Pits.

In 1968 when I was fifteen, the pit opened its secret to me. I breathed, ate, slept, dreamed about the La Brea Tar Pits. I spent summer days working the <u>archaeological</u> dig and in dreams saw the bones glistening, the broken pelvises, the skulls, the vertebrae looped like a woman's pearls hanging on an invisible cord. I welcomed those dreams. I wanted to know where the next

---

Vo•cab•u•lary

archaeological (ar kee uh LAWJ ih kul) relating to the scientific study of prehistory by examining remains

skeleton was, identify it, record its position, discover whether it was whole or not. I wanted to know where to dig in the coarse, black, gooey sand. I lost myself there and found something else.

My mother thought something was wrong with me. Was it good for a teenager to be fascinated by death? Especially animal death in the <u>Pleistocene</u>? Was it normal to be so obsessed by a sticky brown hole in the ground in the center of Los Angeles? I don't know if it was normal or not, but it seemed perfectly logical to me. After all, I grew up in Hollywood, a place where dreams and nightmares can often take the same shape. What else would a child actor do?

"Thank you very much, dear. We'll be letting you know."

I knew what that meant. It meant I would never hear from them again. I didn't get the job. I heard that phrase a lot that year.

I walked out of the plush office, leaving behind the casting director, producer, director, writer, and whoever else came to listen to my reading for a semi-regular role on a family sit-com. The carpet made no sound when I opened and shut the door.

I passed the other girls waiting in the reception room, each poring over her script. The mothers were waiting in a separate room, chattering about their daughters' latest commercials, interviews, callbacks, jobs. It sounded like every Oriental kid in Hollywood was working except me.

My mother used to have a lot to say in those waiting rooms. Ever since I was three, when I started at the Meglin Kiddie Dance Studio, I was dubbed "The Chinese Shirley Temple"—always the one to be picked at auditions and interviews, always the one to get the speaking lines, always called "the one-shot kid," because I could do my scenes in one take—even tight close-ups. My mother would only talk about me behind my back because she didn't want me to hear her brag, but I knew that she was proud. In a

---

Vo•cab•u•lary

Pleistocene (PLYS tuh seen) a long period of time in the earth's history marked by periods of glaciers and recession; also called the Ice Age

way I was proud too, though I never dared admit it. I didn't want to be called a show-off. But I didn't exactly know what I did to be proud of either. I only knew that at fifteen I was now being passed over at all these interviews when before I would be chosen. My mother looked at my face hopefully when I came into the room. I gave her a quick shake of the head. She looked <u>bewildered</u>. I felt bad for my mother then. How could I explain it to her? I didn't understand it myself. We left saying polite good-byes to all the other mothers.

We didn't say anything until the studio parking lot, where we had to search for our old blue Chevy among rows and rows of parked cars baking in the Hollywood heat.

"How did it go? Did you read clearly? Did you tell them you're available?"

"I don't think they care if I'm available or not, Ma."

"Didn't you read well? Did you remember to look up so they could see your eyes? Did they ask you if you could play the piano? Did you tell them you could learn?"

The <u>barrage</u> of questions stopped when we finally spotted our car. I didn't answer her. My mother asked about the piano because I lost out in an audition once to a Chinese girl who already knew how to play.

My mother took off the towel that shielded the steering wheel from the heat. "You're getting to be such a big girl," she said, starting the car in neutral. "But don't worry, there's always next time. You have what it takes. That's special." She put the car into forward and we drove through a parking lot that had an endless number of identical cars all facing the same direction. We drove back home in silence.

I suppose a lot of my getting into show business in the first place was a matter of luck—being in the right place at the right

---

Vo•cab•u•lary

bewildered (bih WIL durd) confused
barrage (buh RAWZH) a rapid outpouring

In the La Brea Tar Pits many of the excavated bones belong to juvenile mammals. Thousands of years ago thirsty young animals in the area were drawn to watering holes, not knowing they were traps. Those inviting pools had false bottoms made of sticky tar, which immobilized its victims and preserved their bones when they died. Innocence trapped by ignorance. The tar pits record that well. **1**

> **1 Infer** How was Cherylene like the young mammals in the tar pits?

time. My sister, seven years older than me, was a member of the Meglin Kiddie Dance Studio long before I started lessons. Once during the annual recital held at the Shrine Auditorium, she was spotted by a Hollywood agent who handled only Oriental performers. The agent sent my sister out for a role in the CBS Playhouse 90 television show *The Family Nobody Wanted.* The producer said she was too tall for the part. But true to my mother's training of always having a positive reply, my sister said to the producer, "But I have a younger sister . . . " which started my show-biz career at the tender age of three.

My sister and I were lucky. We enjoyed singing and dancing, we were natural hams, and our parents never discouraged us. In fact, they were our biggest fans. My mother chauffeured us to all our dance lessons, lessons we begged to take. She drove us to interviews, took us to studios, went on location with us, drilled us on our lines, made sure we kept up our schoolwork and didn't sass back the tutors hired by studios to teach us for three hours a day. She never complained about being a stage mother. She said that we made her proud.

My father must have felt pride too, because he paid for a choreographer to put together our sister act: "The World Famous Lee Sisters," fifteen minutes of song and dance, real <u>vaudeville</u>

Vo•cab•u•lary

vaudeville (VAWD vil) describing a kind of entertainment consisting of various acts (dancers, singers, animal acts, jugglers, etc.)

stuff. We joked about that a lot, "Yeah, the Lee Sisters—Ug-Lee and Home-Lee," but we definitely had a good time. So did our parents. Our father especially liked our getting booked into Las Vegas at the New Frontier Hotel on the Strip. He liked to gamble there, though he said the craps tables in that hotel were "cold," not like the casinos in downtown Las Vegas, where all the "hot" action took place.

In Las Vegas our sister act was part of a show called "Oriental Holiday." The show was about a Hollywood producer going to the Far East, finding undiscovered talent, and bringing it back to the U.S. We did two shows a night in the main showroom, one at eight and one at twelve, and on weekends a third show at two in the morning. It ran the entire summer often to standing-room-only audiences—a thousand people a show.

Our sister act worked because of the age and height difference. My sister then was fourteen and nearly five foot two; I was seven and very small for my age—people thought we were cute. We had song-and-dance routines to old tunes like "Ma, He's Making Eyes at Me," "Together," and "I'm Following You," and my father hired a writer to adapt the lyrics to "I Enjoy Being a Girl," which came out "We Enjoy Being Chinese." We also told corny jokes, but the Las Vegas audience seemed to enjoy it. Here we were, two

The Lee sisters perform on Dinah Shore's TV show.

kids, staying up late and jumping around, and getting paid besides. To me the applause sometimes sounded like static, sometimes like distant waves. It always amazed me when people applauded. The owner of the hotel liked us so much, he invited us back to perform in shows for three summers in a row. That was before I grew too tall and the sister act didn't seem so cute anymore.

> Many of the skeletons in the tar pits are found incomplete—particularly the skeletons of the young, which have only soft cartilage connecting the bones. In life the soft tissue allows for growth, but in death it dissolves quickly. Thus the skeletons of young animals are more apt to be scattered, especially the vertebrae protecting the spinal cord. In the tar pits, the central ends of many vertebrae are found unconnected to any skeleton. Such bone fragments are shaped like valentines, disks that are slightly lobed—heart-shaped shields that have lost their connection to what they were meant to protect.

I never felt my mother pushed me to do something I didn't want to do. But I always knew if something I did pleased her. She was generous with her praise, and I was sensitive when she withheld it. I didn't like to disappoint her.

I took to performing easily, and since I had started out so young, making movies or doing shows didn't feel like anything special. It was part of my childhood—like going to the dentist one morning or going to school the next. I didn't wonder if I wanted a particular role or wanted to be in a show or how I would feel if I didn't get in. Until I was fifteen, it never occurred to me that one day I wouldn't get parts or that I might not "have what it takes."

When I was younger, I got a lot of roles because I was so small for my age. When I was nine years old, I could pass for five or six. I was really short. I was always teased about it when I was in elementary school, but I didn't mind because my height got me movie jobs. I could read and memorize lines that actual five-year-olds couldn't. My mother told people she made me sleep in a drawer so I wouldn't grow any bigger.

But when I turned fifteen, it was as if my body, which hadn't grown for so many years, suddenly made up for lost time. I grew five inches in seven months. My mother was amazed. Even I couldn't get used to it. I kept knocking into things, my clothes didn't fit right, I felt awkward and clumsy when I moved. Dumb things that I had gotten away with, like paying children's prices at the movies instead of junior admission, I couldn't do anymore. I wasn't a shrimp or a small fry any longer. I was suddenly normal.

Before that summer my mother had always claimed she wanted me to be normal. She didn't want me to become spoiled by the attention I received when I was working at the studios. I still had chores to do at home, went to public school when I wasn't working, was punished severely when I behaved badly. She didn't want me to feel I was different just because I was in the movies. When I was eight, I was interviewed by a reporter who wanted to know if I thought I had a big head.

"Sure," I said.

"No, you don't," my mother interrupted, which was really unusual, because she generally never said anything. She wanted me to speak for myself.

I didn't understand the question. My sister had always made fun of my head. She said my body was too tiny for the weight—I looked like a walking Tootsie Pop. I thought the reporter was making the same observation.

"She better not get that way," my mother said fiercely. "She's not any different from anyone else. She's just lucky and small for her age."

The reporter turned to my mother, "Some parents push their children to act. The kids feel like they're used."

"I don't do that—I'm not that way," my mother told the reporter.

But when she was sitting silently in all those waiting rooms while I was being turned down for one job after another, I could almost feel her wanting to shout, "Use her. Use her. What is wrong with her? Doesn't she have it anymore?" I didn't know what I had had that I didn't seem to have anymore. My mother

Hollywood and the Pits

The churning action of the La Brea Tar Pits makes interpreting the record of past events extremely difficult. The usual order of <u>deposition</u>—the oldest on the bottom, the youngest on the top—loses all meaning when some of the oldest fossils can be brought to the surface by the movement of natural gas. One must look for an undisturbed spot, a place untouched by the action of underground springs or natural gas or human interference. Complete skeletons become important, because they indicate areas of least disturbance. But such spots of calm are rare. Whole blocks of the tar pit can become displaced, making false sequences of the past, <u>skewing</u> the interpretation for what is the true order of nature.

had told the reporter that I was like everyone else. But when my life was like everyone else's, why was she disappointed?

That year before my sixteenth birthday, my mother seemed to spend a lot of time looking through my old scrapbooks, staring at all the eight-by-ten glossies of the shows that I had done. In the summer we visited with my grandmother often, since I wasn't working and had lots of free time. I would go out to the garden to read or sunbathe, but I could hear my mother and grandmother talking. **2**

"She was so cute back then. She worked with Gene Kelly when she was five years old. She was so smart for her age. I don't know what's wrong with her."

"She's fifteen."

"She's too young to be an <u>ingenue</u> and too old to be cute. The studios forget so quickly. By the time she's old enough to play an ingenue, they won't remember her."

"Does she have to work in the movies? Hand me the scissors."

My grandmother was making false eyelashes using the hair

> **2 Connect**
> In what ways are Cherylene's upbringing and yours similar and different?

Vo•cab•u•lary

deposition (dep eh ZIH shun) the process in which soil is laid down
skewing (SKYOO ing) distorting or slanting
ingenue (AN juh noo) an innocent young woman

from her hairbrush. When she was young she had incredible hair. I saw an old photograph of her when it flowed beyond her waist like a cascading black waterfall. At seventy, her hair was still black as night, which made her few strands of silver look like shooting stars. But her hair had thinned greatly with age. It sometimes fell out in clumps.

She wore it brushed back in a bun with a hairpiece for added fullness. My grandmother had always been proud of her hair, but once she started making false eyelashes from it, she wasn't proud of the way it looked anymore. She said she was proud of it now because it made her useful.

It was painstaking work—tying knots into strands of hair, then tying them together to form feathery little crescents. Her glamorous false eyelashes were much sought after. Theatrical make-up artists waited months for her work. But my grandmother said what she liked was that she was doing something, making a contribution, and besides it didn't cost her anything. No overhead. "Till I go bald," she often joked.

Hollywood and the Pits

She tried to teach me her art that summer, but for some reason strands of my hair wouldn't stay tied in knots.

"Too springy," my grandmother said. "Your hair is still too young." And because I was frustrated then, frustrated with everything about my life, she added, "You have to wait until your hair falls out, like mine. Something to look forward to, eh!" She had laughed and patted my hand.

My mother was going on and on about my lack of work, what might be wrong, that something she couldn't quite put her finger on. I heard my grandmother reply, but I didn't catch it all: "Movies are just make-believe, not real life. Like what I make with my hair that falls out—false. False eyelashes. Not meant to last."

I spent a lot of time by myself that summer, wondering what it was that I didn't have anymore. Could I get it back? How could I if I didn't know what it was?

That's when I discovered the La Brea Tar Pits. Hidden behind the County Art Museum on trendy Wilshire Boulevard, I found a

The remains in the La Brea Tar Pits are mostly of carnivorous animals. Very few herbivores are found—the ratio is five to one, a perversion of the natural food chain. The ratio is easy to explain. Thousands of years ago a thirsty animal sought a drink from the pools of water only to find itself trapped by the bottom, gooey with subterranean oil. A shriek of agony from the trapped victim drew flesh-eating predators, which were then trapped themselves by the very same ooze which provided the bait. The cycle repeated itself countless times. The number of victims grew, lured by the image of easy food, the deception of an easy kill. The animals piled on top of one another. For over ten thousand years the promise of the place drew animals of all sorts, mostly predators and scavengers—dire wolves, panthers, coyotes, vultures—all hungry for their chance. Most were sucked down against their will in those watering holes destined to be called the La Brea Tar Pits in a place to be named the City of Angels, home of Hollywood movie stars.

Vo·cab·u·lary

scavengers (SKAV en jurz) animals that feed on dead flesh

job that didn't require me to be small or cute for my age. I didn't have to audition. No one said, "Thank you very much, we'll call you." Or if they did, they meant it. I volunteered my time one afternoon, and my fascination stuck—like tar on the bones of a saber-toothed tiger.

My mother didn't understand what had changed me. I didn't understand it myself. But I liked going to the La Brea Tar Pits. It meant I could get really messy and I was doing it with a purpose. I didn't feel awkward there. I could wear old stained pants. I could wear T-shirts with holes in them. I could wear disgustingly filthy sneakers and it was all perfectly justified. It wasn't a costume for a role in a film or a part in a TV sit-com. My mother didn't mind my dressing like that when she knew I was off to the pits. That was okay so long as I didn't track tar back into the house. I started going to the pits every day, and my mother wondered why. She couldn't believe I would rather be groveling in tar than going on auditions or interviews. **3**

3 Infer
What does Cherylene learn about herself in the tar pits?

Hollywood and the Pits

While my mother wasn't proud of the La Brea Tar Pits (she didn't know or care what a fossil was), she didn't discourage me either. She drove me there, the same way she used to drive me to the studios.

"Wouldn't you rather be doing a show in Las Vegas than scrambling around in a pit?" she asked.

"I'm not in a show in Las Vegas, Ma. The Lee Sisters are retired." My older sister had married and was starting a family of her own.

"But if you could choose between. . ."

"There isn't a choice."

"You really like this tar-pit stuff, or are you just waiting until you can get real work in the movies?"

I didn't answer.

At the La Brea Tar Pits, everything dug out of the pit is saved—including the sticky sand that covered the bones through the ages. Each bucket of sand is washed, sieved, and examined for pollen grains, insect remains, any evidence of past life. Even the grain size is recorded—the percentage of silt to sand to gravel that reveals the history of deposition, erosion, and disturbance. No single fossil, no one observation, is significant enough to tell the entire story. All the evidence must be weighed before a <u>semblance</u> of truth emerges.

My mother sighed. "You could do it if you wanted, if you really wanted. You still have what it takes."

I didn't know about that. But then, I couldn't explain what drew me to the tar pits either. Maybe it was the bones, finding out what they were, which animal they belonged to, imagining how they got

Vo•cab•u•lary

semblance (SEM blans) outward appearance

there, how they fell into the trap. I wondered about that a lot.

The tar pits had its lessons. I was learning I had to work slowly, become observant, to concentrate. I learned about time in a way that I would never experience—not in hours, days, and months, but in thousands and thousands of years. I imagined what the past must have been like, envisioned Los Angeles as a sweeping basin, perhaps slightly colder and more humid, a time before people and studios arrived. The tar pits recorded a warming trend; the kinds of animals found there reflected the changing climate. The ones unadapted disappeared. No trace of their kind was found in the area. The ones adapted to warmer weather left a record of bones in the pit. Amid that collection of ancient skeletons, surrounded by evidence of death, I was finding a secret preserved over thousands and thousands of years. There was something cruel about natural selection and the survival of the fittest. Even those successful individuals that "had what it took" for adaptation still wound up in the pits.

I never found out if I had what it took, not the way my mother meant. But I did adapt to the truth: I wasn't a Chinese Shirley Temple any longer, cute and short for my age. I had grown up. Maybe not on a Hollywood movie set, but in the La Brea Tar Pits. ○

**Answer the
BIG Question**

As you do the following activities, consider the Big Question:
How can you become who you want to be?

WRITE TO LEARN Think about childhood stars you know of. Have any of them been successful in Hollywood as adults? Is sacrificing your childhood worth this early career success? Write your ideas in your notebook.

LITERATURE GROUPS Join two or three other students who have read "Hollywood and the Pits." Discuss the connection Cherylene Lee makes between digging in the La Brea Tar Pits and her career as a child performer. What does she learn about Hollywood from her work in the tar pits?

Why share stories?

In this unit, you will discover stories,
folktales, and poems from all over
the world. As you read, you may
find the answer to the question:
Why share stories?

Dead and Gone

by Marie G. Lee

Find out why the frogs have disappeared from Lake Wichigrin.

Chess, my grandson, seems to think I know everything, so he asks me why there are no frogs in Lake Wichigrin.

I knew he was going to ask me that one day. My grandson notices everything. I have an answer prepared, though it's not the whole truth:

"There used to be frogs here when I was a little girl," I say, and I try to sound more like a know-it-all than like a sad person. "But things change. You know, global warming and the thinning of the <u>ozone</u> layer and all that."

Chess is twelve and a science whiz. This explanation seems to satisfy him. I mentally breathe a sigh of relief. ❶

That night when the sun goes down, it settles like a glowing red pea, right on the lake. It reminds me so much—even though I don't want it to—of those nights long ago when my friends and I used to play War.

❶ **Question**
Why doesn't the narrator tell Chess "the whole truth" about the frogs?

My parents brought me up to Lake Wichigrin for summers when I was a little girl. Back then there were only three cabins on our side of the lake; now there are at least ten. Ours was just a one-room box with an outhouse. Now our cabin has five rooms and running water. The old wood stove still has its place of honor in the middle of the cabin, but nowadays we do most of the cooking on an electric range.

It's nice to have all these conveniences in the cabin, but I do miss the sound of the frogs. I used to lie awake at night, listening to the soft bump-bump of the boat against the dock and the frogs croaking. The sounds said to me, summer, summer, summer. It's still pretty-sounding here, with the water and the occasional call of a loon. But I sure do miss those frogs.

The War started over who got Loon Point, the best part of the lake. The Point had many high-branched trees, perfect for attaching a rope so you could swing, Tarzanlike, into the water. And the trees' green leaves cast cool shadows, even during the hottest days of August. Loon Point also had a big rock shaped just like a loon's head—it was perfect for sunning and diving.

Nowadays, I hate this memory so much because the obvious

Vo•cab•u•lary

ozone (OH zohn) a gas in the atmosphere that blocks some of the sun's harmful rays

question is, why didn't we just share Loon Point? Of course we should have shared. It would probably have been fun, all those kids playing together at the Point.

But that wasn't the way it was. We on our side of the lake believed we deserved <u>exclusive</u> rights to the Point—and the other-side kids disagreed. So we devoted all our time to proving our case: Loon Point was ours, and we'd fight for it if necessary.

From the three cabins there were me and my brother John, the Candella twins, and Tanya Foster and her cousin Jon. The other side of the lake was more spread out, so from a wider area came Todd and Max, Georgina, Jamie, and the huge Joey. We were pretty even.

Every summer, John and I were excited to see the our-side kids. When we got there, we made bonfires and roasted marshmallows and had a grand old time talking about what had happened during the school year. Our parents would go to bed, and we'd stay up next to the glow of the fire and start talking serious.

"Are they here yet? Have they been up to the Point?"

We never went up to the Point, except together. Sometimes the first kids to arrive went up to spy to see what was up, but neither side would show up until everything was "official."

The beginning part of the summer was most important. When we were good and ready, we would pack some soda, towels, and swim suits and head up there and make a lot of noise, basically waiting for the other-side kids. When they got there, we would tell them to leave, but of course they wouldn't.

We hated those other-side kids. I can't tell you exactly why. They were just kids, like us. But maybe it was because we thought of them as the other side, against us, so just looking at them would send my blood to boiling. Who did they think they were, anyway? ❷

> ❷ **Understand Cause and Effect**
> What happened when the narrator's side won the War? What happened when they lost?

Vo•cab•u•lary

exclusive (ik SKLOO siv) limited to a certain group

Once War was officially declared, anything could happen. We did things like dump the other-side kids' clothes into the water, steal their food. One day, one of the other-side boys punched my brother John right in the face, so we all rushed in there—even me! We were so mad that no matter how hard they hit, we hit even harder. I got my hair pulled and a big bruise on my arm, but I didn't feel anything—I just wanted to drive them out. And we did. Loon Point was ours for that summer.

Every summer we had to fight for it, though, and sometimes we lost and had to spend a whole summer somewhere else! That, of course, made us want to fight harder next time.

As we got older, the fighting got meaner. We were the first to use weapons—rocks. I actually didn't want to. I saw a movie once about some kids who stood on a bridge over a highway and dumped rocks over the side. The big rocks crashed into a car with a man, his wife, and a little baby. The little baby was on the momma's lap, and he died when the car crashed. I didn't want that to happen, even though there are no bridges on the roads that lead up to the lake.

But everyone else thought rocks would be a splendid idea, so we spent our days collecting them. The night when we met for War (we had started <u>skirmishing</u> at night . . . it was easier to fight when you couldn't see what the person looked like), I threw a rock and I heard it hit something, and someone said "Ow!" I remember feeling very proud of myself for that.

It's kind of strange how all my memories of the beautiful summers here at the lake are somehow attached to War. But I can't unattach them, because that's how my summers really happened.

There was that one summer when both sides decided to use frogs. Frogs didn't hurt as much as rocks, but if you were slapped in the face with one, they were cold and slimy.

In order to win the War, we figured we just had to get more frogs than the other side. Once the other side was "frogged" enough, they'd surrender.

Vo·cab·u·lary

skirmishing (SKUR mish ing) brief fighting between two groups

We spent days collecting frogs, and we kept them in one of those ten-gallon containers that you use for keeping minnows. We kept it <u>tethered</u> at the dock and whenever someone caught a frog, he just threw it in the little door. After a while, though, it got so crowded that some of the frogs drowned. But we didn't mind too much because dead frogs are almost as good weapons as live ones.

And that night the sun set like a glowing red pea on the lake, just as it's doing tonight. It took three of us to lug that huge can of smelly frogs up to the Point. The other side was there, they threw the first bomb.

Splat! The frog hit me full in the face and left my cheek feeling slimy. It made me so mad I grabbed a bunch of frogs from the

Vo•cab•u•lary

tethered (TETH erd) attached with a rope to something else, usually an animal

container and threw them with all my might. The fight was on. Frogs were flying everywhere—in the water, hitting trees, hitting faces.

The other side had a lot of frogs, but we had more. We kept throwing and throwing, and finally, there was a small voice that said, "We give up."

We were so happy that night. We envisioned all the great times we were going to have at Loon Point this summer. Swimming, sunning, playing.

The next day it rained, so we stayed in. The day after that it rained, too. And the day after. We got sick of playing Parcheesi and reading comic books, so we decided to go out to Loon Point in the rain just to look at it, what we'd won. **3**

3 Predict
What do you think the scene at Loon Point will look like?

In our galoshes and rain gear, we trekked out there. We couldn't believe what we saw! There were dead frogs all over the place. Some were lying around with their insides hanging out, some had broken backs. A couple of them had their mouths open—I'd never seen a frog with its mouth open before. Even in the water, there were frogs floating, rain falling on them. On the rock there were dead soggy frogs with red blood on them. For some reason I thought frogs would have green blood, not red blood like ours.

In time, the weather cleared up and we went back and cleaned up. We threw the frog carcasses in the water, or into the woods. Sometimes now I wish we had buried them, or something.

I always wonder if the other frogs saw what happened to their brothers and decided to leave Lake Wichigrin. If you saw this happening to your brothers and sisters and friends, you probably wouldn't want to stay around either. In my imagination, those frogs packed up their bags and made the long march to another lake, Sand Lake, maybe.

Can you believe me? Such an old lady, yet I think so much about those frogs. I guess what bothers me the most is that the frogs were innocent creatures and we made them suffer so we could play War, which was not a very nice game in the first place.

I notice that Chess sometimes stays out late, playing with the other kids. I wonder if he ever plays games like War. I would like to think not, he's too sweet a kid. On the other hand, I was pretty sweet, too, with all my ribbons and lace, but I remember how it felt to throw that frog. I was fighting for something I believed in—not necessarily for Loon Point, but more for us as a group, our honor or something. Of course I see now how foolish it was—when it's too late.

"Chess," I say. He is putting his trunks in a towel. "I want to tell you something about the frogs."

"Not now, Grandma," he says. "I have to meet Steve and Bob."

"Okay," I say. "But remind me. I'll tell you why there aren't any frogs here at this lake."

Chess looks at me, cocks his head as he does when he's a little confused. But then he grabs his towel and runs out the door.

"Remind me to tell you!" I call after him.

"I will," he says. His white form fades away in the dark.

I sit and listen. The swish swish of the lake against the dock. A mosquito buzzes in my ear. ❹ ◯

> ❹ **Analyze**
> What do you think is the message, or point, of this story?

Answer the BIG Question

As you do the following activities, consider the Big Question:
Why share stories?

WRITE TO LEARN Write a brief entry in your notebook about the narrator's reason for telling this story. What do you think she will tell Chess about the frogs?

PARTNER TALK Meet with another student who has read "Dead and Gone." Discuss why the narrator first blames the lack of frogs on global warming and the thinning of the ozone layer. Why is it so difficult for her to tell her grandson the truth?

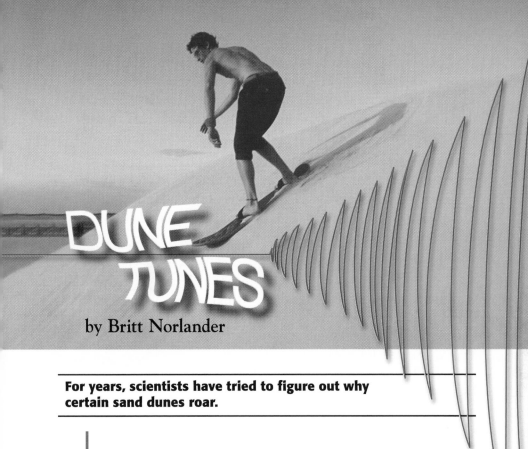

DUNE TUNES

by Britt Norlander

For years, scientists have tried to figure out why certain sand dunes roar.

Lon Beale climbs to the top of a towering sand dune. Then, he straps a board to his feet and leaps off the edge. His sandboard cuts into the dune, sending sand rushing down the slope. As the sand slips, a thunderous boom cracks from the dune. "It roars like a dinosaur," says Beale, director of Sand Master Park—a sandboarding center in Oregon.

This roar has been heard by desert dwellers for centuries. But scientists have never known how it forms. Now, Melany Hunt, a mechanical engineer, and colleagues at California Institute of Technology may have solved the mystery.

When sand on the dunes moves—pushed by strong winds or even sandboarders like Beale—the grains rub together and bounce off each other. These interactions create *sound waves* (vibrating energy waves) that travel through the sand.

Dune Tunes

In booming dunes, the sound waves move downward and hit a layer of wet sand about 2 meters (6 feet) beneath the surface. There, some of the waves get reflected, or bounce back, toward the sandy surface. When the sound waves reach the top of the sand, they get reflected again and travel back downward.

As the waves bounce back and forth through the upper sand layer, waves of a certain *frequency* (number of vibrations per second) become *amplified*, or louder, explains Hunt. These particular waves combine to create a loud boom with a single *pitch* (how high or low a note sounds). "It's like playing one key on the piano," says Hunt. **❶**

This sound can't be created on smaller dunes, Hunt says, possibly because those dunes don't have a wet layer below. But large dunes can form strong waves. "You can even feel the vibrations [travel] up your legs," says Beale. "It's an eerie feeling." ○

❶ Understand Cause and Effect
What causes the sand dunes to boom?

Answer the
BIG Question

As you do the following activities, consider the Big Question:
Why share stories?

WRITE TO LEARN What do you think it would be like to sandboard down a tall, booming sand dune? Write an entry in your notebook describing this experience.

LITERATURE GROUPS Meet with two or three others who have read "Dune Tunes." What explanations might desert dwellers have come up with for the sounds coming out of the dunes? What stories or folktales might those sounds have inspired?

El Inca

by Kagan McLeod

IT WAS 1533, HERE IN PERU, WHERE THE INCAS FOUGHT HARD AGAINST THE EUROPEAN INVADERS.

FOR THEM, IT WAS NOW OR NEVER!

A boy learns about his people's heroic past.

IN THE END, HOWEVER, THE SPANISH WERE TOO MUCH FOR THEM. THEIR CAPITAL, **CUZCO**, WAS LOST.

YOUNG FRIENDS! THE GAMES YOU PLAY ARE FUN AND ADVENTUROUS...

...BUT IN MY TIME, BOYS JUST A FEW YEARS OLDER THAN YOU WOULD BEGIN TRAINING TO BECOME WARRIORS!

A BIT YOUNG, DON'T YOU THINK?

JUST THE PERFECT AGE. ALL OF THE YOUNG NOVICES GATHERED EACH YEAR IN THAT BUILDING. OLDER INCA WARRIORS LIVED THERE AS INSTRUCTORS.

FORTY YEARS AGO, THERE WAS A YOUNG BOY WHO HAD JUST BEGUN HIS TRAINING!

WHAT DID HE DO?

WELL... FIRST, HE FOUND HE COULD HAVE NOTHING BUT A LITTLE WATER AND A FEW HERBS TO EAT FOR SIX DAYS!

AFTER THAT, THE NOVICES WERE DIVIDED INTO TWO GROUPS—ONE TO DEFEND THE GREAT FORTRESS AND ONE TO ATTACK IT!

THE BATTLE LASTED AN ENTIRE DAY!

THE WEAPONS WERE LESS DANGEROUS THAN THE ONES USED IN AN ACTUAL WAR, BUT THAT DIDN'T MEAN THE YOUNG BOY DIDN'T GET HURT!

BONK

NEXT, HE WAS INSTRUCTED IN THE WEAPONS OF WAR.

WRESTLING.

SLING THROWING.

SPEARS.

BOW AND ARROW.

THE INCAS WOULD TEST RESISTANCE TO PAIN BY WHIPPING THE ARMS AND LEGS OF THE STUDENTS! ANYONE SHOWING SIGNS OF SUFFERING WOULD BE SCOLDED!

HOW WILL YOU RESIST THE ENEMY'S WEAPONS IF YOU CAN'T STAND THE CARESS OF MY GENTLE WHIP!?

WHA-PISH

THE BOY WAS ASKED TO GUARD THE CAMP FOR 12 NIGHTS IN A ROW. IF HE WAS CAUGHT WITH DROOPING EYELIDS, HE WOULD BE SCOLDED AGAIN.

THERE WAS ANOTHER TEST, GIVEN BY THE MASTER OF A WEAPON CALLED THE MACANA.

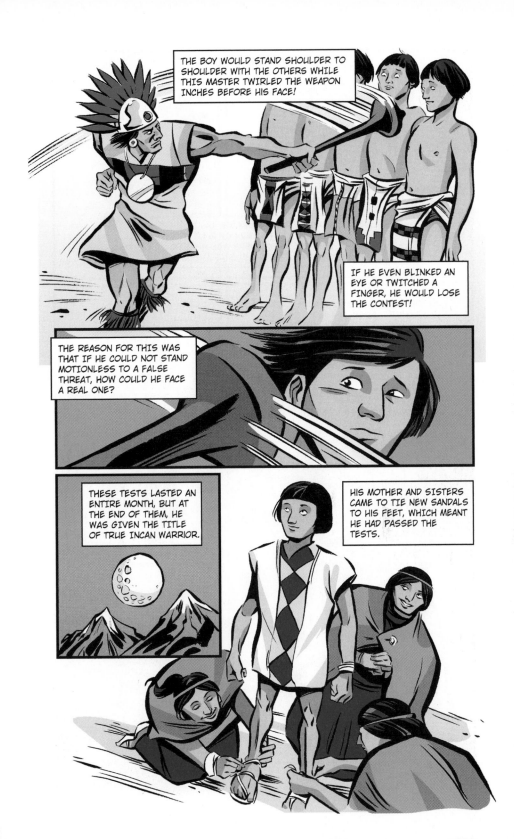

THE BOY WOULD STAND SHOULDER TO SHOULDER WITH THE OTHERS WHILE THIS MASTER TWIRLED THE WEAPON INCHES BEFORE HIS FACE!

IF HE EVEN BLINKED AN EYE OR TWITCHED A FINGER, HE WOULD LOSE THE CONTEST!

THE REASON FOR THIS WAS THAT IF HE COULD NOT STAND MOTIONLESS TO A FALSE THREAT, HOW COULD HE FACE A REAL ONE?

THESE TESTS LASTED AN ENTIRE MONTH, BUT AT THE END OF THEM, HE WAS GIVEN THE TITLE OF TRUE INCAN WARRIOR.

HIS MOTHER AND SISTERS CAME TO TIE NEW SANDALS TO HIS FEET, WHICH MEANT HE HAD PASSED THE TESTS.

NEXT, HE RUSHED BEFORE THE INCAN KING TO RECEIVE THE MARK OF RANK FROM HIM. BUT FIRST, THERE WAS A SPEECH CONGRATULATING THE GRADUATES.

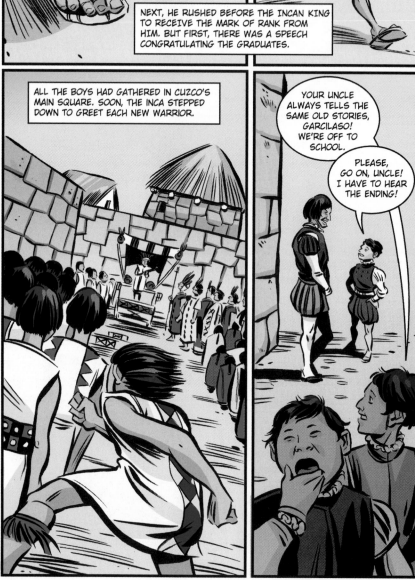

ALL THE BOYS HAD GATHERED IN CUZCO'S MAIN SQUARE. SOON, THE INCA STEPPED DOWN TO GREET EACH NEW WARRIOR.

YOUR UNCLE ALWAYS TELLS THE SAME OLD STORIES, GARCILASO! WE'RE OFF TO SCHOOL.

PLEASE, GO ON, UNCLE! I HAVE TO HEAR THE ENDING!

RIGHT, NOW WHERE WAS I? OH YES, THE INCAN KING APPROACHED THE YOUNG BOY!

RANK WAS SHOWN BY THE PIERCING OF THE EAR. THE INCAN KING WOULD DO THIS PERSONALLY! IT WAS A GREAT HONOR!

THE BOY TRIED NOT TO WINCE AS HE RECEIVED HIS EARRING, BUT IT HURT!

THIS IS YOUR HISTORY TOO, YOUNG GARCILASO. DO NOT LET THE STORY OF YOUR PEOPLE DIE.

PASS IT DOWN TO YOUR CHILDREN. KEEP IT ALIVE IN THEIR HEARTS!

DON'T WORRY, UNCLE. I PROMISE I WILL!

GARCILASO KEPT HIS PROMISE, AND DID EVEN BETTER! BY 1609, HE HAD TAKEN EVERY STORY THAT HIS UNCLE, MOTHER, AND OTHER RELATIVES HAD TOLD HIM AND WROTE THEM DOWN.

THIS ENSURED THAT EVERYONE COULD KNOW THE HISTORY OF THE INCAN PEOPLE.

GARCILASO DE LA VEGA WAS ALSO KNOWN AS *EL INCA*. HE WAS THE SON OF A SPANISH CONQUEROR AND AN INCAN PRINCESS. HE IS REMEMBERED TODAY AS ONE OF THE FIRST AND GREATEST SOUTH AMERICAN WRITERS!

WRITE TO LEARN
What are some stories you have learned about your ancestors? In your notebook, write about them. List some other ways you could get information about your family's history.

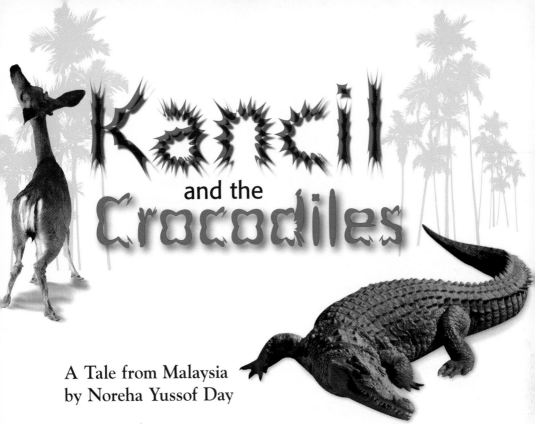

Kancil and the Crocodiles

A Tale from Malaysia
by Noreha Yussof Day

Can a mouse deer trick a hungry crocodile?

Once upon a time, there was a tropical forest full of parrots, <u>orangutans</u>, monkeys, and crocodiles, all of whom could talk.

The parrots talked to the orangutans, the orangutans talked to the monkeys, the monkeys talked to the crocodiles, and the crocodiles talked to anyone who would listen. All the animals lived happily together, as long as they were careful to talk to the crocodiles—who were always hungry—from a distance. Rare arguments were settled by the king.

Kancil, the mouse deer, and Kura-Kura, the tortoise, also lived in this forest, and they were the best of friends.

Vo·cab·u·lary

orangutans (uh RANG uh tangz) a type of ape with long arms and reddish brown hair

Kancil and the Crocodiles

One hot, sunny afternoon, they were walking along the river. Kancil was thirsty. "Wouldn't it be nice to eat some juicy fruit now?" he asked.

Kura-Kura agreed. They walked farther, and passed a few lazy crocodiles floating in the river. "Hello!" called one.

"Hello, Buaya!" answered Kancil. He was always friendly to the crocodiles, because he didn't want to become their lunch.

Suddenly, Kancil saw a <u>rambutan</u> tree on the other side of the river. It was full of ripe, juicy fruit. "Kura-Kura! Look! Rambutans!"

"Oh!" said Kura-Kura. "But how are we going to get them?" he asked, looking at the crocodiles. **1**

1 Predict
How will Kancil and Kura-Kura get the fruit?

Kancil was quiet. Kura-Kura was also quiet. He knew that Kancil was thinking.

Then Kancil exclaimed, "Ah!" And he whispered to his friend.

They walked carefully to the edge of the riverbank. Buaya opened his eyes a little wider and edged closer to the bank himself.

"Hear ye! Hear ye! All the crocodiles in the river: I have a message from the king!" announced Kancil.

"What is the message?" asked Buaya, uncomfortably close to Kancil and Kura-Kura now.

"The king is going to have a party to celebrate the birth of the orangutan twins. He needs to know how many of us live in the forest, and Kura-Kura and I are assigned to count the crocodiles," said Kancil confidently.

The crocodiles began to talk excitedly. No one had ever heard of a party to celebrate the birth of orangutan twins, but no one

Vo•cab•u•lary

rambutan (ram BYOO tun) a type of juicy fruit found in Southeast Asia

had ever heard of there *not* being one. And a party meant food. They all started to count themselves at once.

"Stop! That won't work," yelled Kancil, pleased with himself.

"What do you suggest, Kancil?" asked Buaya.

"Well. If you all make a straight line from here to the other side of the river, we can walk along and count."

"Yes! A good idea," agreed the crocodiles, all pushing to be first.

"Stop pushing!" commanded Buaya. And all the crocodiles formed a neat line and tried to stay still.

"Be careful, Kura-Kura," Kancil whispered. "They won't be interested in us while they think about the party. Count loudly."

And he stepped out onto Buaya and called out, "One crocodile!"

Kura-Kura followed behind and repeated, "One crocodile."

Kancil moved forward and continued, "Two crocodiles!"

Kura-Kura echoed, "Two crocodiles." And on they went.

Finally, they reached the other side. The crocodiles swam close to the bank.

Buaya <u>sidled</u> up and asked, "How many of us are there?" He had been too far away to hear.

"There are twenty-seven greedy crocodiles, Buaya," said Kancil proudly.

"What do you mean?" asked Buaya, upset at being called greedy.

"There is no party. We just wanted to cross the river to get these rambutans. Thank you for helping us," Kancil said.

"We won't forget," added Kura-Kura politely.

"We won't forget, either!" cried Buaya furiously as all the crocodiles grumbled and snapped.

But Kancil and Kura-Kura were already walking toward the rambutan tree with its red, juicy fruit hanging on every branch.

"There is one thing I didn't think of, though," Kancil told his friend. "How are we going to get back?" O

Answer the BIG Question

As you do the following activities, consider the Big Question:
Why share stories?

WRITE TO LEARN Kancil and Kura-Kura lie to get what they want. What lesson do they learn from this experience? Write a brief entry in your notebook.

PARTNER TALK Meet with a classmate who has read this folktale. Share your responses to the characters. Then discuss how the story might continue and how it might end.

Vo•cab•u•lary

sidled (SY duld) to move sideways

A Forest Home

Is it possible for a human to gain the trust of a wild animal?

The rain <u>pelted</u> down heavily as Jane hurried through the forest. Suddenly she froze, almost afraid to breathe. Right there, hunched in front of her, was a large chimpanzee. She knew that if she upset or scared the animal, he could be very dangerous.

A sound <u>rustled</u> above. Jane looked up to see another big chimp. He looked right at her and screamed *WRAAAAH*. This is a chimp's way of threatening a dangerous animal. Branches started shaking all around her and Jane could see another pair of eyes staring through the leaves. A third chimp! Surrounded, Jane <u>crouched</u> down and pretended not to notice them.

Vo•cab•u•lary

pelted (PELT ed) struck again and again
rustled (RUS eld) made a soft, gentle sound
crouched (krowchd) bent forward from the waist; stooped with knees bent

A Forest Home

Suddenly, the animals charged toward her, one at a time. Then, just as suddenly, they turned and ran off. Perhaps they realized this strange creature did not want to hurt them.

To the chimps, Jane was indeed a strange creature. Months before, the young Englishwoman had come to Africa to study animals. Jane had loved animals from the time she was a little girl. And she wanted to learn more about them by watching how they *really* lived—in the wild. Jane's dream came true when she had a chance to live in Gombe National Park in Africa. She worked for a famous scientist named Louis Leakey. It was Jane's job to observe a group of chimps at Gombe and find out more about these amazing animals. And what an experience it turned out to be!

At first, nothing seemed to happen. Jane set up camp in the forest and went on long hikes every day looking for chimps. Her mother lived with her at the camp for a while and ran a small clinic to help African people. An African cook named Dominic and his wife lived at the camp, too, and helped out.

Jane was coming back from one of her hikes one day when she heard Dominic shouting.

"Jane! Jane!" he called excitedly. "While you were gone today a big chimp sat right in that tree. Then he walked over to your tent and took some bananas."

Jane could hardly believe it. It had been so hard to try to get close to the chimps. On her long hikes she had tried to follow them wherever they went. But the chimps usually ran away when they saw her. Or they could threaten her, as she knew. ❶

Now, Dominic's good news was <u>incredible</u>. She decided to stay in camp the next day, just in case the chimp came back. All day she waited. What if he didn't show up a second time? Jane began to worry that

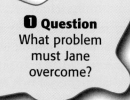

❶ Question
What problem must Jane overcome?

Vo·cab·u·lary

incredible (in KREH duh bul) beyond belief

she had wasted a whole day. But, finally, about 4 o'clock in the afternoon, the chimp came back.

"I know you," she thought at once. She had seen him running around with the others. Jane named this chimp David Greybeard because he had white whiskers growing on his chin. He was a handsome chimp and he was usually calm.

When David walked into the camp, he climbed a tree and began eating nuts. When he had his fill of these, he came down and ate the bananas that Jane set out for him. Three more times that week David visited the camp.

Then one day David took a banana from Jane's hand. When she first held it out to him, he didn't know what to do. He wasn't sure he wanted to get that close to Jane. But he took the banana, reaching for it gently. A wild animal trusted her enough to come within touching distance. Now *this* was progress. From then on, when Jane went into the forest, she brought bananas in case she saw David Greybeard. When she did, David would come and take the banana from Jane's hand and sit next to her while he ate it. When his chimpanzee friends saw David do this, they would stare in wonder!

One day Jane noticed David gathering up <u>termites</u> with a blade of grass. He poked the blade into a mound of soil the insects had built. The termites grabbed onto the grass, and then David would pick them off to eat as he pulled the grass out of the mound. Next, David found a twig, peeled the leaves off, and used that as a sturdier "fishing rod" for his termite dinner. "Think of it!" marveled Jane. A chimp was using, even making, simple "tools."

Scientists hadn't known for sure whether animals ever made tools. But then scientists didn't always know all the facts about animals. They often studied animals in zoos and laboratories. Jane was watching the chimps in their real home.

She made notes on what she had seen, as she did every day.

Dr. Jane Goodall, DBE with Pasa, an orphan chimpanzee at JGI Ngamba Chimpanzee Sanctuary, Uganda. Pasa is a Sanctuary chimpanzee. Jane Goodall does not handle wild chimpanzees.

Vo•cab•u•lary

termites (TUR mytz) small, antlike insects that feed on wood

Then in the evening she would copy the notes over in a journal. This way she could remember all the facts she learned about the chimps.[1]

There would be other discoveries in time. For now, though, Jane was happy just to live quietly in the forest, watching and waiting. She observed the chimps day in and day out and let them become used to her. Her first friend, David Greybeard, sometimes brought other chimps around to the camp. There was the mother chimp she named old Flo, for example. "Maybe I can keep her coming back," Jane thought. She always had bananas in good supply, just in case.

Sure enough, Flo came back again and again. So did her young chimps, Fifi, Figan, and Faben. Jane and the animals got to know each other. And more chimps came. Jane watched the ways they acted and began to get to understand them.

"Imagine this," she thought one day. "Here I am in the middle of the forest. And yet sometimes it's as if I'm living with a strange, different, and wonderful family!" ❷ ○

❷ Analyze
Why is patience so important in Jane's work?

• •

[1]Jane Goodall, a world-known expert on wild chimpanzees, has studied chimps for more than 30 years. Before Goodall's work in Africa, people knew little about these intelligent creatures.

Answer the BIG Question

As you do the following activities, consider the Big Question:
Why share stories?

WRITE TO LEARN Think about the progress Goodall made as she observed the chimps. What did she learn about these animals? Write a brief entry in your notebook.

PARTNER TALK Goodall observed animals in their natural environment. Meet with another student who has read this selection. Discuss how Goodall's experience differs from observing animals in zoos.

The Night the Bed Fell

by James Thurber

Colorful characters and misunderstandings cause a lot of chaos. What fun!

I suppose that the high-water mark of my youth in Columbus, Ohio, was the night the bed fell on my father. It makes a better <u>recitation</u> (unless, as some friends of mine have said, one has heard it five or six times) than it does a piece of writing, for it is almost necessary to throw furniture around, shake doors, and bark like a dog, to lend the proper atmosphere and <u>verisimilitude</u> to what is admittedly a somewhat incredible tale. Still, it did take place.

Vo•cab•u•lary

recitation (res ih TAY shun) the act of repeating memorized material aloud
verisimilitude (ver eh sih MIL ih tood) the appearance of being true or real

It happened, then, that my father had decided to sleep in the attic one night, to be away where he could think. My mother opposed the notion strongly because, she said, the old wooden bed up there was unsafe: it was wobbly and the heavy headboard would crash down on father's head in case the bed fell, and kill him. There was no <u>dissuading</u> him, however, and at a quarter past ten he closed the attic door behind him and went up the narrow twisting stairs. We later heard <u>ominous</u> creakings as he crawled into bed. Grandfather, who usually slept in the attic bed when he was with us, had disappeared some days before. On these occasions he was usually gone six or eight days and returned growling and out of temper, with the news that the Federal Union[1] was run by a passel of blockheads and that the Army of the Potomac[2] didn't have a chance.

We had visiting us at this time a nervous first cousin of mine named Briggs Beall, who believed that he was likely to cease breathing when he was asleep. It was his feeling that if he were not awakened every hour during the night, he might die of suffocation. He had been accustomed to setting an alarm clock to ring at intervals until morning, but I persuaded him to abandon this. ❶ He slept in my room and I told him that I was such a light sleeper that if anybody quit breathing in the same room with me, I would wake instantly. He tested me the first night—which I had suspected he would—by holding his breath after my regular breathing had convinced him I was asleep. I was not asleep, however, and called to him. This seemed to <u>allay</u> his

❶ **Predict**
What do you think might happen to Briggs Beall?

. . . .

[1]Federal Union: The Northern side during the Civil War. He is under the illusion that the Civil War has not yet ended.

[2]Army of the Potomac: One of the Northern armies during the Civil War.

Vo·cab·u·lary

dissuading (dih SWAYD ing) talking someone out of doing something
ominous (AW muh nus) threatening
allay (uh LAY) to calm a worry or an emotion

fears a little, but he took the precaution of putting a glass of spirits of camphor[3] on a little table at the head of his bed. In case I didn't arouse him until he was almost gone, he said, he would sniff the camphor, a powerful reviver. Briggs was not the only member of his family who had his <u>crotchets</u>. Old Aunt Melissa Beall (who could whistle like a man, with two fingers in her mouth) suffered under the <u>premonition</u> that she was destined to die on South High Street, because she had been born on South High Street and married on South High Street. Then there was Aunt Sarah Shoaf, who never went to bed at night without the fear that a burglar was going to get in and blow <u>chloroform</u> under her door through a tube. To avert this calamity—for she was in greater dread of <u>anesthetics</u> than of losing her household goods—she always piled her money, silverware, and other valuables in a neat stack just outside her bedroom, with a note reading: "This is all I have. Please take it and do not use your chloroform, as this is all I have." Aunt Gracie Shoaf also had a burglar phobia, but she met it with more fortitude. She was confident that burglars had been getting into her house every night for forty years. The fact that she never missed anything was to her no proof to the contrary. She always claimed that she scared them off before they could take anything,

· ·

[3]spirits of camphor: A liquid with a powerful odor.

Vo·cab·u·lary

crotchets (KROCH itz) peculiar or stubborn ideas
premonition (pree muh NIH shun) advance warning of a future event
chloroform (KLOR uh form) type of medicine that used to be used as a painkiller
anesthetics (an is THET iks) medicine to dull pain

by throwing shoes down the hallway. When she went to bed she piled, where she could get at them handily, all the shoes there were about her house. Five minutes after she had turned off the light, she would sit up in bed and say "Hark!" Her husband, who had learned to ignore the whole situation as long ago as 1903, would either be sound asleep or pretend to be sound asleep. In either case he would not respond to her tugging and pulling, so that presently she would arise, tiptoe to the door, open it slightly and heave a shoe down the hall in one direction, and its mate down the hall in the other direction. Some nights she threw them all, some nights only a couple of pairs. ❷

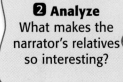

❷ Analyze
What makes the narrator's relatives so interesting?

But I am straying from the remarkable incidents that took place during the night that the bed fell on father. By midnight we were all in bed. The layout of the rooms and the <u>disposition</u> of their occupants is important to an understanding of what later occurred. In the front room upstairs (just under father's attic bedroom) were my mother and my brother Herman, who sometimes sang in his sleep, usually "Marching Through Georgia" or "Onward, Christian Soldiers." Briggs Beall and myself were in a room adjoining this one. My brother Roy was in a room across the hall from ours. Our bull terrier, Rex, slept in the hall.

My bed was an army cot, one of those affairs which are made wide enough to sleep on comfortably only by putting up, flat with the middle section, the two sides which ordinarily hang down like the sideboards of a drop-

---

Vo·cab·u·lary

disposition (dis puh ZIH shun) arrangement

leaf table. When these sides are up, it is <u>perilous</u> to roll too far toward the edge, for then the cot is likely to tip completely over, bringing the whole bed down on top of one, with a tremendous banging crash. This, in fact, is precisely what happened about two o'clock in the morning. (It was my mother who, in recalling the scene later, first referred to it as "the night the bed fell on your father.")

Always a deep sleeper, slow to arouse (I had lied to Briggs), I was at first unconscious of what had happened when the iron cot rolled me onto the floor and toppled over on me. It left me still warmly bundled up and unhurt, for the bed rested above me like a canopy. Hence I did not wake up, only reached the edge of consciousness and went back. The racket, however, instantly awakened my mother, in the next room, who came to the immediate conclusion that her worst dread was realized: the big wooden bed upstairs had fallen on father. She therefore screamed, "Let's go to your poor father!" It was this shout, rather than the noise of my cot falling, that awakened Herman, in the same room with her. He thought that mother had become, for no apparent reason, <u>hysterical</u>. "You're all

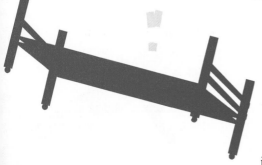

right, Mamma!" he shouted, trying to calm her. They exchanged shout for shout for perhaps ten seconds: "Let's go to your poor father!" and "You're all right!" That woke up Briggs. By this time I was conscious of what was going on, in a vague way, but did not yet realize that I was under my bed instead of on it. Briggs, awakening in the midst of loud shouts of

---

Vo·cab·u·lary

perilous (PER uh lus) very dangerous
hysterical (hih STAIR ih kul) displaying uncontrollable emotions (crying, laughing, etc.)

fear and apprehension, came to
the quick conclusion that he
was suffocating and that we
were all trying to "bring him
out." With a low moan,
he grasped the glass of
camphor at the head of his
bed and instead of sniffing
it poured it all over himself.
The room reeked of camphor.
"Ugf, ahfg," choked Briggs, like
a drowning man, for he had almost
succeeded in stopping his breath under
the <u>deluge</u> of <u>pungent</u> spirits. He leaped out of bed and groped
toward the open window, but he came up against one that
was closed. With his hand, he beat out the glass, and I could
hear it crash and tinkle on the alleyway below. It was at this
juncture that I, in trying to get up, had the uncanny sensation
of feeling my bed above me! Foggy with sleep, I now suspected,
in my turn, that the whole uproar was being made in a frantic
endeavor to extricate me from what must be an unheard-of and
perilous situation. "Get me out of this!" I bawled. "Get me out!"
I think I had the nightmarish belief that I was entombed in a
mine. "Gugh," gasped Briggs, floundering in his camphor.

By this time, my mother, still shouting, pursued by Herman,
still shouting, was trying to open the door to the attic, in order to
go up and get my father's body out of the wreckage. The door was
stuck, however, and wouldn't yield. Her frantic pulls on it only
added to the general banging and confusion. Roy and the dog
were now up, the one shouting questions, the other barking.

Father, farthest away and soundest sleeper of all, had by
this time been awakened by the battering on the attic door. He
decided that the house was on fire. "I'm coming, I'm coming!"

Vo•cab•u•lary

deluge (DEL yooj) sudden, heavy downpour
pungent (PUN jent) strong smelling or tasting

he wailed in a slow, sleepy voice—it took him many minutes to regain full consciousness. My mother, still believing he was caught under the bed, detected in his "I'm coming!" the mournful, resigned note of one who is preparing to meet his Maker. "He's dying!" she shouted.

"I'm all right!" Briggs yelled to reassure her. "I'm all right!" He still believed that it was his own closeness to death that was worrying mother. I found at last the light switch in my room, unlocked the door, and Briggs and I joined the others at the attic door. The dog, who never did like Briggs, jumped for him—assuming that he was the culprit in whatever was going on—and Roy had to throw Rex and hold him. We could hear father crawling out of bed upstairs. Roy pulled the attic door open, with a mighty jerk, and father came down the stairs, sleepy and irritable but safe and sound. My mother began to weep when she saw him. Rex began to howl. "What in the name of God is going on here?" asked father. **3**

> **3 Understand Cause and Effect**
> The narrator's bed falls on top of him. What events follow this cause?

The situation was finally put together like a gigantic jigsaw puzzle. Father caught a cold from prowling around in his bare feet but there were no other bad results. "I'm glad," said mother, who always looked on the bright side of things, "that your grandfather wasn't here." ○

Answer the BIG Question

As you do the following activities, consider the Big Question:
Why share stories?

WRITE TO LEARN Thurber's story introduces you to many quirky characters. In your notebook, write a brief description of someone you know who is colorful, unusual, or funny.

LITERATURE GROUPS Meet with two or three others who have read "The Night the Bed Fell." Discuss the unusual characters in the story. Why do you think Thurber chose to write this story?

THE PUZZLE OF PAN AM
FLIGHT 103

from *Forensic Scientists*

by Rose Inserra

How did fragments collected from the wreckage of an airplane help explain why it exploded in flight?

On December 21, 1988, Pan Am Flight 103 exploded like a fireball over the town of Lockerbie in Scotland, destroying 21 houses on impact and killing 259 people aboard the plane and 11 on the ground. The flight had taken off earlier from a London airport, headed for New York. More than four million pieces of the wreckage were traced and the airplane was reconstructed. All material that had been collected was put together like a jigsaw puzzle.

The wreckage trail <u>sifted</u> through by investigators included

---

Vo·cab·u·lary

sifted (SIFT ed) sorted carefully

Police sort through the wreckage of Pan Am Flight 103.

engines, control surfaces, landing gear, fuel tanks, doors, instruments, panels from inside the airplane, and the flight data recorder (black box).

The flight data recorder records everything happening in the cockpit. It showed that the control settings on the airplane were correct at the time of flight. It also showed that the engine and bodywork of the plane were normal. There had been no radio message giving a <u>distress</u> call.

A reconstruction of the wreckage showed that an explosion happened at the neck of the plane, behind the cockpit. The explosion did not blow the plane apart. It blew a hole about 10 inches (25 cm) wide. The force of the shock waves blew the plane apart. These waves rushed through the body of the plane and blew out at weak points. In three seconds the plane was in several pieces falling to the ground. With the fuel tanks almost full, the plane hit the town with the force of an earthquake measuring 1.6 on the <u>Richter scale</u>. ❶

> ❶ **Understand Cause and Effect**
> What happened as a result of the initial explosion?

Vo•cab•u•lary

distress (dih STRES) a condition requiring immediate help
Richter scale (RIK ter skayl) a scale that measures the force of an earthquake

Other evidence about the explosion was also found:

- The flight data recorder had recorded a sound that may have been a bomb exploding.
- One of the engines had suffered damage from the blast.
- There were burn marks in the luggage compartment.
- There was explosive damage in the luggage compartment, which meant that the explosion had happened next to a luggage container floor.
- Traces of an electric <u>device</u> that can be used to explode bombs were found.
- Particles from a plastic explosive were found in the luggage compartment walls.

Investigators have concluded that an explosive device was planted in the luggage compartment of the plane. ○

Answer the BIG Question

As you do the following activities, consider the Big Question:
Why share stories?

WRITE TO LEARN Museums often create displays that show what life was like in the past. Why do you think people are so fascinated with looking back into time? Write a brief entry in your notebook.

PARTNER TALK Meet with a classmate who has read "The Puzzle of Pan Am Flight 103." Discuss the different purposes served by reconstructions.

Vo·cab·u·lary

device (dih VYS) an invention that serves some specific purpose

Too Many

MUMMIES?

by Mark Rose

**Can a museum have too
many mummies?**

Highway construction near Lima, Peru, has turned up 26 Inca mummy bundles. The bundles—each holding the remains of more than one adult—date from the 60 years just before the Spanish Conquest in 1533. They are the remains of middle-class farmers and craftsmen (most of the tools found with them are related to making textiles). But the mummies are creating a problem. Space! In 2002, nearly 2,000 mummies were dug up near Lima. The local museum is running out of space and may not be able to take care of newcomers properly. One solution that has been proposed: placing the new road in a tunnel that would run beneath the Inca cemetery. ○

Answer the BIG Question

As you do the following activities, consider the Big Question:
Why share stories?

WRITE TO LEARN Imagine 2,000 mummies in one museum. In your notebook, write a brief entry about how you would handle the problem.

PARTNER TALK Meet with a partner who has read "Too Many Mummies." Brainstorm ways to deal with the problem. What do you think of the solution mentioned in the article?

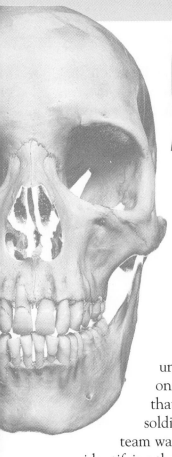

GRINNER
A FACE FROM THE PAST

An excerpt from *Talking Bones:*
The Science of Forensic Anthropology

by Peggy Thomas

**Find out what scientists discovered when
they dug up an old burial site.**

In 1987, an unmarked cemetery was uncovered during the construction of a new house on the shores of Lake Erie in Canada. It turned out that the site had once been a burial ground for dead soldiers during the War of 1812. An archaeological team was assigned the job of recovering the bodies and identifying them as best they could. Twenty-eight skeletons were <u>exhumed</u> and from the <u>insignias</u> on the buttons found among the bones it appeared that they were American soldiers. Each skeleton showed signs of battle injuries or medical treatment such as musket fire, cannon blasts, and <u>amputation</u>.

The second soldier to be uncovered had a full set of teeth that gleamed white against the dark brown dirt, and as it is with all skeletons, after the <u>ligaments</u> of the jaw decayed, his heavy <u>mandible</u> dropped to the chest giving him a gaping grin. The

---

Vo•cab•u•lary

exhumed (ig ZOOMD) removed from a grave
insignias (in SIG nee uz) official symbols or identifying marks
amputation (am pyoo TAY shun) removal of a limb by a surgeon
ligaments (LIG uh mentz) bands of tough tissue connecting body parts
mandible (MAN dih bihl) lower jawbone

archaeological team nicknamed him Grinner.

Grinner had been buried with his feet bound and hands folded across his stomach. Under his right shoulder blade was a copper pin that may have held closed a bandage, suggesting that Grinner had been in a military hospital before he died.

Of all of the skeletons, Grinner's skull was in the best shape; some of the other skulls had been destroyed by cannon fire or were missing altogether. ❶ Grinner was a good candidate for a <u>reconstruction</u>. The anthropologist chose to give Grinner blue eyes and reddish brown hair because U.S. Army records indicated that these were the most common features among the soldiers at that time. Now visitors to Fort Erie, Canada, can actually see the face of one of the soldiers who slept in the barracks, stood guard in the towers, and fought and died in the War of 1812.

❶ Analyze
What can museum visitors learn by viewing reconstructions?

Museums all over the world use reconstructions to put faces on the past. At a reconstructed Norse village in York, England, there is a reconstruction of a Viking man who lived 1,000 years ago, and at the New York State Museum in Albany, New York, there are reconstructions of early Native Americans <u>depicting</u> what life was like in America long before Europeans arrived.

Perhaps the most <u>intriguing</u> reconstructions are the ones at the American Museum of Natural History in New York City. In the Hall of Human Biology and Evolution there are <u>dioramas</u> that depict early man and woman as they may have looked walking across an African plain more than 3 million years ago. Inspired by a set of footprints found in 1976 that had been fossilized in the mud for 3 million years, paleoanthropologists at the museum

---

Vo•cab•u•lary

reconstruction (ree kun STRUK shun) the act of putting something back together
depicting (dih PIKT ing) portraying or showing
intriguing (in TREEG ing) arousing the interest of
dioramas (dy uh RAM uz) three-dimensional displays

speculated about how the ancestors who left those tracks might have looked. Because the couple did not trip and fall into the mud leaving facial impressions, the scientists had to rely on skeletal data such as the 4-foot-tall skeleton known as "Lucy," and other fragments of 3-million-year-old skulls as models for the reconstruction. ○

Beetle on a String

by Vince Gotera

What is it like to hold a life of another in your hands?

When I was a kid, I walked bugs on a leash.
This was in the Philippines, where my parents
and I moved when I was a toddler, trading
foggy San Francisco for Manila's typhoons.

Actually, it was an <u>idyllic</u> place for a child—
warm evenings <u>drenched</u> in the sweet scent
of <u>sampaguita</u> flowers, but most of all,
a huge universe of <u>enthralling</u> insects

Vo•cab•u•lary

idyllic (eye DIL ik) simple and carefree
drenched (drencht) spread throughout something
sampaguita (sam pah GEE tah) national flower of the Philippines grown for its beauty and fragrance
enthralling (en THRAWL ing) so interesting as to hold complete attention

filling the night with buzzing and clicks, strobe
flashes of their glow-in-the-dark wingflicks.
It was my father who showed me how to catch
a scarab beetle in the cup of your hand, wait

for the wings to subside and close, then loop a thread
between <u>thorax</u> and <u>carapace</u>, tying it off—
not too tight—to allow the insect to fly
on a two-foot-long lasso. I remember

how I would smile and laugh, maybe five
or six years old, as a beetle would circle my head
like a whirring kite, <u>iridescent</u> green in the sun,
the thread stretched almost to the breaking point.

At night, I would tie my beetles to the round knobs
on my dresser drawers and be soothed to sleep
by a lullaby of buzzing. By morning, the beetles
were always dead, weights hung on string.

Those long nights must have been horrible.
Straining your body to shift an immovable weight,
unable to <u>evade</u> the swooping flight
of predators, banging again and again hard
against the dead wood, brought up short
by that unforgiving tether, cutting off
your pulsing blood every time, the long
   tube
of your heart quivering. It makes me
   shiver now

to wonder what thoughtless boy holds my string? ❶

❶ Analyze
What message do you think the speaker of this poem wants to share?

Vo·cab·u·lary

thorax (THOR aks) part between the head and the abdomen of an animal or insect
carapace (KAR ah pays) animal or insect shell
iridescent (eer ih DES ent) having radiant rainbowlike colors
evade (ih VAYD) cleverly escape or avoid

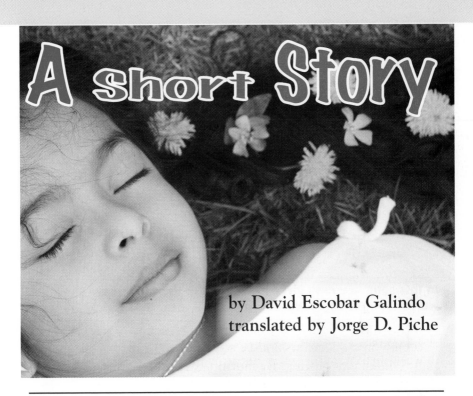

A short Story

by David Escobar Galindo
translated by Jorge D. Piche

Read to see how an ant inspires a young girl's vivid imagination.

The ant climbs up a trunk
carrying a petal on its back;
and if you look closely
that petal is as big as a house
especially compared to the ant that
carries it so olympically.

You ask me: Why couldn't I carry
a petal twice as big as my body and my head?
Ah, but you can, little girl,
but not petals from a dahlia,
rather boxes full of thoughts
and loads of magic hours, and
a wagon of clear dreams, and
a big castle with its fairies: **2**
all the petals that form the soul of
a little girl who speaks and speaks . . .!

2 Question
What are the "petals" that the little girl can carry, according to the speaker?

Travelin' Soldier

written by Bruce Robison
performed by the Dixie Chicks

**In this song, a young girl meets a boy in the café where she
works.** *Songs are poems set to music.*

Two days past eighteen
He was waitin' for the bus in his army greens
Sat down in a booth at a café there
Gave his order to the girl with a bow in her hair
He's a little shy so she gave him a smile
So he said would you mind sittin' down for a while
And talkin' to me I'm feelin' a little low
She said I'm off in an hour and I know where we can go

So they went down and they sat on the pier
He said I bet you got a boyfriend but I don't care
I've got no one to send a letter to
Would you mind if I sent one back here to you?

Chorus:
I cried
Never gonna hold the hand of another guy
Too young for him they told her
Waitin' for the love of the travelin' soldier
Our love will never end
Waitin' for the soldier to come back again
Never more to be alone
When the letter says a soldier's coming home

So the letters came
From an army camp
In California then Vietnam
And he told his heart
It might be love
And all of the things he was so scared of
Said when it's gettin kinda tough over here
I think about that day sittin' down at the pier
And close my eyes and see your pretty smile
Now don't worry but I won't be able to write for a while

Chorus:
One Friday night at a football game
The Lord's Prayer said and the anthem sang
A man said folks would you bow your heads
For the list of local Vietnam dead
Cryin' all alone under the stands
Was the <u>piccolo</u> player in the marching band
And one name read and no one really cared
But a pretty little girl with a bow in her hair **3** ○

3 Understand Cause and Effect
Why is the piccolo player crying?

Answer the
BIG Question

As you do the following activities, consider the Big Question:
Why share stories?

WRITE TO LEARN Each poem tells a brief story in someone's life. Choose one of the three poems. Which images in the poem best tell that story? Write a brief entry in your notebook.

LITERATURE GROUPS Meet with two or three others who have read these poems. Discuss the story in each poem and how the poet told it.

Vo•cab•u•lary

piccolo (PIK eh loh) a small flute with a high pitch

Hosni the Dreamer

An Arabian Tale
by Ehud Ben-Ezer

Find out what happens when a shepherd refuses to follow the crowd.

*H*osni was a shepherd who worked for a <u>sheikh</u>. He was alone during the day, and since he had no one to talk to, he would sometimes talk to his sheep.

After work, the shepherds liked to spend their evenings joking with one another, or discussing what they would buy if they had money. All but Hosni.

Vo•cab•u•lary

sheikh (sheek) a leader of an Arabian family or village

He preferred to spend his evenings listening to the tribal elders' tales of travel and adventure in faraway cities. Hosni had always lived in the desert, and their stories filled him with dreams.

One night, Hosni dreamed that he was in a city. The dream seemed so real to him that he felt he had actually been there. ❶ He wanted to tell the other shepherds about it, but he was afraid they would laugh at him.

Instead, he told his dream to his sheep.

One of the shepherds overheard him and said to the others, "Hosni talks nonsense to his sheep!"

"How strange," said one.

"How stupid," said another. Soon all the shepherds were making fun of him.

One day, the sheikh wanted to sell some of his camels in the city. He decided to take several of his shepherds on this journey, but Hosni wasn't one of them.

When Hosni begged the sheikh to let him go, the sheikh said, "Sorry, Hosni. Maybe next time."

Then, just when they were ready to leave, one of the shepherds fell ill. The sheikh decided to let Hosni take the sick man's place.

They traveled for days, going through canyons, passing over mountains. Hosni felt so lucky to be going to the city that he didn't even notice how hot and dry it was.

After crossing a large wadi—a riverbed that was dry—they finally reached the city.

The sheikh sold his camels. He paid each shepherd a gold <u>dinar</u> and gave them the rest of the day off to enjoy the wonders of the city.

> ❶ **Predict**
> Will Hosni's dream come true? Will he actually travel to a city?

Vo•cab•u•lary

dinar (dih NAR) a form of Arabian money

The shepherds hurried off together, leaving Hosni on his own.

Hosni wandered through the city's streets, amid the noisy crowd. The more he walked, the more the city felt like his dream, and like the tribal elders' tales. Only now it was real, and even more exciting than he had imagined.

He went to the city's market, passing by the shops and stands with their colorful cloth, embroidered robes, carpets, shiny pots and plates. The scent of <u>pilaf</u>, <u>kebab</u>, <u>falafel</u>, <u>couscous</u>, and sweet <u>halvah</u> filled the air. But Hosni didn't buy anything.

Then he noticed a sign on a small shop: "One verse for one gold dinar."

Hosni felt he must go in.

When he entered, he found himself in a different world, where he could no longer hear the noise and <u>commotion</u> of the market.

An old man was sitting alone.

Hosni gave the old man his gold dinar. The man took the coin, studied Hosni carefully, then slowly pronounced, "Don't cross the water until you know its depth." Hosni waited. Finally, he asked, "Is that all, sir?"

The old man said no more.

The next morning, Hosni, the sheikh, and the shepherds left the city and rode into the desert.

On the way, the shepherds talked about all they had eaten and all they had bought in the city. They asked Hosni what he bought. Hosni didn't respond. They began teasing him for not purchasing anything and for wasting his trip to the city.

Finally, Hosni blurted out, "I did buy something. A verse!"

Vo•cab•u•lary

pilaf (pi LAWF) a steamed rice dish
kebab (kah BAHB) cubes of meat and vegetables on a stick
falafel (fuh LAW ful) a dish made from ground spiced chickpeas
couscous (KOOS koos) a North African pasta dish
halvah (hawl VAH) a treat made with honey and sesame seeds
commotion (kuh MOH shun) noisy disturbance or disorder

"A verse?" They could hardly believe their ears. He told them the verse, and they burst out laughing. "He spends all his money on worthless nonsense," said one.

"What a foolish fool," said yet another, laughing. And the sheikh laughed, too.

The shepherds were still laughing when they noticed dark rain clouds in the distance. They knew from the lightning and thunder that there must be a violent downpour in the mountains above them. But the rain was far away, and not a single drop fell on them.

They soon came to the wadi that had been dry on their way to the city, and now rainwater from the mountains was flowing in it.

The sheikh and the shepherds didn't hesitate. They entered the water with their loaded-down camels and began crossing.

Hosni thought about the verse he had bought, and stopped. *"Don't cross the water until you know its depth,"* he repeated to himself. Hosni called to the sheikh and the shepherds to come back. But the sheikh replied impatiently, "Hurry up, Hosni!" **2**

2 Predict
Do you think Hosni will obey the sheikh? Why or why not?

Now, a richly dressed man was also standing by the wadi. He was leading a camel by a long rope. On top of the camel was a <u>luxurious</u> <u>canopy</u>.

When the man saw the sheikh and the shepherds begin to cross the wadi, he, too, entered the water. Hosni tried to warn him, but the man just shrugged his shoulders and kept going.

Though Hosni did not want to be left behind, he kept thinking about the verse and couldn't bring himself to cross.

The others hadn't gone far when suddenly a swift and powerful undercurrent swept them away and the rushing water

Vo·cab·u·lary

luxurious (lug ZHUR ee us) costly; plush; rich
canopy (KAN uh pee) a tent-like cloth covering

swallowed them up.

Hosni was horrified by what had happened.

Then he heard a voice from inside the canopy on the camel's back. "My poor, poor servant! Oh, how awful!"

Hosni approached the canopy and discovered a young maiden in it.

"Gracious sir," she said. "I'm Zobeide. Now that my servant has <u>perished</u>, I'm lost. Please, help me."

"Don't worry," Hosni said gently. "I can take you back to the city."

"Oh, no! Not there," she said. "I don't want to return to the Emir. Against my wishes, he has sent me as a present to a prince I don't know. Where are you heading?"

"I have no family," said Hosni. "Now that the sheikh is dead, I have no work either. Besides, I'd rather go to an entirely new place than return to one where I was unhappy."

"Please, let me travel with you," said Zobeide.

Hosni tied the rope of Zobeide's camel to his. He didn't attempt to cross the rushing waters. Instead, he went around the entire length of the wadi.

They traveled for a long time.

Vo·cab·u·lary

perished (PAIR isht) died

The days were very hot and the nights were cold.

Hosni told Zobeide what he had learned from the tribal elders, of his dream about a city he had never seen before, and how the old man sold him a verse that saved him from the terrible tragedy they had witnessed.

Zobeide told Hosni, "My father had worked for the Emir. After I became an orphan, I was raised in the Emir's palace. Life there wasn't as happy as you would think. Although I am most disturbed by what happened at the wadi, I believe it was a sign that I wasn't meant to live in another palace with an unknown prince."

Finally, they came to another city. Hosni and Zobeide grew to love each other.

Soon they were married. With the silver and gold that Zobeide's camel carried, they bought a large house and fields.

In time, they raised a family, and lived happily for many years. Hosni never forgot the old man and his verse. **3** ○

3 Analyze
How does Hosni prove that the other shepherds were wrong about him?

Answer the
BIG Question

As you do the following activities, consider the Big Question:
Why share stories?

WRITE TO LEARN Has anyone ever laughed at one of your stories, ideas, or dreams? How did this make you feel? Write a brief entry in your notebook about this experience.

LITERATURE GROUPS Meet with two or three others who have read this folktale. Discuss how Hosni differs from the other shepherds. What effect did Hosni's decisions have on the path his life takes?

It's a Small E-mail World After All

by E. Sohn

How many e-mails will it take for two randomly selected people to connect? ❶

❶ Question
What do you think the answer to this question is?

W e're all connected. You can send an e-mail message to a friend, and your friend can pass it on to one of his or her friends, and that friend can do the same, continuing the chain. Eventually, your message could reach just about anyone in the world, and it might take only five to seven e-mails for the message to get there.

Scientists recently tested that idea in a study involving 24,000 people. Participants had to try to get a message forwarded to one of 18 randomly chosen people. Each participant started by sending one e-mail to someone they knew. Recipients could then forward the e-mail once to someone they knew, and so on.

Targets, who were randomly assigned by researchers from Columbia University in New York, lived in 13 countries. They included an Australian police officer, a Norwegian veterinarian, and a college professor.

Out of 24,000 chains, only 384 reached their goal. The rest petered out, usually because one of the recipients was either too busy to forward the message or thought it was junk mail.

The links that reached their goal made it in an average of 4.05 e-mails. Based on the lengths of the failed chains, the researchers estimated that two strangers could generally make contact in five to seven e-mails.

The most successful chains relied on casual acquaintances rather than close friends. That's because your close friends know each other whereas your acquaintances tend to know people you don't know. The phenomenon, known as the strength of weak ties, explains why people tend to get jobs through people they know casually but aren't that close to.

So, start networking and instant messaging now. As they say in show business: It's all about who you know. ○

Answer the BIG Question

As you do the following activities, consider the Big Question:
Why share stories?

WRITE TO LEARN What are the advantages and disadvantages of e-mail? Do you prefer to contact friends by phone or e-mail? Write a brief response in your notebook.

PARTNER TALK Meet with a partner who has read "It's a Small E-mail World After All." Discuss the ideas presented in the article. Do you think e-mail has brought people closer together? Why or why not?

Darkness at Noon
Solar Eclipse

by Shonto Begay

What happened when the sun died?

I was ten years old when the stars came out at noon. After penning the sheep and goats in the corral for their noon rest, I felt a strange sense of uneasiness. The chirping of birds was absent, the buzzing of insects stopped, even the breeze died down.

My toes felt the sand still warm through the holes in my sneakers. The landscape fell under a shadow on this cloudless day. As I hurried through the tumbleweed and rabbitbrush, it got darker. I looked up and saw twinkling stars far above. The dogs were lying in the doorway.

I ran into the darkened <u>hogan</u>. Immediately I was told to sit down and remain quiet. I couldn't even eat or drink. My aunt said the sun had died. *The sun had died.* The words hit me like thunder. How could this happen? What did we do? I had only started to live. My brothers sat nearby, silent in their own <u>turmoil</u>. The hogan was dark. Only occasional whispers broke the silence.

Outside toward the east, up on the hill, I heard the rising and

---

Vo•cab•u•lary

hogan (HOH gawn) a one-room Navajo house
turmoil (TUR moyl) a confused disturbance

falling of prayer song. My father was up there boldly standing in the face of darkness, calling back the sun. I prayed silently with him.

As we sat in the darkness for what seemed like eternity, little crescents of light began to appear on the hogan floor, faint at first, then brighter. The sun was returning. It was coming back to life. I prayed harder as the stars disappeared and faint blue washed over the sky. The crescents of light on the floor, coming in from the smokehole, started to round themselves out, becoming half circles, then slowly one full, bright whole. The sun had regained its form. The holy cycle. The sacred symbol of all creation was reborn this day for me.

My father came down from the hill exhausted and happy. We ran out to meet him before the <u>elders</u> could contain us.

That day and all the days since, I appreciate even more the sun we thought we'd lost. The colors are richer and the warmth of the sun, more comforting. The days are brighter. The summer heat is welcome.

Each day, I rise just before the sun does, to sprinkle my corn pollen, and to thank the coming day for its gift of light. **❶** ○

> **❶ Understand Cause and Effect**
> What effect has the solar eclipse had on the narrator?

Answer the BIG Question

As you do the following activities, consider the Big Question:
Why share stories?

WRITE TO LEARN Recall a time when you were young and something in life seemed magical because it was a complete mystery. Write a brief entry in your notebook.

LITERATURE GROUPS Meet with two or three others who have read "Darkness at Noon." Why do you think the author wrote this story?

Vo•cab•u•lary

elders (EL derz) those who are superior due to age

IN THE BLOOD

by Pat Mora

A grandfather and grandchild share a special connection.

The brown-eyed child
and the white-haired grandfather
dance in the silent afternoon.
They snap their fingers
to a rhythm only those
who love can hear.

SUPPLE cord

by Naomi Shihab Nye

What comforted you when you were a small child?

My brother, in his small white bed,
held one end.
I tugged the other
to signal I was still awake.

Vo·cab·u·lary

supple (SUP el) capable of bending easily; flexible

We could have spoken,
could have sung
to one another,
we were in the same room
for five years,
but the soft cord
with its little <u>frayed</u> ends
connected us
in the dark,
gave comfort
even if we had been <u>bickering</u>
all day.
When he fell asleep first
and his end of the cord
dropped to the floor,
I missed him terribly,
though I could hear his even breath
and we had such long and separate lives
ahead. ❶ ○

> **❶ Analyze**
> Think about the relationship between the two brothers. What does the cord symbolize, or stand for?

Answer the BIG Question

As you do the following activities, consider the Big Question:
Why share stories?

WRITE TO LEARN How does each poet show the closeness of the family relationships? Which poem did you like the best? Write a brief entry in your notebook.

PARTNER TALK Meet with a classmate who has read these poems. Discuss the importance of the family relationship presented in each poem. If you wish, share a story about a special connection you have with a family member.

Vo·cab·u·lary

frayed (frayd) worn; coming apart at the ends
bickering (BIK ur ing) petty arguing

once a Good man

by Jane Yolen

Climb aboard an angel's wings for a glimpse of both Heaven and Hell.

Once a good man lived at the foot of a mountain. He helped those who needed it and those who did not. And he never asked for a thing in return.

Now it happened that one day the Lord was looking over his records with his Chief Angel and came upon the Good Man's name.

"*That* is a good man," said the Lord. "What can we do to reward him? Go down and find out."

The Chief Angel, who was nibbling on a thin cracker, swallowed hastily and wiped her mouth with the edge of her robe.

"Done," she said.

So the Chief Angel flew down, the wind feathering her wings, and landed at the foot of the mountain.

"Come in," said the man, who was not surprised to see her.

For in those days angels often walked on Earth. "Come in and drink some tea. You must be aweary of flying."

And indeed the angel was. So she went into the Good Man's house, folded her wings carefully so as not to knock the furniture about, and sat down for a cup of tea.

While they were drinking their tea, the angel said, "You have led such an <u>exemplary</u> life, the Lord of Hosts has decided to reward you. Is there anything in the world that you wish?" **1**

The Good Man thought a bit. "Now that you mention it," he said, "there is one thing."

"Name it," said the angel. "To name it is to make it yours."

The Good Man looked slightly embarrassed. He leaned over the table and said quietly to the angel, "If only I could see both Heaven and Hell I would be completely happy."

The Chief Angel choked a bit, but she managed to smile nonetheless. "Done," she said, and finished her tea. Then she stood up and held out her hand.

"Hold fast," she said. "And never lack courage."

So the Good Man held fast. But he kept his eyes closed all the way. And before he could open them again, the man and the angel had flown down, down, down, past moles and mole hills, past buried treasure, past coal in seams, past layer upon layer of the world, till they came at last to the entrance to Hell.

The Good Man felt a cool breeze upon his lids and opened his eyes.

"Welcome to Hell," said the Chief Angel.

The Good Man stood amazed. Instead of flames and fire, instead of mud and <u>mire</u>, he saw long sweeping green meadows

1 Predict
What do you think the Good Man might ask for?

Vo•cab•u•lary

exemplary (ig ZEM pluh ree) beyond excellent; serving as a model
mire (myr) wet, soggy, muddy ground

edged around with trees. He saw long
wooden tables piled high with food.
He saw chickens and roasts, fruits and
salads, <u>sweetmeats</u> and sweet
breads, and goblets of wine.

Yet the people who sat at
the table were thin and pale.
They <u>devoured</u> the food only
with their eyes.

"Angel, O angel," cried the
Good Man, "why are they hungry?
Why do they not eat?"

And at his voice, the people all
set up a loud <u>wail</u>.

The Chief Angel signaled him
closer.

And this is what he saw: The people
of Hell were bound fast to their chairs with
bands of steel. There were sleeves of steel from
their wrists to their shoulders. And though the tables were
piled high with food, the people were starving. There was no way
they could bend their arms to lift the food to their mouths.

The Good Man wept and hid his face. "Enough!" he cried.

So the Chief Angel held out her hand. "Hold fast," she said.
"And never lack courage."

So the Good Man held fast. But he kept his eyes closed all the
way. And before he could open them again, the man and the angel
had flown up, up, up, past eagles in their <u>eyries</u>, past the plump clouds,
past the streams of the sun, past layer upon layer of sky, till they came

Vo•cab•u•lary

sweetmeats (SWEET meetz) sugary treats, such as candy or crystal-
lized fruit
devoured (dih VOWRD) consumed or ate quickly or greedily
wail (wayl) a long cry
eyries (AYR eez) bird's nests on a cliff or mountaintop

at last to the entrance to Heaven. ❷

The Good Man felt a warm breeze upon his lids and opened his eyes.

"Welcome to Heaven," said the Chief Angel.

❷ **Predict**
How will Heaven be different from Hell?

The Good Man stood amazed. Instead of clouds and choirs, instead of robes and rainbows, he saw long sweeping green meadows edged around with trees. He saw long wooden tables piled high with food. He saw chickens and roasts, fruits and salads, sweetmeats and sweet breads, and goblets of wine.

But the people of Heaven were bound fast to their chairs with bands of steel. There were sleeves of steel from their wrists to their shoulders. There seemed no way they could bend their arms to lift the food to their mouths.

Yet these people were well fed. They laughed and talked and sang praises to their host, the Lord of Hosts.

"I do not understand," said the Good Man. "It is the same as Hell, yet it is not the same. What is the difference?"

The Chief Angel signaled him closer.

And this is what he saw: Each person reached out with his steel-banded arm to take a piece of food from the plate. Then he reached over—and fed his neighbor.

When he saw this, the Good Man was completely happy. ○

Answer the BIG Question

As you do the following activities, consider the Big Question:
Why share stories?

WRITE TO LEARN Write a brief entry in your notebook about the main lesson in this story. How did the story affect you when you read it?

LITERATURE GROUPS Join with two or three others who have read this story. Discuss how it relates to the idea of sharing our stories.

Index of Authors and Titles

Index of Authors and Titles

Acknowledgments

Literature credits

Unit 1

Lou Gehrig's farewell speech and "To Lou Gehrig" TM/© Estate of Eleanor Gehrig by CMG Worldwide/www.LouGehrig.com. Reprinted by permission.

"Sister/Friend" from *Girl Coming in for a Landing: A Novel in Poems* by April Halprin Wayland and illustrated by Elaine Clayton, copyright © 2002 by April Halprin Wayland. Illustrations copyright © 2002 by Elaine Clayton. Used by permission of Alfred A. Knopf, an imprint of Random House Children's Books, a division of Random House, Inc.

"Poem" from *The Collected Poems of Langston Hughes* by Langston Hughes, copyright © 1994 by The Estate of Langston Hughes. Used by permission of Alfred A. Knopf, a division of Random House, Inc.

"Tales of a Seventh Grade Nada" by Bizet Kizcorn.

Excerpt from *The Fellowship of the Ring* by J. R. R. Tolkien. Copyright © 1954, 1965 by J. R. R. Tolkien. Copyright © renewed 1982 by Christopher R. Tolkien, Michael H. R. Tolkien, John F. R. Tolkien, and Priscilla M. A. R. Tolkien. Reprinted by permission of Houghton Mifflin Company. All rights reserved.

"Hobbit-Like Human Ancestor Found" by Hillary Mayell. *National Geographic Kids News*, November 22, 2004. Reprinted by permission of the National Geographic Society.

From *The Diary of a Young Girl: The Definitive Edition* by Anne Frank. Otto H. Frank and Mirjam Pressler, Editors, translated by Susan Massotty, copyright © 1995 by Doubleday, a division of Random House, Inc. Used by permission of Doubleday, a division of Random House, Inc.

"Baby Hippo Orphan Finds a Friend" by Catherine Clarke Fox. *National Geographic Kids News*, March 4, 2005. Reprinted by permission of the National Geographic Society.

"Finding a Way" by Jan Klinkbeil.

When the Rattlesnake Sounds: A Play About Harriet Tubman by Alice Childress, copyright © 1975, renewed 2003. Used by permission of Flora Roberts, Inc.

Unit 2

"The Calamity Kids in: The Bermuda Triangle Terrarium!" by Jerzy Drozd and Sara Turner.

"To Young Readers" by Gwendolyn Brooks. Reprinted by consent of Brooks Permissions.

"Invitation" from *Where the Sidewalk Ends* by Shel Silverstein. Copyright © 1974 by Evil Eye Music. Reprinted by permission of HarperCollins.

"Real Spider Superpowers" by Sarah Ives. *National Geographic KidsNews*, July 6, 2004. Reprinted by permission of the National Geographic Society.

"Blues for Bob E. Brown" by T. Ernesto Bethancourt, copyright © 1993 by T. Ernesto Bethancourt, from *Join In, Multiethnic Short Stories* by Donald R. Gallo, ed. Used by permission of Dell Publishing, a division of Random House, Inc.

"Hurricane Emily bad news for endangered turtles" by Eloise Quintanilla. From the *Chicago Sun-Times* Friday, July 22, 2005.

"Naked Animals" by David George Gordon. *National Geographic KidsNews*. Reprinted by permission of the National Geographic Society.

"Animal House" by Heather Herman, as told to Louise Jarvis. From *Teen Vogue* September 2004. Edited by Alyssa Giacobbe.

"Short Circuit" by Ben Shannon.

"King Tut's Mysterious Death" by Kristin Baird Rattini. *National Geographic KidsNews*. Reprinted by permission of the National Geographic Society.

Unit 3

"The Boy with Yellow Eyes" by Gloria Gonzalez, from *Visions*, Dell Publishing Company. Copyright © 1987 by Gloria

Acknowledgments

Gonzalez. Reprinted by permission of Brandt and Hochman Literary Agents, Inc.

"Ode to Weight Lifting" from *Neighborhood Odes*, copyright © 1992 by Gary Soto, reprinted by permission of Harcourt, Inc.

"Look Around and See Only Friends" by Samantha Smith, from *Great American Speeches for Young People*. Published by John Wiley & Sons, Inc. Used by permission of Jane Smith.

"Roller Coaster Thrills" by Emily Sohn, from *Science News for Kids*, June 16, 2004. Reprinted with permission from *Science News for Kids*, copyright © 2004.

"Skate Park" by Alec Zobrame.

"Macavity: The Mystery Cat" from *Old Possum's Book of Practical Cats*. Copyright © 1939 by T. S. Eliot and renewed 1967 by Esme Valerie Eliot, reprinted by permission of Harcourt, Inc.

"Survival of the Fittest" from *Stories for When You're Home Alone* by Allen B. Ury. Copyright © 1996 by RGA Publishing Group. Reprinted by permission of the author.

"Learning English" by Luis Alberto Ambroggio, translated from Spanish by Lori M. Carlson. Copyright © by Luis Alberto Ambroggio. From *Cool Salsa: Bilingual Poems on Growing Up Latino in the United States*, edited by Lori M. Carlson. Published by Henry Holt and Company. Collection copyright © 1994 by Lori M. Carlson.

"What Makes Me Me?" by Robert Winston; DK Publishing 2004.

"Worry Seems to Shorten a Timid Rat's Life" by Emily Sohn, from *Science News for Kids*, December 17, 2003. Reprinted with permission from *Science News for Kids*, copyright © 2003.

"Laugh" by Mark Rafenstein, from *Current Health*, February 2000. Copyright © 2000 Weekly Reader Corporation. Reprinted by permission.

Unit 4

"The Day I Ran with Lance Armstrong" by Samuel Brook Douglas. *Skipping Stones* March-April 2005. Reprinted by permission of *Skipping Stones* Magazine.

From "Ice Cube—Actor/Musician" by McClain J. and Angela R. Reprinted with permission of *Teen Ink* and TeenInk.com.

"Third Down and Forever" by Douglas Holgate.

"Dealing with Peer Pressure" by Kevin J. Took, M.D. This information was provided by KidsHealth, one of the largest resources online for medically reviewed health information written for parents, kids, and teens. For more articles like this one, visit www.KidsHealth.org or www.TeensHealth.org.

"Thanking the Birds" by Joseph Bruchac. Reprinted by permission of Barbara S. Kouts.

"Jimmy Jet and His TV Set" from *Where The Sidewalk Ends* by Shel Silverstein. Copyright © 1974 by Evil Eye Music. Reprinted by permission of HarperCollins.

"Waiting for the War" by Graham Salisbury, copyright © 1999 by Graham Salisbury, from *Time Capsule: Short Stories About Teenagers Throughout the Twentieth Century* by Donald R. Gallo. Used by permission of Dell Publishing, a division of Random House, Inc.

"The Struggle to Be an All-American Girl" by Elizabeth Wong. Reprinted by permission of the author, www.elizabethwong.net.

"A Crush" from *A Couple of Kooks and Other Stories About Love* by Cynthia Rylant. Published by Scholastic Inc./Orchard Books. Copyright © 1990 by Cynthia Rylant. Reprinted by permission.

"A Gold Miner's Tale" from *We The People* by Bobbi Katz. Text copyright © 2000 by Bobbi Katz. Used by permission of HarperCollins Publishers.

Unit 5

"The No-Guitar Blues" from *Baseball in April and Other Stories*, copyright © 1990 by Gary Soto, reprinted by permission of Harcourt, Inc..

"Merrick Johnston: Mountain Climber" from *Gutsy Girls: Young Women Who Dare* by Tina Schwager, P. T. A., A. T. C., and Michele Schuerger © 1999. Used with permission from Free Spirit Publishing Inc., Minneapolis, MN; 1-866-703-7322; www.freespirit.com. All rights reserved.

"Krumping: If You Look Like Bozo Having Spasms, You're Doing It Right" by Shaheem Reid with additional reporting by Mark Bella for MTV News. Copyright © 2005 by MTV Networks.

"Chicago Kids Sink Their Teeth Into Dino Camp" by Sarah Ives. *National Geographic KidsNews*, July 20, 2004. Reprinted by permission of the National Geographic Society.

"Asteroid Belt" by Steven Maxwell.

"The Dog Diaries" copyright © 1992 by Merrill Markoe. From *What the Dogs Have Taught Me*. Reprinted with permission by Melanie Jackson Agency, LLC.

"It's Not A Crime To Love Science" by Juliann F. Willey, from *33 Things Every Girl Should Know: Stories, Songs, Poems, and Smart Talk by 33 Extraordinary Women*, edited by Tonya Bolden. Copyright © 1998 by Tonya Bolden. Reprinted by permission of Crown Publishers, a division of Random House, Inc.

"Hollywood and the Pits," copyright © 1992 by Cherylene Lee. Reprinted by permission of Bret Adams Ltd.

Unit 6

"Dead and Gone" by Marie G. Lee. Reprinted by permission of the author.

From "Dune Tunes Physical" by Britt Norlander. Published in *Scholastic Science World*, June 7/21, 2005. Copyright © 2005 by Scholastic Inc. Reprinted by permission.

"El Inca" by Kagan McLeod.

Reprinted with the permission of Simon & Schuster Books for Young Readers, an imprint of Simon & Schuster Children's Publishing Division, from *Kancil and the Crocodiles* by Noreha Yussof Day. Text copyright © 1996 by Noreha Yussof Day.

"A Forest Home" from People to Know, A supplement to *Childcraft—The How and Why Library*; published by World Book, Inc.

"The Night the Bed Fell," copyright © 1933 by James Thurber. Copyright © renewed 1961 by Helen Thurber and Rosemary A. Thurber. Reprinted by arrangement with the Barbara Hogenson Agency.

"The Puzzle of Pan-Am Flight 103," from *Scientists at Work: Forensic Scientists* by Rose Inserra. Copyright © 2004 by Rose Inserra. Reprinted by permission of The Creative Company.

"Too Many Mummies" by Mark Rose, from DIG's September 2004 issue: *Monstrous Megaliths*, copyright © 2004, Carus Publishing Company, published by Cobblestone Publishing, 30 Grove Street, Suite C, Peterborough, NH 03458. All rights reserved. Used by permission of the publisher.

"Grinner: A Face From the Past" by Peggy Thomas, from *Talking Bones: The Science of Forensic Anthropology*; Publisher Facts on File, An Infobase Holdings Company; ISBN 0816 031142; Copyright © 1995 by Peggy Thomas.

"Beetle on a String" by Vince Gotera. Reprinted by permission of the author.

"A Short Story" by David Escobar Galindo, translated by Jorge D. Piche.

"Travelin' Soldier" by Bruce Robison. Copyright © 1996 Tiltawhirl Music (BMI)/Bruce Robison music (BMI) 100% (Administered by Bluewater Music Corp).

Hosni the Dreamer by Ehud Ben-Ezer. Copyright © 1997 by Ehud Ben-Ezer. Reprinted by permission of the author.

"It's a Small E-mail World After All" by Emily Sohn, from *Science News for Kids*, August 20, 2003. Reprinted with permission from *Science News for Kids*, copyright © 2003.

"Darkness at Noon: Solar Eclipse" from *Navajo: Visions and Voices Across the Mesa* by Shonto Begay. Copyright © 1995 by Shonto Begay. Reprinted by permission of Scholastic Inc.

"In the Blood" reprinted with permission from the publisher of *My Own True Name* by Pat Mora (Houston: Arte Publico Press-University of Houston © 2000).

"Supple Cord" from *A Maze Me: Poems for Girls* by Naomi Shihab Nye. Copyright © 2005 by Naomi Shihab Nye. Reprinted by permission of the author.

"Once a Good Man" by Jane Yolen. Copyright © 1977 by Jane Yolen. First appeared in *The Hundredth Dove*, published by T. Y. Crowell. Reprinted by permission of Curtis Brown, Ltd.

Acknowledgments

Glencoe would like to acknowledge the artists who participated in illustrating this program: Sara Turner and Jerzy Drozd; Donovan Foote; Steven Murray; Bizet Kizcorn; Douglas Holgate.

Photo credits

Cover i (cl)Jupiter Images, (cr)Ben Shannon, (t)Index Stock Imagery, (bl)Brand X Pictures/PunchStock, (br)Nick Koudis/Getty Images; iv v Cut and Deal Ltd./Index Open; 0 Jupiter Images; 1 © PhotoAlto/Alamy Images; 2 Bettmann/CORBIS; 4 Don Tremain/Getty Images; Trinette Reed/Brand X Pictures/Jupiter Images; 5 Rubberball/Getty Images; 6 CORBIS; 19 Kurt Strazdins/Knight-Ridder/Tribune Media Information Services; 24 Knight-Ridder/Tribune Media Information Services; 29 Stephen Hird/Reuters/CORBIS; 31 Reuters/CORBIS; 33 Comstock; 35 49 CORBIS; 55 Louie Psihoyos/CORBIS; 59 CORBIS; 60 Keith Philpott/Time Life Pictures/Getty Images; 62 (inset)Rubberball/Getty Images, (bkgd)MBCheatham/iStock International, Greg Paprocki/Getty Images; 76 Medioimages/Getty Images; 78 Jupiter Images; 79 80 Index Stock Imagery, 81 Index Stock Imagery; © CORBIS Premium RF/Alamy Images; 85 Stockbyte/Getty Images; 87 Darren Hopes/Getty Images; 90 CORBIS; 94 Darren Hopes/Getty Images, © Blend Images/Alamy Images; 97 Index Stock Imagery; 100 NOAA; 101 DigitalVision/Getty Images; 102 Henry Ausloos/Animals Animals; 104 (bkgd)Index Stock Imagery, Diane Diederich/iStock Photo; 107 David Zalubowski/AP Images; 108 Ryan McVay/Getty Images; 121 Brand X Pictures/PunchStock, (bkgd)CORBIS, Brand X Pictures/PunchStock; 124 PhotoAlto/PunchStock; 125 Jose Luis Pelaez, Inc./Blend Images/CORBIS; 126 (l)Andersen Ross/Getty Images, (r)Getty Images; 128 FogStock, LLC/Index Open; 130 (b)Jupiter Images, (inset)Jupiter Images, (bkgd)Index Open; 132 (c)DesignPics/Index Open; (l r)AbleStock/Index Open; 134 Photomondo/Getty Images; 139 SW Productions/Getty Images; 140 (bkgd)Image Source, (inset)© Comstock/Jupiter Images; 141 CORBIS; 143 Hot Ideas/Index Open; 145 Brand X Pictures/PunchStock; 147 Jupiter Images; 149 Javier Pierini/Getty Images; 163 Jupiter Images; 177 Index Open, Photodisc/PunchStock; 178 Photodisc/PunchStock; 181 James Woodson/Getty Images, Mel Curtis/Getty Images; 183 © Hola/SuperStock; 185 Getty Images; 187 Creatas; 189 DigitalVision/Getty Images; 190 Jupiter Images; 193 © Somos Images/CORBIS;

194 Brant Sanderlin/Atlanta Journal-Constitution; 196 C Squared Studios/Getty Images; 197 Jules Frazier/Getty Images; 198 Index Stock Imagery, Karl Walter/Getty Images; 200 Peter Kramer/Getty Images; 215 Stockbyte; 217 Maria Taglienti-Molinari/Brand X Pictures/Jupiter Images; 220 Jupiter Images; 221 Rubberball; 229 Hot Ideas; 231 233 Getty Images; 237 Marjory Collins/Getty Images; 239 Getty Images; 241 243 Jupiter Images; 245 Siede Preis/Getty Images; 246 (bkgd)Siede Preis/Getty Images, (inset)© Blend Images/Alamy Images; 247 Siede Preis/Getty Images; 248 CORBIS; 251 Siede Preis/Getty Images; 253 Jules Frazier/Getty Images; 254 S. Solum/PhotoLink/Getty Images; 256 SW Productions/Getty Images; 258 Rubberball; 263 (r)Getty Images, (l)Rubberball; 266 Alan Pappe/Getty Images; 267 (bkgd)Comstock, Courtesy Merrick Johnston; 273 Dynamic Graphics/Jupiter Images; 275 Courtesy Tommy the Clown; 277 Kevork Djansezian/AP Images; 279 CORBIS; 280 281 Conor Barnes/Project Exploration; 294 (inset)Digital Vision, Rubberball; 297 (l)Ryan McVey/Getty Images, (cr)Getty Images; 300 Creatas; 303 (bkgd)DigitalVision, Nick Koudis/Getty Images; 305 (bkgd)Comstock, CORBIS; 308 CORBIS; 309 Courtesy Cherylene Lee; 310 312 313 314 CORBIS; 315 Nicholas Pitt/Getty Images; 316 CORBIS; 318 Design Pics/PunchStock; 319 Barbara Penoyar/Getty Images; 320 DigitalVision, Doug Menuez/Getty Images; 324 Tim Hall/Getty Images; 325 Nick Koudis/Getty Images; 327 Javier Pierini/Getty Images; 341 (l)Getty Images, (r)Ingram Publishing/PictureQuest, (bkgd)Joseph Mule/PictureQuest; 343 (l r)Getty Images, (bkgd)Creatas Images/PictureQuest; 345 Michael Neugebauer; 347 Photo 24/PictureQuest; 348 JGI Uganda/Dr. Jane Goodall, DBE Founder, Jane Goodall Institute UN Messenger of Peace; 357 Gillianne Tedder/PictureQuest; 358 AP Images; 360 Silvia Izquierdo/AP Images; 361 Jupiter Images; 363 Creatas/PunchStock; 365 © Blend Images/Alamy Images; 366 CORBIS; 368 (inset)The Studio Dog, (bkgd)Peter Adams/Getty Images; 370 Artville, LLC; 372 (inset)Pankai Shah/Getty Images, DigitalVision/Getty Images; 376 Photolink/Getty Images; 378 Medioimages/Getty Images; 380 (br)Rubberball, (bkgd)Photolink/Getty Images, © Comstock.